Additional Praise for

WASHINGTON'S
FAREWELL

"It's hard to tell which is more nearly perfect—John Avlon's argument or his timing. In the wake of a dispiriting campaign, Avlon finds in Washington's Farewell Address a stunningly topical antidote to excessive partisanship and greedy self-interest. His book is a stake through the heart of political extremism"

—Richard Norton Smith, author of *On His Own Terms:
A Life of Nelson Rockefeller*

"George Washington's long, formal farewell address once held enormous power among Americans, and John Avlon summons and contextualizes that relevance in this captivating book. At once a biography of George Washington at his zenith and a chronicle of a new nation still crafting its traditions, this book makes a powerful case that the first president's last public message deserves again to hold iconic status in the pantheon of our greatest founding documents."

—Harold Holzer, author of *Lincoln and the Power of the Press:
The War for Public Opinion*, winner of the Lincoln Prize

"*Washington's Farewell* sweeps us into a timeless and humanizing story. Shining a revelatory spotlight on a long forgotten document, more than 220 years old, Avlon melds gloriously raw insight with the Farewell Address, revealing prophetic wisdom into contemporary American politics and the evolving Great American Experiment."

—Mark Santangelo, chief librarian and archivist, Fred W. Smith
National Library for the Study of George Washington

"In this lucidly rendered and insightful portrait of George Washington, John Avlon deconstructs the great man's famous Farewell Address, one of the most influential documents of our political heritage, and employs the component parts as entry points into an illuminating exploration of the first president's character and legacy. Thus does Avlon give us the real-life Washington and a compelling narrative of his time."

—Robert W. Merry, author of *Where They Stand: The American Presidents in the Eyes of Voters and Historians* and *A Country of Vast Designs: James K. Polk, the Mexican War, and the Conquest of the American Continent*

"Absorbing . . . Avlon's book could hardly have come at a more opportune time. . . . Avlon compellingly argues that the Farewell Address is not a document only for presidents but rather for all Americans to read and know."

—*The East Hampton Star*

ALSO BY JOHN AVLON

Independent Nation: How the Vital Center Is Changing American Politics

Wingnuts: How a Lunatic Fringe Is Hijacking America

Deadline Artists: America's Greatest Newspaper Columns
(editor with Jesse Angelo and Errol Louis)

Deadline Artists: Scandals, Tragedies and Triumphs
(editor with Jesse Angelo and Errol Louis)

WASHINGTON'S
FAREWELL

THE FOUNDING FATHER'S WARNING
TO FUTURE GENERATIONS

───────────── ★ ─────────────

JOHN AVLON

SIMON & SCHUSTER PAPERBACKS
New York London Toronto Sydney New Delhi

Simon & Schuster Paperbacks
An Imprint of Simon & Schuster, Inc.
1230 Avenue of the Americas
New York, NY 10020

First Simon & Schuster trade paperback edition January 2018

SIMON & SCHUSTER PAPERBACKS and colophon are registered trademarks of Simon & Schuster, Inc.

For information about special discounts for bulk purchases, please contact Simon & Schuster Special Sales at 1-866-506-1949 or business@simonandschuster.com.

The Simon & Schuster Speakers Bureau can bring authors to your live event. For more information or to book an event, contact the Simon & Schuster Speakers Bureau at 1-866-248-3049 or visit our website at www.simonspeakers.com.

Interior design by Renato Stanisic

Manufactured in the United States of America

10 9 8 7 6 5 4 3 2

The Library of Congress has cataloged the hardcover edition as follows:

Names: Avlon, John P., author.

Title: Washington's farewell : the founding father's warning to future generations / by John Avlon.

Description: New York : Simon & Schuster, 2017. | Includes bibliographical references and index.

Identifiers: LCCN 2016045258 (print) | LCCN 2016048212 (ebook) | ISBN 9781476746463 (hardback) | ISBN 9781476746470 (paperback) | ISBN 9781476746487 (ebook)

Subjects: LCSH: Washington, George, 1732–1799. Farewell address. | Washington, George, 1732–1799—Influence. | National characteristics, American. | BISAC: HISTORY / Military / United States. | POLITICAL SCIENCE / Government / General. | HISTORY / United States / Revolutionary Period (1775–1800).

Classification: LCC E312.952 .A94 2017 (print) | LCC E312.952 (ebook) | DDC 973.4/1092—dc23

LC record available at https://lccn.loc.gov/2016045258

ISBN 978-1-4767-4646-3
ISBN 978-1-4767-4647-0 (pbk)
ISBN 978-1-4767-4648-7 (ebook)

To the past, present, and future
With endless appreciation:
My parents, John and Dianne
My bride, Margaret
And our children, Jack and Toula Lou

CONTENTS

★

The moderation and virtue of a single character probably pre-vented this revolution from being closed, as most others have been, by a subversion of the liberty it was intended to establish.

—THOMAS JEFFERSON ON GEORGE WASHINGTON.

INTRODUCTION

This is the story of the most famous American speech you've never read.

Once celebrated as civic scripture, more widely reprinted than the Declaration of Independence, George Washington's Farewell Address is now almost forgotten. Our first founding father intended it to be his last political will and testament—the sum of his hard-won wisdom from a half-century of public service in war and peace.

Most political speeches are full of promises, New Deals and New Covenants. Washington's Farewell was "a warning from a parting friend," written for future generations of Americans about the forces he feared could destroy our democratic republic. Chief among these were hyper-partisanship, excessive debt and foreign wars—dangers we still struggle with today.

Washington also used his Farewell Address to proclaim first principles that could offer enduring solutions: the pursuit of peace through strength, the wisdom of moderation, the importance of virtue and education to a self-governing people, as he established the precedent of the peaceful transfer of power. This was Washington's final revolutionary act: an open letter to the American people, not formally delivered in front of legislators, but published in a newspaper on September 19, 1796.

When he announced his retirement after two bruising terms as president, the success of the American experiment was far from certain. Just twenty years after the Declaration of Independence and less than a decade since the Constitution's adoption, the country was erupting into opposing factions, even within Washington's cabinet. Civil war seemed to be a real possibility.

The Articles of Confederation had been too weak to sustain the nation in the years after independence, requiring the triage of a closed-door Constitutional Convention and the election of Washington as the first president. There was no guarantee this incarnation of the republic would survive.

Already there were riots, insurrections and threats of secession. A sin tax on liquor provoked an armed "Whiskey Rebellion" in the western wilderness of Pennsylvania. Overseas, our revolutionary allies in France were overcome by a revolution of their own, as guillotine enthusiasts in the Jacobin regime dispatched ambassadors to undermine Washington's government, with near-treasonous assistance from his own cabinet officers. In the president's home state of Virginia, political opponents offered up a chilling toast: "a speedy death to Washington!"

Through sheer force of will and a gritty commitment to the governing principle of moderation, Washington kept these forces at bay while our infant independent nation gained enough strength to stand on its own.

None of it was easy. The old lion wanted to retire.

At age sixty-four, he still stood a head taller than most men, but his health was beginning to fail, sparking gossip among rivals that Washington was "growing old, his bodily health less firm, his memory always bad, becoming worse." Always an uncomfortable public speaker, low-voiced and halting, his lack of oratorical confidence was at least in part a function of physical discomfort. The president was down to a single tooth, with a set of dentures hanging around a lonely left bicuspid. His artificial teeth were state-of-the-art for the time, but the man had a menagerie in his mouth: teeth carved from walrus tusks and hippopotamus bone (then sonorously known as "sea horse") as well as the repurposed teeth of nine slaves. This required a clenched jaw and a minimum of smiles.

The most self-monitoring of men in public, Washington was becoming brittle and short-tempered in private, occasionally erupting into towering rages. Unaccustomed to direct criticism as a general on the battlefield, he was surprisingly thin-skinned when attacked in the political arena, complaining to Thomas Jefferson that he was being slandered by the press "in such exaggerated and indecent terms as could scarcely be applied to a Nero; a notorious defaulter; or even to a common pickpocket."

Washington knew his time was running out, writing with uncharacteristic flourish to a friend that "the cares of office will I have no doubt hasten my departure for that country from whence no traveler returns."

His sense of personal urgency was compounded by events. Storm clouds threatened our snug harbors on the Atlantic. Revolutions everywhere seemed to be devolving toward anarchy and terror. Washington understood that utopian dreams often turn into nightmares.

The implosion of democratic republics overseas sent shock waves: the idealism of the French Revolution turned to tyranny; Poland's attempt at a parliamentary democracy became polarized and paralyzed; St. Domingue's Caribbean slave rebellion was equal parts liberation and slaughter.

These stories filled the newspapers, adding pressure to America's attempt to find a durable middle ground between monarchy and the mob. "Standing, as it were, in the midst of falling empires," Washington wrote his secretary of war, Henry Knox, "it should be our aim to assume a station and attitude which will preserve us from being overwhelmed in their ruins."

The founding fathers' fascination—obsession is not too strong a word—with ancient Greece and Rome offered cautionary tales, warning about the forces that brought down past republics. Edward Gibbon's *The History of the Decline and Fall of the Roman Empire* was a contemporary bestseller, sold in bookstores from Boston to Charleston, and was one of the most popular books in the congressional library.

Washington's vice president, John Adams, believed "there never was a democracy yet that did not commit suicide." Civilization was understood to be fragile, barbarians always at the gate.

George Washington had set his mind on a Farewell Address at the end of his first term. He assembled the greatest team of ghostwriters in history to help flesh out his ideas. First James Madison and then Alexander Hamilton—the once-friendly coauthors of the Federalist Papers—were summoned to work on the speech in secret, even as both schemed to create opposing political parties, against Washington's wishes and in contradiction of the warning they helped him write. In bringing their words together, Washington hoped to create a document beyond partisanship, able to unite the nation.

To Washington, the success of a nation, like the success of an individual, was a matter of independence, integrity, and industry. The character of a nation mattered as much as the character of a man or woman. His Farewell Address represented lessons taken from his time as a surveyor, soldier, farmer, revolutionary general, entrepreneur, and president, drawing on sources as diverse as the Bible, the Constitution, and his favorite play, *Cato*. It was the work of a lifetime, an autobiography of ideas.

The 6,088-word, fifty-four-paragraph text—longer than the original draft of the Constitution—had been written and rewritten over five years. His beloved step-granddaughter Nelly Custis would recall decades later, in a previously unpublished letter, watching "President Washington repeatedly in the act of writing the 'Farewell Address' in the day time, and also at night by the candlestick."

Washington's Farewell Address was not read aloud before an audience. Instead of delivering the news like a European king, he delivered it directly to the American people through one of the 100 newspapers in the nation. He chose the independent-minded *American Daily Advertiser*, whose offices were five blocks down the street from the executive mansion in Philadelphia. He submitted it almost nine years to the day after the Constitution was signed.

Addressed to his "friends and fellow citizens," the news of Washington's decision not to run for reelection, establishing the two-term tradition, was unceremoniously bunched between advertisements for slaves, rum and tobacco.

This book tells the story of the Farewell Address: its secret composition, deeper meanings, and outsized impact from Washington's time to our own. It offers an intimate look into both the Founding Fathers' bitter personal battles and the values they fought to secure. Then, as now, politics is history in the present tense. It is a tale of intrigue amid the founding of the two-party system and the struggle of the first president to save the United States from self-destruction. Through it all, Washington worked to establish "a standard to which the wise and honest can repair."

★

THERE ARE FOUNDING FATHERS WHO are famous for their writing. Washington is not one of them. Jefferson had the heroic rhythm and flow of the Declaration. Adams could be acerbic, puffed up, pretentious and funny. Hamilton was a live wire of insights and attitude. Madison was all about ideas, philosophy in form and function.

Washington took a soldier's approach to his correspondence, direct and mission driven. He declared "with me it has always been a maxim rather to let my designs appear from my works than by my expressions." He was nonetheless prolific with his pen, cutting the quills himself and writing in his enviably neat, rightward-leaning script.

"Few men who had so little leisure have written so much," attested his friend and first Supreme Court chief justice, John Jay. "His *public* letters alone are voluminous, and public opinion has done justice to their merits."

"His education had been confined," acknowledged his frequent dining companion, Henrietta Liston, the vivacious wife of the postwar British ambassador. "He knew no language but his own, and expressed himself in that rather forcibly than elegantly. . . . Letter writing seemed in him a peculiar talent. His style was plain, correct, and nervous."

Washington was painstakingly modest but not without a sense of his place in history. He kept his papers carefully organized at Mount Vernon—totaling more than 100,000 letters, manuscripts, drafts, and diaries—so mindful of history's eyes that he reached back to edit some of his early letters during his retirement. He knew posterity was watching, considering his papers "a species of public property, sacred in my hands." The Farewell Address was his greatest work.

It did not emerge in a single moment of inspiration. The Farewell Address's essential insights can be found in Washington's previous farewell to the nation, when he resigned his commission as general of the Continental Army in 1783, while offering parting advice for the nation he saw poised between greatness and great danger.

The maxims that he established after the Revolutionary War remained his bedrock throughout the presidency: a strong central government led by an independent chief executive, the transformative power of trade and commerce, and the importance of religion and education in building the character of the country.

At his death in December 1799, two weeks before the end of the century, Washington completed his Farewell Address with a personal coda—a written will that announced his intention to free his slaves—finally confronting, inartfully and incompletely, the core contradiction of slavery.

As the nation mourned, a new struggle began over the afterlife of Washington's ideas. From the torching of the White House in the War of 1812 to the fraying ties between North and South, the Farewell Address helped reconcile competing factions for generations.

Supreme Court chief justice John Marshall regarded Washington's Farewell as a source of "precepts to which the American statesmen cannot too frequently recur." Washington's sometime friend and frequent rival Thomas Jefferson, who devoted so much subterranean energy to attacking his presidential policies, nonetheless directed the newly formed University of Virginia to assign the Farewell Address to all law school students as one of "the best guides" to "the distinctive principles of the government . . . of the United States." The Monroe Doctrine codified its advice in foreign affairs. A generation later, President Andrew Jackson devoted his own Farewell Address to a meditation on the "voice of prophecy" of Washington's Farewell and its warnings against secession.

As the Civil War approached, both North and South used the Farewell Address as a rhetorical weapon, the ultimate patriotic primary source. Advocates for Union, such as Henry Clay and Daniel Webster, cited the speech under the Capitol dome, warning southern colleagues not to give in to the temptation of secession, lest they violate Washington's Farewell advice. Abraham Lincoln repeatedly referred to it in his 1860 campaign stump speech. Mississippi senator Jefferson Davis, the future president of the Confederacy, tried to twist Washington into a partisan figure, refusing to pay for drafts of the Farewell Address to be enshrined in the Library of Congress at taxpayer expense, cloaking the snub in arguments for fiscal discipline. He and other Confederates claimed Washington as one of their own, a slave-owning southern rebel.

In the wake of the Civil War, the Farewell Address was quoted to bind the wounds between the states through the power of public education. It became required reading, a benign form of civic indoctrination, taught in schools and recited in public squares on Washington's birthday.

The Farewell Address was quoted on stamps, slapped on postcards and baseball cards; it was used to sell candlesticks. When Thomas Edison pioneered recorded cylinders, a reading of the Washington's Farewell was among the first recordings sent to market. In *The Power of Myth*, Joseph Campbell recalled, "When I was a boy, we were given George Washington's Farewell Address and told to outline the whole thing, every single statement in relation to every other one. So I remember it absolutely."

But in the wake of the First World War, the Farewell Address began to fall out of favor. Two Washington scholars—President Woodrow Wilson and Senator Henry Cabot Lodge—squared off on whether the United

States should enter the League of Nations, debating the meaning and applicability of the Farewell.

By the Second World War, Americans had turned from Washington's advice about the dangers of permanent foreign alliances out of practical necessity. A parade of conservatives, cranks and conspiracists picked up its banner, the lowlight being a Nazi front group known as the German American Bund, which made the Farewell the centerpiece of a sinister rally in Madison Square Garden in which they proclaimed George Washington "the first Nazi."

Over time, the Farewell was eclipsed by the Gettysburg Address as America's go-to civic scripture. Lincoln's speech is approachable: a rhythmic, flowing 272 words, rather than 6,088 words at a steep incline. Which would you rather memorize? The Gettysburg Address was the New Testament to Washington's Old Testament, a poetic promise of life after death, rather than rules of behavior dispatched by a distant god.

★

WASHINGTON'S INSISTENCE ON SELF-MASTERY CAN make him seem cold and unapproachable. His birthday, once celebrated as "America's Political Christmas," is now distinguished primarily by a long winter weekend, bundled up with other presidents. Few films dramatize his life, even as popular attention is lavished upon his surrogate sons of the revolution. But behind the dutiful portraits that show a dour face dotted with impassive eyes was a passionate, ambitious man who worked tirelessly to achieve independence for his country and himself.

The Farewell Address is still read aloud each year in the U.S. Senate, the honor alternating between Democrats and Republicans, intended to serve as a reminder of the obligations Washington imposed on his inheritors—a tribute given to no other speech in our nation. It has inspired other presidents, most famously Dwight D. Eisenhower, to encapsulate their own farsighted farewell warnings about the existential threats facing our republic. But the only contemporary hardcover edition of the Farewell Address currently in print misstates the date of publication—it's labeled September 17 rather than 19—and declares that the speech was "delivered to the assembled members of Congress." The Farewell's most famous dictum—no entangling alliances—never actually appears in the address, while its core warning against hyper-partisanship has been ignored. Basic details have been lost alongside its central place in the civic debates of our nation.

Now, in the early decades of the twenty-first century, there is renewed anxiety about America's future, a tendency to view our nation in decline as other empires rise overseas. The same anxiety might drive us to reflect on first principles and there is no better primary source than our first president's lessons for future generations.

The durable wisdom of the Farewell Address deserves greater appreciation and it is just beginning to receive wider recognition. In recent years it has been cited by *The Daily Show* on election night and inspired a song in the hip-hop musical *Hamilton*.

In the Farewell, liberals and conservatives can both find evidence to buoy their political faiths while challenging their claims to represent the "real" beliefs of the founding fathers. Our first and only independent president, Washington steered clear of the partisan fray. He refused to be subjected to an ideological straitjacket, preferring to walk a centrist path that avoided excesses and the unintended consequences of overextension in politics, finance and foreign policy. The Farewell expresses a set of foundational principles so deeply embedded in our national character that they do not seem as distinct on the surface as the partisan clashes that echo on in the name of Jefferson and Hamilton.

Washington's influence endures in a political philosophy of independence. It is based on a belief in a strong and inclusive government, led by an independent-minded executive, pursuing military and economic strength to avoid a dangerous dependence on foreign nations.

Washingtonians believe in the governing principle of moderation, balancing idealism with realism, rejecting overextension and separatism from whatever the source. They strive to find a wise balance between individual liberty and generational responsibility.

Today, we need only take the Farewell Address down from the shelf and dust it off to make this old story new again, connecting the past and present with the future. It can still achieve Washington's aim by helping us to reunite our nation and re-center our politics. It can teach lessons rooted in Washington's life.

As historian Daniel Boorstin wrote: "The heirs of Jefferson and Madison would be the Democratic-Republicans, the heirs of Hamilton and Adams would be the Federalists. But the heirs of Washington would be all Americans."

SECTION I

THE CRISIS OF CREATION

★

If you travel to Philadelphia and stand at the corner of Market and Sixth Streets, you'll see the bare bones of an outdoor exhibit on the site where George Washington lived and worked during the last six years of his presidency. Except for the white spire of Independence Hall looming a block away, it is an uninspiring installation. But even this half-hearted marker, officially designated as a memorial to America's original sin of slavery, is an improvement over the public toilet, slapped with a small brass plaque, that squatted here for a half century.

The indignity came after the three-and-a-half-story red-brick building—occupied by two presidents and their families, senior staff, nine slaves, and seventeen servants—was briefly repurposed as a hotel, then a storefront topped by a boardinghouse.

The executive mansion was torn down in 1832 and replaced by a series of shops, including a ladies' shirtwaist factory, a party provision store named Zorn's, and a Laundromat loftily called "Washington Hall," at the heart of a busy downtown business district. The only suggestion of the original presence was a whisper of its outline visible on an adjoining brick building. In 1954, the block was demolished to accommodate the creation of the Liberty Mall.

But once upon a time, this was the place where the precedent of the American presidency was established every day amid tumultuous fights that threatened the young republic's life just twenty years after its birth.

So set your mind to 1796, as the sounds of cars and sirens give way to horse hooves and wagon wheels on cobblestone. The streets smell of manure, the rooms of tobacco. Americans are celebrating the twentieth anniversary of the Declaration of Independence as Tennessee becomes the sixteenth state to join the Union. The first U.S. passport is issued, the first American cookbook is published, and the first elephant arrives on American soil, as a curiosity from India. Most momentous, George Washington announces he is walking away from the power of the presidency, kicking off the first real presidential campaign.

By the end of his second term, two party factions had emerged, fighting for dominance as the president struggled to stay above the fray. Attacked on all sides, while keeping faith with what he called the "arduous trust of the presidency," Washington delivered his country to his successors in far better condition than he found it. As Supreme Court chief justice and New York governor John Jay wrote, "His administration raised the nation out of confusion into order; out of degradation and distress into reputation and prosperity; it found us withering; it left us flourishing."

Two blocks from the Philadelphia executive mansion were the offices of warring partisan newspapers, getting into the groove of freedom by hurling insults at the president. And on one stormy Monday, this spot was the hinge upon which American history turned.

On the afternoon of September 19, 1796, readers of *Claypoole's American Daily Advertiser* paid six cents and scanned the front page to find the customary catalogue of want-ads and items for sale: Irish linens; Madeira wine, and runaway slaves.

When they opened the paper to the second and third pages, they found the space almost entirely occupied by a single item of dense text, addressed to "The People of the United States," beginning with the words "Friends and Fellow Citizens," and signed simply at the end in small type, *G. Washington.*

It was the scoop of a century—a retirement notice that would change the world. President Washington, the father of the unruly nation, announced that he would not seek a third term. With his decision, fears about American democracy devolving into a dictatorship were ended, but an uncertain future now lay ahead.

George Washington was not a chatty man and his farewell could have been as brisk and cordial as much of his official correspondence. He announced his intended departure right at the top, then writing after six taut paragraphs: "Here, perhaps, I ought to stop."

But he did not stop there. "A solicitude for your welfare, which cannot end but with my life, and the apprehension of danger, natural to that solicitude, urge me, on an occasion like the present, to offer to your solemn contemplation, and to recommend to your frequent review, some sentiments which are the result of much reflection, of no inconsiderable observation, and which appear to me all-important to the permanency of your felicity as a people."

They were, he wrote, "the disinterested warnings of a parting friend."

And so Washington laid out his vision for the nation he believed was in danger from forces within and without. In uncommonly personal language, he summed up a lifetime in his nation's service. The Farewell Address captured Washington as a man in full—a soldier, farmer, entrepreneur and statesman, an autodidact insecure in his professional talents but supremely confident in his personal pursuit of character.

Washington worked for months on the document with his mercurial former Treasury secretary Alexander Hamilton, building on an earlier draft written with his once close ally turned adversary, Congressman James Madison, and finally edited by John Jay—reuniting the rowdy band of brothers who had written the Federalist Papers arguing for ratification of the Constitution.

Before publication, Washington made final line edits by candlelight and closed the address on a personal note: "I anticipate with pleasing expectation that retreat in which I promise myself to realize, without alloy, the sweet enjoyment of partaking, in the midst of my fellow-citizens, the benign influence of good laws under a free government, the ever-favorite object of my heart, and the happy reward, as I trust, of our mutual cares, labors, and dangers."

As the news spread on the streets of Philadelphia, George and Martha Washington were already gone, their bags packed by slaves in the shadow of Independence Hall, rolling on the three-day journey toward their beloved Mount Vernon on the banks of the Potomac.

The First Farewell

★

He had a genius for goodbyes. Washington's first farewell occurred thirteen years before, in June 1783, as he prepared to resign his commission as commander in chief of the victorious Continental Army to return to his farm. Like a modern-day Cincinnatus, the modesty of the move guaranteed his greatness. It was a revolutionary gesture, causing King George III to remark, "If he does that, he will be the greatest man in the world."

After proclaiming a day of jubilee, complete with an extra ration of rum for soldiers, bonfires on mountain-tops and fireworks thundering above the Hudson River, Washington set his mind to retirement, writing a friend that "before I retire from public life, I shall with the greatest freedom give my sentiments to the States on several political subjects."

He marked the moment by writing a 4,000-word address to the American people, scratching out the text in a stone Dutch farmhouse perched above the Hudson in the hamlet of Newburgh, New York. Washington had lived there in something close to comfort for two years with Martha after the upheaval of combat on the run required him to sleep in more than 200 homes over eight years.

It was a time of celebration but the general called it a moment of "crisis." Washington offered his parting advice on how to establish the foundation of an independent nation absent the common enemy that had united the thirteen colonies. The ideas flowed from his wartime experiences—struggles with a divided, dysfunctional Congress, insufficient funds, and crippling debt, compounded by a lack of resolve by the new citizens of the United States.

Washington asked that his letter be read aloud by the governors of the thirteen colonies at the commencement of the next session of their state legislatures—a means of distribution known as a Circular Letter to the States, of which he had availed himself eleven times during the course of the war.

General Washington intended *this* to be his Farewell Address—and it was alternately called his "Legacy" and "Farewell Address" in the decade that separated it from the end of his presidency. Here he established the roots of his concerns and remedies, articulating many of the principles and policies he would execute as president and enshrine in his final farewell.

Yes, this was a time for celebration and appreciation, but the success of the revolution had only brought the American people a heavier responsibility: "At this auspicious period, the United States came into existence as a nation, and if their citizens should not be completely free and happy, the fault will be entirely their own."

"This is the moment to establish or ruin their national character forever," Washington continued. "It is yet to be decided whether the Revolution must ultimately be considered as a blessing or a curse: a blessing or a curse, not to the present age alone, for with our fate will the destiny of unborn millions be involved."

And so he delineated "four things, which I humbly conceive are essential to the well being, I may even venture to say, to the existence of the United States as an independent power."

The first was "an indissoluble Union of the States under one federal head." Washington wanted to ensure that the states would resist any separatist impulse, believing that a strong central government led by a president was the surest way to preserve the republic. He wrote this without any assumption or intimation that he would be the nominee for this national office.

Second came "a sacred regard to public justice," by which he meant not only a fair judicial system, but more specifically a congressional commitment to pay the revolutionary soldiers what they were owed. Already, states were skirting their larger commitments once the war had been won. Paying debts was essential to the stable credit of a nation and Washington believed those debts should begin at home with the heroes whose sacrifice had made independence possible.

Third, Washington called for "the adoption of a proper peace establishment," which was an ornate way of calling for a standing American army. This was controversial. Throughout history republics had been undone by overgrown military establishments, but in a earlier dispatch titled "Sentiments on a Peace Establishment," Washington had counteracted this conventional wisdom by arguing that a permanent continental army, supplemented by state militias, could curtail individual state expense while making the prospect of reconquest less attractive to the British and other aggressive colonizers.

Fourth and finally, Washington made a passionate case for cultivating an identity as American citizens that would elevate national unity over local loyalties, inducing "them to forget their local prejudices and policies, to make those mutual concessions which are requisite to the general prosperity, and in some instances, to sacrifice their individual advantages to the interest of the community." In the eternal balance between individual rights and community obligations, Washington believed that there were times that the national interest trumped individual self-interest, especially in the early, unstable years of the young republic, when the failure of one could bring the destruction of the other.

"These are the pillars on which the glorious fabric of our independency and national character must be supported," Washington wrote. He was declaring his personal political credo that would guide him for the rest of his life: the elevation of the common good over narrow self-interest, aided by an energetic central government, animated by the pursuit of justice through moderation.

The response was rapturous. One newspaper correspondent wrote,

"When I read General Washington's circular letter, I imagine myself in the presence of the great General of the twelve United States of Israel."

Five months later, on November 25, Washington led his troops on a triumphant march from Newburgh into the city of New York—then just 4,000 homes on the southern tip of Manhattan—timing his victorious arrival with the departure of the final British troops on ships packed with loyalists and their furniture headed for the chilly hinterlands of Nova Scotia. The anniversary was celebrated for more than a century as "Evacuation Day."

They met the first celebrating group of New Yorkers at what is today Union Square, where a statue of Washington on horseback still stands. He traveled down the Boston Post Road and sought a quick break at the Bull's Head Tavern, a stagecoach stop and cattle market just north of the city limits near the corner of Bowery and Delancey Streets, where he raised a glass to liberty and New Yorkers did the same. A young woman who witnessed the event recalled decades later, "[As] I looked at them, and thought upon all they'd done and suffered for us, my heart and eyes were full, and I admired and gloried in them all the more, because they were weather-beaten and forlorn."

The party continued for more than a week. On December 4, hours before he was scheduled to resign his commission and return home, Washington summoned Continental Army officers to Fraunces Tavern on Pearl Street for a "turtle feast" and heartfelt farewell to his patriotic band of brothers.

The tavern had been the meeting place for an early group of revolutionaries known as the Sons of Liberty, and its owner—a West Indian immigrant named Samuel Fraunces—had helped stop a poisoning plot against Washington by a member of his own security detail, a group known quite literally as "Life Guards." Now, in the long room of his restaurant, Fraunces hosted the officers who had won the war and Washington raised a glass: "With a heart full of love and gratitude, I now take leave of you: I most devoutly wish that your latter days may be as prosperous and happy, as your former ones have been glorious and honorable." Grown men cried and even the famously self-controlled Washington got a bit teary-eyed. The scope of the party took some of the sting out of the sorrow: the 120 guests drained 135 bottles of Madeira and 60 bottles of beer.

After an early morning departure, Washington made his way by boat to Annapolis, Maryland, where he officially resigned his commission to the members of the Continental Congress, then rode to Mount Vernon.

Washington at Home

★

He arrived on Christmas Eve, determined to enjoy his first holiday at home in eight years.

Over four days of celebration, there were thousands of pounds of bacon consumed, gallons of homemade rye whiskey, and what he called an "attack of Christmas pies": layers of meat heaped inside a sturdy crust— turkey, goose, fowl, partridge and pigeon—seasoned with nutmeg, cloves, mace, pepper and salt and slathered with four pounds of butter, all cooked together for at least four hours. For dessert, there was Martha's "great cake"—containing 40 eggs, 4 pounds of butter, 4 pounds of powdered sugar, 5 pounds of fruit and a half pint of wine and brandy thrown in for good measure. Stir in Washington's extended family and more than a handful of friends and it was a welcome end to nearly a decade on the run. Martha hoped that "from this moment we should have been left to grow old in solitude and tranquility together."

There was reason for Martha to hope. Washington's seldom seen playful side emerged at Mount Vernon. As one measure of whimsy, his dogs' names included Sweetlips, Truelove, Drunkard, Music, Mopsey and Vulcan.

As a young man, after nursing the hurt of an unrequited love for his best friend's wife, he had opted for a practical match with Martha, a wealthy widow. Decades later, he counseled a friend that "more permanent and genuine happiness is to be found in the sequestered walks of connubial life, than in the giddy rounds of promiscuous pleasure."

But in the prime of life, he was no prude, appreciating attractive women and indulging in the occasional bawdy joke among close friends. He loved dancing, horseback riding, attending the theater, fishing and fireworks.

Washington rose around 4 a.m.* in the blue-black predawn and breakfasted at 7 a.m. on Indian cakes with honey and tea. He shared the founders' comforting mania for self-improvement and punctuated his day with long horseback rides, surveying his four farms. He took his dinner promptly at 4 p.m. (fish was a favorite dish), which he washed down with "from half a pint to a pint of Madeira wine." One visitor to Mount Vernon recounted, "The General with a few glasses of champagne got quite merry, and being with his intimate friends laughed and talked a good deal. Before strangers he is very reserved, and seldom says a word."

If there is a degree of defensiveness in this recounting of Washington's sense of humor, it's because history hasn't recorded him cracking many jokes or even cracking much of a smile. There's a famous story about Washington's insistence on personal distance: Alexander Hamilton bet their friend Gouverneur Morris that he couldn't saddle up to the general at a party and put his arm around him in a display of easy familiarity. When Morris walked up, draped an arm over Washington's shoulder, and exclaimed, "My dear general, how happy I am to see you looking so well," Washington greeted the arm with cold alarm and removed the offending appendage. Morris beat a quick retreat, to Hamilton's amusement.

"Washington was not fluent nor ready in conversation, and was inclined to be taciturn in general society," agreed James Madison in an interview with Washington's early biographer, Harvard president Jared Sparks. Yet "in the company of two or three intimate friends, he was talkative, and when a little excited was sometimes fluent and even eloquent." "The story so often repeated of his never laughing," Madison continued, was "wholly untrue; no man seemed more to enjoy gay conversation, though he took

---

* When asked by General Henry Lee about the secret to his enormous efficiency, Washington replied, "Sir, I rise at four o'clock, and a great deal of my work is done while others are still asleep."

little part in it himself. He was particularly pleased with the jokes, good humor, and hilarity of his companions."

Behind the mask of command, Washington could be earthy and inquisitive. Among his hobbies was animal husbandry, breeding the mules that would one day become synonymous with the South. He requested a jackass from the Spanish king and dubbed it "Royal Gift." But when a mare was placed in a paddock, with Washington urging on the breeding from an arm's length away, the Spanish jackass looked askance after a sniff or two and declined to consummate the relationship.

For all his accomplishments, what really inspired Washington was the life of a farmer. "It is honorable, it is amusing, and with judicious management, it is profitable," he wrote a friend in 1788. "To see plants rise from the Earth and flourish by the superior skill and bounty of the laborer fills a contemplative mind with ideas which are more easy to be conceived than expressed."

But the life of a gentleman farmer was made possible by slavery. Washington was one of the largest slave owners in Virginia, having inherited most of his 300 slaves from his wife's first husband.

As a budding revolutionary, he had taken a surprising antislavery stand as a leading member of the Virginia House of Burgesses, backing a sternly worded resolution: "During our present difficulties and distress, no slaves ought to be imported into any of the British colonies on this continent, and we take this opportunity of declaring our most earnest wishes to see an entire stop forever put to such a wicked, cruel, and unnatural trade."

Whatever progress was marked by those words was undercut, not just by a lack of follow-through from Washington and his fellow legislators, but also by the moral myopia of the planter elite. After all, Washington and his fellow Virginia freemen told the Crown: "we will use every means which Heaven hath given us to prevent our becoming its slaves." Washington went to war against the metaphorical slavery of British rule while practicing literal slavery himself.

During the war, Washington approved the enlistment of free blacks into the Continental Army, reversing his previous opposition, and witnessed the bravery of black soldiers in battle. His closest personal aide during the war was a biracial slave named Billy Lee, who accompanied him into conflicts and earned a place alongside the general in multiple portraits. But Billy Lee was the exception and not the rule.

After the war's end, Washington increasingly found his slaves both a moral and financial burden, privately writing that it was "a great repugnance" for him to buy more slaves, describing them as "that species of property which I have no inclination to possess." He wanted to see the United States evolve out of the injustice of slavery, but he was captive to its cruel economy.

At Mount Vernon, he busied himself with the business of the farm and enthusiastically obsessed over a scheme to spur interstate commerce through a series of canals as a way of spreading prosperity and mutual dependence that could curtail any separatist impulses.

But Washington's retirement from public service did not last. A weak central government under the Articles of Confederation accelerated his anxieties about whether the United States was ready for the responsibilities of liberty. An impotent Congress was treated with contempt by its members, who rarely showed up for meetings as debts piled high without the collective will to pay them.

Washington wrote in frustration to Virginia governor Benjamin Harrison, who was married to Martha's cousin, that "the disinclination of the individual States to yield competent powers to Congress for the federal government—their unreasonable jealousy of that body and of one another . . . will, if there is not a change in the system, be our downfall as a nation. This is as clear to me as the A, B, C; and I think we have opposed Great Britain, and have arrived at the present state of peace and independency, to very little purpose, if we cannot conquer our own prejudices."

Washington reached for a poetic metaphor to describe the self-indulgence of the states: "Like a young heir, come a little prematurely to a large inheritance, we shall wanton and run riot until we have brought our reputation to the brink of ruin, and then like him shall have to labor with the current of opinion when *compelled* perhaps, to do what prudence and common policy pointed out as plain as any problem in Euclid, in the first instance."

Threats came from the right and left. The states' failure to pay their debts led to the promiscuous printing of paper currency, which fueled inflation that sunk debtors even deeper in the hole and added to the insult of increased local land taxes. This hit farmers the hardest.

In August 1786, Continental Army captain Daniel Shays had enough. The veteran of the Battle of Bunker Hill was deep in debt, anxious that the taxman would seize his meager Massachusetts farm. Local jails were full of otherwise honest debtors and this didn't feel like the liberty he'd been promised. So he donned his old uniform and began armed drills with a homegrown agrarian army. Their local tax rebellion consisted of fellow veterans determined to derail bankruptcy proceedings amid rumbles about common property. Judges faced the armed protestors and fled.

As the drumbeat spread throughout New England, Shays won converts and there was talk of marching on Boston. Congress again proved impotent to raise funds to tamp down the insurgency. Only when some 1,500 supporters tried to storm the armory in Springfield, Massachusetts, was there organized response from local militias that put Shays's rebellious band on the run.

Washington watched Shays' Rebellion with alarm, writing General Henry Knox, "If three years ago any person had told me that at this day, I should see such a formidable rebellion against the laws and constitutions of our own making as now appears I should have thought him a bedlamite—a fit subject for a mad house."

Here was the mobocracy that democratic skeptics warned against. Madison believed that Shays' Rebellion "contributed more to that uneasiness which produced the [Constitutional] Convention, and prepared the public mind for a general reform" than all the failings of the Articles of Confederation.

Washington agreed. "We have probably had too good an opinion of human nature in forming our confederation," he wrote. "Experience has taught us that men will not adopt and carry into execution measures the best calculated for their own good without the intervention of a coercive power." A strong central government led by an effective executive was needed, as Washington had warned.

Amid the drift, whispers of monarchy were returning. The German-born revolutionary veteran General Steuben wrote Prussia's Prince Henry at the request of a member of Congress to ask whether he would consider becoming the constitutional monarch of the United States, replacing one inbred king with another.

To Washington, this longing for a monarch was as threatening as Shays' Rebellion. "I am told that even respectable characters speak of a monarchal form of government without horror," he wrote to John Jay. "From thinking proceeds speaking, thence to acting is often but a single step. But how irrevocable and tremendous! What a triumph for the advocates of despotism to find that we are incapable of governing ourselves, and that systems founded on the basis of equal liberty are merely ideal and fallacious!" They had come too far to die by suicide.

While Washington insisted, "it is not my business to embark again on a sea of troubles," he had already begun work with James Madison. Dour and dressed like a tiny pilgrim, Madison was a small and sickly legislator blessed with a sharp mind and tireless work ethic that allowed him to outshine more charismatic colleagues. Together they created a new vision of self-government, one in which "a liberal and energetic Constitution, well guarded and closely watched . . . might restore us to that degree of respectability and consequence to which we had a fair claim, and the brightest prospect of attaining."

Despite the obvious deficiencies of the Articles of Confederation, there did not seem to be much urgency on the part of most delegates to the first Constitutional Convention, in Annapolis. Only five showed up on time. After a follow-up meeting was announced at Independence Hall in Philadelphia for "the sole and express purpose of revising the Articles of Confederation," Washington had to wait thirteen days for the minimum seven states' representatives to appear so that he could gavel the proceedings to order as the convention's president.

Washington's stature gave the private proceedings legitimacy. He was enormously tall for his time, more than six feet two inches. He enhanced his presence with an eye toward dignified dress, wearing his wartime uniform to the opening of the Constitutional Convention. Experience expanded his aura of authority: more than half of the fifty-five representatives had served under his command in the war.

With delegates ranging in age from 26 to 81—their average age was 42—Washington took time to lobby members over tea and at taverns after the day's work had ended. Even in the closed-door sessions, where he refrained from speaking, his eyes betrayed his judgments and delegates sought his approval.

It is not an exaggeration to say that the Constitutional Convention succeeded because of Washington's place at the helm and his universally presumed presence as the first chief executive. A South Carolina delegate, Pierce Butler, testified to his impact: "Many of the members cast their eyes towards General Washington as President, and shaped their ideas of the powers to be given to a President by their opinions of his virtue."

In the end, after reversals of fortune and the division of the Virginia delegation, compromise reigned with the creation of three equal branches of government and a two-tiered legislature that balanced the needs of small and large states. Contentious moral issues such as the legality of slavery were shelved in favor of securing support from southern states. The new Constitution passed with 39 votes of the 55 delegates present. Not everyone was happy with the outcome. Washington's neighbor, George Mason, threatened to cut off his hand rather than sign the document, while Patrick Henry, the man who proclaimed "Give me liberty or give me death," compared the Constitution to the tyranny of King George III. But the deed was done and now subject to state ratification.

On the ride home to Mount Vernon after five long months away from Martha, accompanied by a four-volume set of *Don Quixote* he purchased the day the Constitution was signed, Washington's stagecoach nearly slipped off a treacherous bridge in a torrential storm. One horse fell fifteen feet, almost pulling the coach and occupant into the murky and turbulent Elk River.

The fight for state ratification of the Constitution was more fierce than the negotiations over drafting it. Washington accepted many of his friends' opposition even as he defended his decision, explaining in nearly identical letters to Patrick Henry and Benjamin Harrison, "I wish the Constitution which is offered had been made more perfect, but I sincerely believe it is the best that could be obtained at this time." He notably did not believe that the Constitution should be seen as an infallible document, telling his nephew Bushrod, a future Supreme Court justice, "I do not conceive that we are more inspired—have more wisdom—or possess more virtue than those who will come after us."

Washington was careful to seem above the political fray, watching the fights from afar, reading local papers, and exchanging letters to get the latest gossip on its chances for passage. But in reading over the pro and con arguments, he became more convinced that the Constitution had struck the right balance. The overheated objections arguing that it carried the seeds of tyranny were specious and self-interested: "It is clear to my conception that no government before introduced among mankind ever contained so many checks and such efficacious restraints to prevent it from degenerating into any species of oppression."

The debates over the Constitution seeded the first partisan divides in the nation—the Federalists, who were in favor of ratification, versus the Anti-Federalists (though as Congressman Elbridge Gerry slyly noted, it would have been far more favorable for opponents of the Constitution to frame the debate as being between the "Rats" and "Anti-Rats"). Underlying the battles was an enduring ideological conflict: advocates of a more centralized government against advocates for states' rights, urban versus rural America, split broadly between North and South.

Support for the Constitution was bolstered by arguments supplied by Madison, Hamilton, and Jay in the Federalist Papers. The three framed the debate at a breakneck pace, publishing eighty-seven articles under the byline "Publius"—taking the name of an ancient Roman aristocrat who toppled the monarchy and established the republic—between October 1787 and the following August.

"It seems to have been reserved to the people of this country," explained Hamilton in the first dispatch for New York's *Independent Journal,* "to decide the important question, whether societies of men are really capable or not of establishing good government from reflection and choice, or whether they are forever destined to depend, for their political constitutions, on accident and force." The founders knew they were playing for history's highest stakes.

The great gamble paid off. One by one, state conventions fell into line. First came Delaware, followed by Pennsylvania and New Jersey. With the mid-Atlantic states secure, most southern states came next, though tiny, perpetually problematic Rhode Island and North Carolina declined to ratify. New York and Virginia were in effect the two biggest swing states. But with New Hampshire's vote on June 21, 1788, the Constitution was adopted to the clanging of church bells that Washington could hear from his portico at Mount Vernon.

Looking back on the moment years later, Washington pronounced it "the new constellation of this hemisphere" and "a new phenomenon in the political and moral world, and an astonishing victory gained by enlightened reason over brutal force."

A Reluctant President

★

H igh-minded moments of self-congratulation were short-lived. With ratification came calls for Washington to assume the office of president. Even before the official vote, he was busy trying to tie up his affairs at Mount Vernon, struggling to secure a loan to pay off his debts while preparing an inaugural address.

Washington worried that he had more to lose than gain by becoming the first president of the United States. He was uncertain of his capacity to serve as a head of state and always covetous of his most precious possession, his reputation. All was not well on the home front, either. Martha was not pleased about the prospective move to New York City undercutting her dreams of a well-deserved retirement. She never cared for politics. Pleading domestic responsibilities, she declined to accompany her husband to his inaugural.

Against this anxious backdrop, Washington began working on the first inaugural address in the winter of 1789. He entrusted the task to his wartime aide-de-camp David Humphreys, a Yale-educated schoolteacher and sometime poet who irritated his colleagues with late-night poetry readings. Humphreys had the advantage of proximity. After the war he lived at Mount Vernon, serving as Washington's personal secretary. But Humphreys did not have the gift of brevity, and his first draft of the inaugural ran seventy-three pages, a rolling rumination of patriotic aphorisms, prayer, directions to Congress and denials of dynastic ambition.

Included in the draft were some memorable lines that have survived the scissors of early biographers and admirers, most notably when Washington was to declare, "I rejoice in the belief that mankind will reverse the absurd position that the many were made for the few; and that they will not continue slaves in one part of the globe, when they can be freemen in another."

Washington copied the speech into his own hand and sent the draft off to James Madison to review in early January 1789 after asking for the most secure means of delivering such a "private and confidential" letter. Madison pronounced it "so strange a production" and quickly decamped to Mount Vernon for a week, where they worked on a new, slimmer draft.

On April Fool's Day, 1789, Washington wrote General Knox, "my movements to the chair of government will be accompanied by feelings not unlike those of a culprit who is going to the place of his execution." Two weeks later, he left Mount Vernon, confessing to his diary that he possessed "a mind oppressed with more anxious and painful sensations than I have words to express." The *Pennsylvania Packet* described his departure for duty in dramatic terms: Washington had chosen to "bid adieu to the peaceful retreat of Mount Vernon, in order to save his country once more from confusion and anarchy."

On the seven-day, 240-mile trip to New York, Washington was greeted with petal-strewn streets and triumphal arches, finding it all a bit embarrassing. He crossed the Hudson into the capital city on a barge surrounded by tall ships and celebratory cannon fire, accompanied by the strains of "God Save the King." The city boasted a population of 50,000 people, but the character of the city was already established. As John Adams complained, "They talk very loud, very fast and altogether. If they ask you a question, before you can utter three words of your answer they will break out upon you again and talk away."

New York transformed its old City Hall into a national capital at the hands of French-born revolutionary veteran Pierre Charles L'Enfant, who fitted the structure with marble columns and sixteen-foot windows, establishing the Federalist style of architecture for the cost of $32,000 raised by local citizens. Inside, the walls were adorned with thirteen stars to symbolize the states and a motif of arrows and olive branches underneath forty-six-foot-high ceilings where the House and Senate met.

On the morning of April 30, Washington took the oath of office in the second-floor portico at the top of Broad Street. He wore white stockings and a modest brown broadcloth suit specially ordered from the Hartford Woolen Manufactory in Connecticut, with metal buttons adorned with eagles, while a ceremonial sword hung by his side. The city overflowed with tourists from across the nation, some sleeping in hastily erected tents. A sea of upturned faces packed every street and alley spread out before him.

Washington spoke in such a low voice that even those close craned their necks to hear him. After improvising "So help me God" and kissing a Bible from a local Masonic temple placed on a crimson pillow, he was proclaimed president of the United States, received a thirteen-gun salute amid deafening cheers and then walked into the Senate Chamber to deliver his inaugural address, interposing the personal and the political, the opportunities and the responsibilities of the moment:

> There is no truth more thoroughly established, than that there
> exists in the economy and course of nature, an indissoluble union
> between virtue and happiness, between duty and advantage,
> between the genuine maxims of an honest and magnanimous policy,
> and the solid rewards of public prosperity and felicity. . . . And
> since the preservation of the sacred fire of liberty, and the destiny
> of the republican model of Government, are justly considered as
> deeply, perhaps as finally staked, on the experiment entrusted to the
> hands of the American people.

It was the first statement of presidential perspective. But a trenchant if often unkind observer, Senator William Maclay of Pennsylvania, described an awkward scene in his dishy diary:

This great man was agitated and embarrassed more than he ever was by the leveled cannon or pointed musket. He trembled, and at several times could scarce make out to read, though it must be supposed he had often read it before. He put part of the fingers of his left hand into the side of what I think the tailors call the fall of the breeches, changing the paper into his left hand. After some time he then did the same with some of the fingers of his right hand. When he came to the words "all the world," he made a flourish with his right hand which left rather an ungainly impression. I sincerely, for my part, wished all set ceremony in the hands of the dancing masters, and that this first of men had read off his address in the plainest manner, without ever taking his eyes from the paper, for I felt hurt that he was not first in everything.

It took Washington twenty minutes to read the 1,400-word speech. Once the inaugural was completed, with the streets too crowded to accommodate coaches, Washington waded through the cheering crowd to give a prayer of thanksgiving at St. Paul's Chapel, then attended a private dinner at New York chancellor Robert Livingston's house followed by a night of fireworks in a strange city that he would now call his own.

"Good government, the best of blessings, now commences under favorable auspices," crowed one newspaper. But the path was dimly lit. The Constitution required the separation of powers and presented a broad structure of government guided by republican principles. Its actual operation was a blank slate. And so Washington's first term was preoccupied by establishing the precedent of being president. "Few who are not philosophical spectators can realize the difficult and delicate part which a man in my situation had to act," he wrote. "I walk on untrodden ground."

Washington selected forty-six-year-old John Jay to serve as chief justice of the Supreme Court, which would not hear a case for over a year. It was not initially known whether Washington's choice for secretary of state, forty-four-year-old Thomas Jefferson, was in France or en route to the

United States. His department consisted of only five full-time staffers. Secretary of War Henry Knox, the lone holdover from the Articles of Confederation era, had only a clerk and assistant. Attorney General Edmund Randolph was considered a consultant, without staff, and encouraged to represent private clients on the side. The Treasury Department dwarfed them all, led by thirty-four-year-old Alexander Hamilton, with a staff of thirty-nine clerks in New York and dozens of collectors and inspectors along the coast.

Washington's cabinet meetings were modeled on his senior staff military meetings during the war. He solicited a wide range of opinions and then made up his mind. At the same time, the first Congress was clustered in Federal Hall, paid a then-princely sum of two dollars a day and set about fitfully passing new laws and fighting among themselves.

Party lines were not defined. Madison initially served as both a speechwriter to the president and a congressman who drafted the official responses to those presidential declarations. The rough coalitions reflected regional differences: urban versus rural, North versus South, with rural southerners feeling particularly persecuted.

Senator Butler of South Carolina raged against the division and dysfunction. "Never was a man more egregiously disappointed than I am," he wrote. "I came here full of hopes that the greatest liberality would be exercised; that the consideration of the whole, and the general good, would take place of every other object; but here I find men scrambling for partial advantages, State interests and in short, a train of those narrow, impolitic measures that must, after a while, shake the Union to its very foundation."

Vice President John Adams was also disappointed in the quality of men in the first Congress: "You might search in vain for the flashes of Demosthenes, or for the splendid illumination of Cicero," he complained. To Connecticut's John Trumbull "everything seems conducted by Party, Intrigue & Cabal," while Maryland's William Smith despaired, "It is truly distressing to be detailed here so long & do so little good."

These complaints about Congress would echo across the centuries. But despite the fights, the first Congress and first administration were productive partners for a time. The federal judiciary and the patent office were established. Treason, piracy, counterfeiting, and murder on government property were declared the first federal crimes. Washington signed legislation calling for "the encouragement and protection of manufacturing in America" and signed a proclamation declaring a day of Thanksgiving in November. At the behest of James Madison and approval of President Washington, Congress began debating ratification of the Bill of Rights, the unfinished business of the Constitutional Convention. The first national census was also conducted, which determined that among America's 4 million citizens, only 5 percent lived in towns with a population of more than 2,500.

From his rented three-story mansion on Cherry Street, Washington indulged in a morning ride and afternoon walk along the Battery, overlooking New York Bay, but was otherwise occupied with setting an executive example that could outlast him. He refused all social invitations, even to funerals, for fear of creating favoritism or the equivalent of court intrigues. On Tuesday afternoons, he received unscheduled visitors, formal affairs during which he would stand by the fireplace with a ceremonial sword to greet his guests.

Some citizens bristled at the trappings of pomp and circumstance that seemed more befitting of a monarchy than a republic. Jefferson railed in private against the "mimicry of royal forms and ceremonies" he saw at Federal Hall. Some New Yorkers fumed when a portrait of the president was commissioned to hang in City Hall. Others mocked his ornate carriage, led by six white horses. At the homespun state suppers, always served promptly at three o'clock, Washington came under criticism for his stoic silence, punctuated by his odd habit of occasionally drumming his silverware on the table.

He put on a brave face, but Washington's body was rebelling under the pressure of the presidency. Months after assuming the office, he was bedridden with a golf-ball-sized malignant carbuncle on his left thigh, which had to be cut out without anesthesia, resulting in six weeks of bed rest.

He confessed to David Humphreys, "I know it is very doubtful whether ever I shall arise from this bed and God knows it is perfectly indifferent to me whether I do or not." Humphreys responded: "If, Sir, it is indifferent to you, it is far from being so to your friends and your Country. For they believe it has still great need of your services."

Whether he liked it or not, Washington was the glue that held the new nation together. "While we had a Washington and his virtues to cement and guard the union, it might be safe," Congressman John Vining of Delaware despaired, "but when he should leave us, who would inherit his virtues, and possess his influence? Who would remain to embrace and draw to a centre those hearts which the authority of his virtues alone kept in union?"

The individual states were rebellious and jealous. Indian attacks in the western wilderness led to complaints that the government was permitting "the distant members of the Empire to be robbed, murdered, scalped, and carried away into captivity by an insignificant herd of tawny banditti."

The Congress was dispirited and frequently deadlocked, consumed by petty rivalries. Talk of secession already festered. And inside Washington's cabinet, the philosophical divisions were growing bitter and personal.

The Seeds of the Two-Party System

★

The Constitution was written without mentioning political parties. There was an idealistic assumption among the founders that elected representatives would reason together as individuals and their differences would reflect their constituents' interests. The separation of powers between the president, the Supreme Court and Congress would supply the necessary checks and balances.

But there was no pure, pre-partisan Eden in America. The fault lines that erupted into our two-party system extended directly from the fractious fights over the Constitution.

When the first Congress convened in New York, the states' rights advocates who had opposed ratifying the Constitution remained suspicious of the new government, anxious about any further encroachment of federal power. Beneath these political resentments the deeper divisions were regional—North versus South, urban versus rural—and they represented long-standing local prejudices rooted in class and perceptions of privilege.

Two debates from Washington's first term shaped our democracy in fundamental ways: Alexander Hamilton's centralized financial plan for the federal government to assume state war debts, and the location of the final capital of the federal government. Beneath policy preferences were intense political rivalries. Power, money and ambition drive resentments among men and these passions also helped form the foundation of our partisan system.

Thomas Jefferson's reentry into American society after a decade as ambassador to France had been rocky. This brilliant Virginia aristocrat—a lover of books, fine wine and his slave Sally Hemings—fancied himself a populist devoted to the international expansion of liberty. Acclimating himself to the new administration, he was offended by what he saw as the trappings of monarchy surrounding President Washington and the drift toward corrupt British systems.

In the early months of 1790, when he emerged from the painful fog of one of his periodic migraines, Jefferson was shocked to see the details of Hamilton's financial plans. This young immigrant upstart, who had been an obscure artillery officer when Jefferson was writing the Declaration of Independence, seemed to be trying to roll back the revolution by centralizing economic power in the hands of an urban elite.

While Jefferson affected a ramshackle republican persona, casually dressed and often professing his lack of political ambition, he enjoyed its subterranean machinations. Behind the scenes, he rallied his fellow southerners in Congress to oppose the administration's efforts. And no ally was more important than James Madison.

Madison and Jefferson had first met in the fall of 1776 as members of the Virginia assembly, with Madison a bit in awe of the older, taller author of the Declaration. They became close friends and corresponded frequently throughout Jefferson's overseas deployment during the debacle of the Articles of Confederation.

But in the years between the war and inauguration, with Jefferson in Paris, Madison became Washington's most trusted aide for all things legislative and lyrical. More than any man, he'd formed the intellectual foundation of the Constitution while he and Hamilton became brothers in arms as the principle coauthors of the Federalist Papers.

But Madison's focus on creating a stronger central government began to fade as the reality of politics took the place of theory. Passed over for an appointed Senate seat from Virginia because of lingering bitterness from Patrick Henry over the fight for ratification, Madison successfully ran for a congressional seat in a district dominated by Anti-Federalists, whose skepticism about the Constitution had morphed into skepticism about the Washington administration and soon hardened into outright opposition.

Madison did not shift his loyalties overnight. At first, he successfully balanced advocating for the administration's legislative agenda with representing his rural constituents. But when Hamilton unveiled his vision for a more centralized economic system, Madison began to feel that Anti-Federalist anxieties had been justified.

While Hamilton saw his financial plan as a means of securing independence by establishing credit and paying down debts, opponents saw it as aping the British system, creating an overly centralized government that would protect urban financiers at the expense of small towns and farmers.

Representatives from rural southern states had long feared the creation of an economic aristocracy modeled on what they saw as the worst of corrupt European society. Now it seemed to be coming to pass. The rights of individual states were falling further away as the federal government grew even stronger.

At first, the debates were high-minded, with Madison making the case that Hamilton was seeking to assume powers that were never granted by the Constitution. The specter of debt, however deployed, was an abomination to Madison's sense of fiscal responsibility ("a public debt is injurious to the interests of the people, and baneful to the virtue of government") and seemed to ignore the cycle of war, debt and taxation that had sparked the revolution.

The Treasury secretary stressed that the debt would be temporary: he "ardently" wished to "see it incorporated, as a functional maxim, in the system of public credit of the United States, that the creation of debt should always be accompanied by the means of extinguishment."

This was a difference of opinion, not a difference of ideals. Nonetheless, Hamilton was blindsided by his former ally's opposition, concluding

"Mr. Madison cooperating with Mr. Jefferson is at the heart of a faction decidedly hostile to me."

Hamilton's power over administration policy also drove personal resentment. Madison's complaints about "satellites and sycophants" surrounding the president betrayed a bit of an outsider's envy. But if Madison was an insider on the outside of the administration's executive actions, then Hamilton was the ultimate outsider on the inside.

The unelected immigrant had accumulated the largest budget and bureaucracy in the federal government. Opponents sneered about his common Caribbean roots and spread rumors that he was a mixed race Creole, but there was no denying he had the ear of the president. To make matters worse, his assumption of state debt elevated speculators over soldiers in an attempt to strengthen the new nation's credit. Unsurprisingly, this proved politically unpopular. The backlash fueled (ill-founded) suspicions that Hamilton was personally corrupt, spurring a series of congressional investigations by political opponents loyal to Madison and Jefferson. A brief economic panic fueled by speculators only further increased anxieties.

Working in concert, Madison and Jefferson lobbied against the proposal and for a time it seemed as though they might succeed in blocking Hamilton's ambitions. Alarmed at the prospect of his financial plan's looming defeat in Congress, Hamilton set about politicking with representatives, using New York City's position as the temporary capital of the new nation as a bargaining chip. Then the most famous horse-trading in American political history took place over dinner between the feuding founding brothers. Invited to Jefferson's apartment at 57 Maiden Lane on June 20, 1790, Hamilton sat down to a high-stakes wine-and-dine negotiation with Jefferson and Madison. By the end of the night, New York lost the capital to Virginia and America had strong central government.

Congress passed the banking bill and the assumption of state debt, as well as a measure to move the capital to Philadelphia while a permanent capital was built on the banks of the Potomac. Jefferson blithely described it as "the least bad of all the turns the thing could take." But the deal could not conceal the growing contempt between the former friends, who now considered themselves political enemies.

Sometimes history turns on a hinge and in the fateful nine months between the fall of 1791 and the summer of 1792, America's fitful partisan impulses exploded into full-fledged combat.

The proliferation of the partisan press was largely to blame. Always uncomfortable with direct conflict, Jefferson believed that John Fenno's slavishly pro-administration newspaper, the *Gazette of the United States*—to which Hamilton often anonymously contributed and Jefferson described as "a paper of pure Toryism, disseminating the doctrine of monarchy, aristocracy and the exclusion of the influence of the people"—needed to be counteracted with a steadfast administration critic to ensure dissent and diversity of opinion.

On a famed botany excursion up the Hudson in May and June of 1791, Jefferson and Madison, accompanied by two slaves, observed maple trees and Hessian flies while hatching the Democratic-Republican Party. In New York, they met with sympathetic politicos—including future vice president to Jefferson and Hamilton-assassin Aaron Burr—and sought out one of Madison's old college classmates, a newspaper editor and political poet named Philip Freneau. His hatred of the British stemmed from his service in the revolutionary war and subsequently being captured by English sailors on the high seas. Jefferson and Madison wanted Freneau to move to Philadelphia and start a new national newspaper that would hold the administration to account. Freneau wanted more money, and so Jefferson arranged for him to simultaneously work as a translator in the State Department, actively undermining the administration within which he served.

On Halloween of 1791, the *National Gazette* began publishing. With a platform now in place, Jefferson encouraged his allies to attack Hamilton in the press, exhorting Madison, "For god's sake, my dear sir, take up your pen, select the most striking heresies, and cut him to pieces in the face of the public."

Four years before, in the Federalist Papers, Madison had denounced factions, the spirit of self-interested partisanship, which had corrupted previous democracies. Now, in one of the most impactful flip-flops in American history, he became convinced that only a loyal opposition could save the republic from usurpers like Hamilton. In a series of eighteen essays written under pseudonyms for the *National Gazette* over five months, Madison argued that the rise of political parties was inevitable and the natural framework of parties was not multiple—as in many parliamentary systems—but two, in effect creating a duopoly. "By making one party a check on the other, so far as the existence of parties cannot be prevented, nor their views accommodated," Madison wrote. "If this is not the language of reason, it is that of republicanism."

This logic allowed Madison, Jefferson and their growing number of followers to believe that their opposition to the Washington administration was not partisan at all, but instead a populist pushback against a small cabal that was corrupting the promise of the revolution. In their eyes, Hamilton was manipulating Washington. "I am extremely afraid that the [president] may not be sufficiently aware of the snares that may be laid for his good intentions by men whose politics at bottom are very different from his own," Madison wrote, while denouncing "an assumption of prerogatives not clearly found in the Constitution and having the appearance of being copied from a monarchical model."

Over time, the Madison-led, Jefferson-inspired Democratic-Republicans in Congress increasingly acted as a political coalition in opposition to the administration. Initially, the allies of President Washington were known informally as "friends of the government," unhelpfully adopting the same term British Loyalists used during the war. Confronted by an organized opposition, they soon began calling themselves Federalists, recalling their support for ratifying the Constitution and its call for a strong central government, communicating their commitment to national unity or, at least, the policies of the Washington administration.

The battle between self-styled Democratic-Republicans and the Federalists they called "monocrats" had begun. Dueling essays attacking Hamilton and Jefferson soon proliferated in the partisan press. A cold war was being conducted within Washington's cabinet. It would soon turn hot.

The Death of the One-Term Dream

★

By the end of his first term, Washington had enough. He'd established the precedent of presidential leadership and traveled across the states of the North and South on goodwill tours to unite the nation. From Portsmouth, New Hampshire, to Savannah, Georgia, Washington stayed in taverns and inns to avoid the appearance of personal favoritism that could come from choosing local homes, but otherwise mingled with his fellow citizens over food and festivities, toasted as a founding father in the flesh. He moved the executive mansion from New York to Philadelphia, as construction on the final capital that would bear his name commenced amid mud and mosquitoes. For all the accolades, he was physically exhausted and deeply frustrated by the rise of partisanship.

On Sunday, February 19, 1792, Washington dropped a note to James Madison—apparently still unaware of the full extent of his partisan intrigues—asking him to drop by the Philadelphia executive mansion at eleven o'clock that morning, if he "could make it convenient to spare half an hour from other matters." In their meeting, Washington explained that he wanted to make a permanent return home to Mount Vernon at the end of his term, which expired in March of the following year.

The news must have come as a shock. After all, the Constitution was written without limits on presidential terms. But it was little more than a trial balloon at the time: nothing more seems to have been said about the request until May 5, when Washington followed up by asking Madison's advice on the "*mode* and *time* most proper for making known that intention." According to Madison's notes of their subsequent conversation, Washington was debating not *if* to decline a second term but *how* to do it, wanting to choose a method "which would be most remote from the appearance of arrogantly presuming on his re-election" and a time "as would be most convenient to the public in making the choice of his successor."

Washington explained that "he could not believe or convince himself anywise necessary to the successful administration of the government" and again confessed his insecurities that "he had from the beginning found himself deficient in many of the essential qualifications, owing to his inexperience in the forms of public business, his unfitness to judge of legal questions, and questions arising out of the Constitution."

A torrent of complaints followed. Washington was irritated by the "spirit of party" in his government and expressed concerns about his health, both physical and mental. He was "in the decline of his life, his health becoming sensibly more infirm, and perhaps his faculties also." He'd "rather go to his farm, take his spade in his hand, and work for his bread, than remain in the present situation."

This was a breathtaking confession by the first president of the United States. Madison began privately arguing against Washington's wishes, telling him, "However novel or difficult the business might have been to him, it could not be doubted that with the aid of the official opinions and informations within his command, his judgment must have been as competent in all cases, as that of any one who could have been put in his place, and in many cases certainly more so; that in the great point of conciliating and uniting all parties under a government which had excited such violent controversies and divisions, it was well known that his services had been in a manner essential."

Moreover, Madison made the case that "the conciliating influence of a temperate and wise administration would, before another term of four years should run out, give such a tone and firmness to the Government as would secure it against danger" from enemies foreign and domestic.

Washington took in Madison's argument and turned to other subjects. But as the meeting was ending, he repeated his wish for a draft of a farewell address to be finished before the adjournment of Congress.

Four days later, Madison called on Washington to recommend "a direct address of notification to the public in time for its proper effect on the election," but again pleaded with Washington to not take such a momentous step. Washington sidestepped the advice and asked Madison to "suggest any matters that might occur as proper to be included in what he might say to Congress."

From Mount Vernon, Washington wrote Madison on May 20, explaining that he appreciated his efforts to dissuade him: "I have not been unmindful of the sentiments expressed by you. . . . On the contrary, I have again and again revolved them with thoughtful anxiety." He expressed concern that a "declaration to retire, not only carries with it the appearance of vanity and self-importance, but it may be construed into a maneuver to be invited to remain. And, on the other hand, to say nothing implies consent; or at any rate, would leave the matter in doubt, and to decline afterward might be deemed as bad, & uncandid."

Despite this self-doubt, rooted in questions about perception, Washington declared that "nothing short of conviction that my dereliction of the Chair of Government (if it should be the desire of the people to continue to me in it) would involve the country in serious disputes respecting the chief magistrate and the disagreeable consequences which might result there from in the floating and divided opinions which seem to prevail at present, could, in any wise, induce me to relinquish the determination I have formed."

And so Washington asked Madison to "turn your thoughts to a valedictory address from me to the public, expressing in plain and modest terms—that having been honored with the Presidential chair, and to the best of my abilities contributed to the organization and administration of the government—that having arrived at the period of life when the private walks of it, in the shade of retirement, becomes necessary and will be most pleasing to me; and the spirit of government may render a rotation in the elective officers of it more congenial with their ideas of liberty and safety, that I take my leave of them as a public man."

In this note, Washington also drew direct parallels between his postwar Circular to the States and the present: "I take the liberty at my departure from civil, as I formally did at my military exit, to invoke a continuation of the blessings and Providence upon it—and upon all those who are supporters of its interest and the promoters of harmony, order, and good government."

In a handoff worthy of a spy novel, Washington declined to trust the postal service with the news and arranged a shadowy transfer of the letter to Madison on the road between Mount Vernon and Philadelphia, near present-day Georgetown.

Twenty-six days later, Madison sent back his first draft of the Farewell Address, building squarely on Washington's extensive suggestions. It was a straightforward document, devoted primarily to explaining Washington's decision to leave the presidency, and otherwise focused exclusively on his admonition to elevate national unity over all other concerns:

> We may all be considered as the children of one country. We have
> all been embarked on one common cause. We have all had our
> share in common sufferings and common successes. The portion
> of the Earth allotted to the theater of our fortunes, fulfils our most
> sanguine desires. All of its essential interests are the same; while its
> diversities arising from climate from soil and other local and lesser
> peculiarities, will naturally form a mutual relation of the parts, that
> may give the whole a more entire independence than has perhaps
> fallen to the lot of any other nation.

Like the texts prepared by modern presidents and their speechwriters, it was a collaborative effort—but in this case, the speechwriter was the primary author of the Constitution and a future president himself.

As requested, Madison recommended a date for the public announce-ment—mid-September 1792—and suggested the means of delivery: "a simple publication in the newspapers" addressed "to the people," who were "his only constituents."

This suggestion to bypass a formal address to Congress was revolu-tionary: a departure from the precedent that saw kings and heads of state addressing their parliaments from thrones. The American president was accountable only to the people.

But while Washington seemed to have made up his mind to finally retire beneath his oft-cited "vine and fig tree," his surrogate sons at the highest levels of the young government weren't done lobbying him to avert what they saw as a looming disaster for the republic.

Jefferson fired off a preemptive shot, presumably in collusion with Madi-son. "The confidence of the whole union is centered in you," he wrote. "Your being at the helm will be more than an answer to every argument which can be used to alarm and lead the people in any corner into violence or secession. North and South will hang together, if they have you to hang on."

The volleys came in quick succession. Alexander Hamilton field-tested the prospect of Washington's resignation among what he termed "the opin-ions of persons whose opinions were worth knowing"—and appealed to Washington's sense of duty and vanity. "The impression is uniform—that your declining would be to be deplored as the greatest evil that could befall the country at the present juncture, and as critically hazardous to your own reputation," Hamilton wrote. "I pray God that you will determine to make a further sacrifice of your tranquility and happiness to the public good. I trust, that it need not continue above a year or two more"—holding out the possibility of a midterm resignation more suited to a prime minister than what we now see as a president's fidelity to full terms.

Finally, Attorney General Edmund Randolph wrote a blunt letter to the president. "We must gain time for the purpose of attracting confidence in the government by experience of its benefits. . . . The public deliberations require stability. You alone can give them stability. You suffered to yield, when the voice of your country summoned you to the administration. Should a civil war arise, you cannot stay at home. And how much easier it will be to disperse the factions which are rushing to this catastrophe, than to subdue them after they shall appear in arms?"

The specter of civil war was invoked to Washington by all three of his closest cabinet confidants. This was not an abstract concern. It appeared likely without the unifying presence of Washington at the helm.

During this critical period of decision, Washington began to understand the extent to which partisanship had infected his cabinet through furious proxy wars in the press. Now aware of Philip Freneau's role as both State Department employee and editor of the *National Gazette*, he asked Jefferson and Hamilton about their respective roles in the anonymous back-and-forth attacks.

Hamilton quickly copped to writing his essays under assumed names, an honesty perhaps made easier by the fact that he had been defending the president's positions. But Jefferson instinctively evaded the truth, denying that he had known Freneau would start up a newspaper, while proclaiming "I can protest in the presence of heaven" that he had not tried to influence the paper's contents, let alone endorse their anti-administration editorials. His only rooting interest was in the "chastisement of the aristocratical and monarchical writers, and not to any criticisms of the proceedings of government."

As huge as Jefferson's and Hamilton's conflicting ambitions were, even these seemed briefly insignificant in the late summer of 1792, in the face of the disastrous consequences they knew they could not forestall should the president leave office. What was needed was time. What was needed was Washington.

And so, slowly, Washington reconsidered. He did not give up his one-term dream in a moment of resolve or epiphany. The suggested mid-September deadline came and went. By the start of October, with the next scheduled election weeks away, Washington was still playing faint lip service to the idea of retirement, but the uniform reaction of associates outside his family was clearly shifting his calculus. By October 20, Hamilton was assured by his revolutionary-era friend (and future secretary of war) James McHenry that "[h]appily for public tranquility the present incumbent, after a serious struggle intends, if I mistake not, to submit to another election."

Washington may have been reluctant, but members of the Electoral College were not. They unanimously reelected him in December, while John Adams fought off a challenge from Anti-Federalist New York governor George Clinton to remain vice president.

A sense of duty once again outweighed his personal preferences. Washington's second inaugural address, on March 4, 1793, was the shortest in American history—135 words, half the length of the Gettysburg Address. There was none of the eloquence that can come with economy of language. Instead, this was a terse and reluctant recognition of the ceremony—with Washington wasting precious words by taking the time to laconically state that "the Constitution requires an oath of office. This oath I am now about to take, and in your presence."

Four years earlier, Washington confessed to his friend General Knox that he was going to his inauguration like a criminal to the place of his execution. Now more than ever, he looked and sounded the part. He only knew half of what was ahead.

Second-Term Blues

★

In second terms, promises of hope and change turn to hard facts and consequence. But there was no precedent to guide Washington over the tumultuous events of his second term that would inform his Farewell Address.

Washington, who famously declared "I was no party man myself, and the first wish of my heart was, if parties did exist, to reconcile them," was forced to fully confront the factions within his cabinet, fueled by duplicity bordering on treason and enflamed by the rise of a partisan press that infuriated him with its unaccountable and often manic attacks on his character.

The partisan divisions were deeper than rivalries for power and regional perspectives: they were rooted in suspicions over international loyalties. The government was divided between those who were enamored of the French Revolution, and those who favored neutrality in the latest war between France and Britain. These political fights threatened to throw the country into paroxysms of separatism and secession, encouraging armed rebellion in distant regions and even the possibility of a foreign-backed coup d'état.

The flashpoints of this crisis have become the dusty stuff of history classes: a litany of names such as Citizen Genêt, the Whiskey Rebellion and the Jay Treaty. All carried with them the force of drama in real time, as enemies within and without pushed America to the brink of disunion.

The resolutions of Washington's Farewell Address would be forged from these fires.

The second term sapped Washington's remaining strength, as he had known it would. Forced to confront a dizzying array of attacks against his character and his country, an exhausted Washington grew more irritable. The mask of command slipped more often and the real man shone through, emotionally raw but still determined to steel himself against the storm.

At sixty-four, Washington was already well beyond the average life expectancy of the time. His impressive physical attributes are so well known as to drive biographers' descriptions to blur into one broad man-crush. The portraitist Gilbert Stuart told a colleague that had Washington "been born in the forests . . . he would have been the fiercest man among the savage tribes." But a handful of descriptions from Washington's second term break free of the hero worship to reveal the real man up close, as in the following dossier-like sketch from the secretary to the British minister:

> His person is tall and sufficiently graceful; his face well formed,
> his complexion rather pale, with a mild philosophic gravity in the
> expression of it. In his air and manner he displays much *natural*
> dignity; in his address he is cold, reserved, and even phlegmatic,
> though without the least appearance of haughtiness or ill nature;
> it is the effect, I imagine, of constitutional diffidence. That caution
> and circumspection which formed so striking and well known
> feature in his military, and indeed in his political character, is very
> strongly marked in his countenance, for his eyes retire inward . . .
> and have nothing of the fire of animation or openness in their
> expression. If this circumspection is accompanied by discernment
> and penetration, as I am informed it is, and I should be inclined to
> believe from the judicious choice he has generally made of persons
> to fill public stations, he possesses the two great requisites of the
> statesman, the faculty of concealing his own sentiments and of
> discovering those of other men. A certain degree of indecision,

however, a want of vigor and energy, may be observed in some of
his actions, and are indeed the obvious result of too refined caution.

Henrietta Liston, the blue-eyed wife of the British ambassador, was a
favorite of Washington and often selected to sit by his side at state dinners.
She offered her own description from an intimate distance:

Naturally grave and silent, his mode of life had rendered him
frugal and temperate. Vanity in him was a very limited passion,
and prudence his striking trait. Most people say and do too much.
Washington, partly from constitutional taciturnity, but still more
from natural sagacity and careful observation, never fell into
this common error. Nature had been liberal to him. To a majestic
figure was added a native unaffected gracefulness of deportment
and dignity of manner, which was rather improved by a liking—I
will not say a fondness—for dress. . . .
    Though neither a man of learning, nor of much acquired
knowledge, he possessed, not only great good sense and a sound
judgment, but was a man of observation and of deep reflection.
. . . Naturally hot-tempered, cold-hearted, and guarded, he
acquired a uniform command over his passions on public
occasions, but in private and particularly with his servants, its
violence sometimes broke out. His countenance was peculiarly
pleasant when he laughed, which he apparently did with good
humor at the jests of others, and he told his own occasionally
with gaiety; but it was the flash of a moment; gaiety was not
natural to him. He rose at all seasons early. It was his constant
practice to reply to every letter he received, whether the contents
were of more or less importance, agreeable or otherwise. His
first and last pleasure appeared to be farming; on that theme he
always talked freely, being on other topics extremely cautious not

to commit himself, and never spoke on any subject of which he was not master.

These two descriptions of President Washington toward the end of his second term in Philadelphia are admiring but not uncritical, capturing the degree of distance and lack of fiery wit that made some of his contemporaries both underestimate and resent him.

Washington's formality bred respect more than affection. But the upstart nation was loved as well as respected by many around the world. The revelation of America's revolution enflamed imaginations. Reformers in Poland were inspired to pass Europe's first written constitution. As far away as Mozambique, rebellions against Arab masters were justified to passing British privateers by locals declaring, "America is free. Could we not be?"

So it was a bitter irony that many of the dramas surrounding Washington's second term were set against the backdrop of the French Revolution. It all began as a hopeful bit of flattery—America's revolutionary fire of liberty lit a spark in France. And while the French monarchy had been our ally in the war for independence, it seemed at first that international liberalism was simply carrying its march across the Atlantic, insisting on liberty, fraternity and equality.

Washington watched these upheavals with hope, especially as it seemed at first that his protégé Lafayette, who'd left the homeland he once called the "lap of sensual pleasure" to fight alongside American rebels, might lead his country's revolution in an enlightened direction. After the storming of the Bastille, Washington wrote Gouverneur Morris, "The revolution which has been effected in France is of so wonderful a nature that the mind can hardly realize the fact . . . but I fear that though it has gone triumphantly through the first paroxysm, it is not the last it has to encounter before matters are finally settled. . . . To forbear running from one extreme to another is no easy matter, and should this be the case, rocks and shoals not visible at present may wreck the vessel."

The vessel was wrecked. Steering between extremes was not the French Revolution's strong suit. Lafayette was imprisoned as the radical Jacobins' list of "enemies of the revolution" encompassed an ever-widening circle of citizens. The angled blade of the guillotine was introduced as an efficient means of mass execution, and soon heads were rolling every day in the center of Paris for "crimes against liberty," slicing through the sinew and spine of royal neck and common man alike. The Terror had begun.

The French Revolution's rush to mobocracy especially horrified Washington, Adams and Hamilton, who perceived the extremes of liberty lurching from anarchy to tyranny. The chaos was compounded when the revolutionary government in France declared war on Britain and Holland eleven days after beheading America's old ally, King Louis XVI, whose portrait still hung in the executive mansion.

With British frigates still seizing American ships on the high seas, Washington was determined to declare neutrality between the warring powers to avoid becoming ensnared in their costly European conflicts. He called a cabinet meeting to discuss the proposition and despite intense debate it was decided that the United States' wartime treaty with France was invalidated by the execution of the head of state who signed it.

On April 22, 1793, the Proclamation of Neutrality was issued over Washington's signature without consulting Congress, declaring the United States at peace with warring Britain and France and pledging that America would engage in "conduct friendly and impartial towards the belligerent powers" while warning citizens against "committing, aiding or abetting hostilities against any of the said powers." This controversial commitment to neutrality, with the goal of strengthening our independence, would become a major theme of Washington's Farewell Address.

But for many Americans, declaring neutrality between Britain and France was an insult to our French wartime allies and the wider cause of liberty. Jefferson remained enthralled by the French Revolution, despite its now obvious excesses. "The liberty of the whole earth was depending on the issue of the contest, and was ever such a prize won with so little innocent blood?" he wrote in 1793. "My own affections have been deeply wounded by some of the martyrs to this cause, but rather than it should have failed, I would have seen half the earth desolated. Were there but an Adam and an Eve left in every country, and left free, it would be better than as it now is."

This was a bloody utopianism. The secretary of state viewed the violence that flowed from populist rebellion with a philosophical detachment available to one who never served as a soldier (a distinction he shared with Madison). Jefferson could dispatch letters proclaiming that "a little rebellion now and then is a good thing" without having to worry that his own house might be burned to the ground or his life threatened by an angry mob.

When the chaos of the French Revolution sparked a slave uprising on the Caribbean trading outpost of St. Domingue, part of present-day Haiti, Jefferson was missing in action. Gone was the rhetoric of liberation. Instead there was talk of limited aid for the French plantation owners and a concern about stemming a tide of refugees to the southern states. Jefferson considered slave rebellions a step too far for freedom.

Hating George Washington

*

Today, George Washington occupies a lofty place in the American political pantheon, a unifying figure standing far above the partisan fray. He wanted it to be that way. But during his administration, Washington was pilloried like any other president. It's a reminder that even the founding fathers had to contend with critics: some justified, some overheated and others unhinged.

As a general, George Washington was widely admired but he came under fire from rival officers and congressional critics who groused that he was indecisive, too quick to retreat; they also accurately pointed out that he'd lost more battles than he'd won. Their efforts to undermine confidence in General Washington were aided by British Loyalists who spread rumors, along with forged documents, purporting to show that Washington was a traitorous double agent on the British payroll, trying to twist the hero into the kind of monstrous fraud that always attracts conspiracy theorists. His critics bubbled up most dangerously during a near-coup orchestrated by senior officers after the war in which they plotted to seize power, Congress having repeatedly failed to pay their soldiers.

Once Washington resigned his commission and relinquished power, he basked in broad popularity. He was a national hero and attacking him outright was near heresy. That's one reason Washington was so reluctant to risk his reputation again by entering the political arena.

Days after his election, critics began chipping away at his reputation.

A cartoon titled "The Entry" was published in New York depicting Washington entering the capital city on a jackass, led by his worshipful aide David Humphreys paired with the couplet: "The glorious time has come to pass / When David shall conduct an Ass." These sorts of disrespectful witticisms would soon seem quaint.

Political opposition and a partisan press proved to be a combustible combination. "Something or other is always wrong, and they never appear perfectly satisfied," recounted a British tourist in the 1790s. "If any measure is before Congress for discussion, seemingly distrustful of abilities or the integrity of the men they have elected, they meet together in their towns or districts." A great driver of that debate and dissatisfaction was newspapers, which proliferated during the early decades of the republic, growing from roughly 100 in 1790 to more than 300 in 1810. "In America, a great number of people read the Bible," explained gunpowder magnate Pierre Samuel duPont de Nemours, "and all the people read a newspaper." Freedom of the press was enshrined in the First Amendment to the Constitution in the Bill of Rights, but the founding fathers had a complicated relationship with the early journalists Washington called "infamous scribblers."

Before the presidency, Washington declared, "If freedom of speech is taken away, then dumb and silent we may be led, like sheep to the slaughter." But the constant anti-administration attacks of the secretly Jefferson and Madison-backed *National Gazette* got under his skin, with three copies delivered daily to his front door. When Secretary of War Henry Knox brought a copy of the paper into a cabinet meeting containing a broadside called "The Funeral of George Washington" which described a tyrannical executive on a guillotine, the president exploded in one of his rare but memorable rages.

"The President was much inflamed," recounted Jefferson, "[and he] got into one of those passions when he cannot command himself; ran on much on the personal abuse which had been bestowed on him; defied any man on earth to produce one single act of his since he had been in the government which was not done on the purest motives . . . that *by God* he had rather be in his grave than in the present situation; that he would rather be on his farm than to be made *Emperor of the world*."

When the *National Gazette* expired due to unprofitability, compounded by a yellow fever epidemic in Philadelphia, its mantle was eagerly taken up by the *Aurora*. It was published by Benjamin Franklin's grandson, Benjamin Franklin Bache, a onetime administration office-seeker nicknamed "Lightning Rod Jr.," who never took to heart his grandfather's admonition that we all must doubt a little bit in our own infallibility.

The *Aurora* delighted in personal attacks against the president, with Bache declaring it his mission to "destroy undue impressions in favor of Mr. Washington." Among the president's alleged sins were arrogance, stupidity, and a love of monarchy. He was called a lousy general, a lukewarm patriot and an incompetent executive, enthralled with Britain and determined to sell out our revolutionary saviors in France while intentionally undermining the U.S. Constitution. As one of the *Aurora*'s correspondents wrote: "If ever a nation was debauched by a man, the American nation has been debauched by WASHINGTON! . . . Let the history of the federal government instruct mankind that the mask of patriotism may be worn to conceal the foulest designs against the liberties of a people."

Anti-Washington screeds demanded the president "point out one single act which unequivocally proves you a friend to the independence of America" and argued, "Will not the world be led to conclude that the mask of political hypocrisy has been alike worn by a CAESAR, a CROMWELL, and a WASHINGTON?"

Washington was attacked as an economic royalist for ultimately supporting Hamilton's plan to create a national bank, accused of backing "the greatest good for the least number possessing the greatest wealth," while Bache railed against his supposed mediocrity, declaring there "are thousands among [us] who equal you in capacity and excel you in knowledge."

To a nation so recently separated from a king, there seemed to be the danger of monarchy reemerging, with one New York newspaper writing; "We have given him the powers and prerogatives of a King. He holds levees like a King, receives congratulations on his birthday like a King, employs his old enemies like a King, shuts himself up like a King, shuts up other people like a King, takes advice of his counselors or follows his own opinions like a King."

This riff about Washington isolating himself from public opinion was particularly pungent and seemed to reflect historical precedent. "Is our president, like the grand sultan of Constantinople, shut up in his apartment and unacquainted with all the talents or capacities but those of the seraskier or mufti that just happen to be about him?" asked administration critics. Political opponents became increasingly bold in their attacks on the president, with some of Washington's fellow Virginians raising a glass to offer up a chilling toast, "a speedy death to President Washington!"

For Washington, a personal casualty of the partisan divide was the friendship of Thomas Paine. The pamphleteer had once been a favorite of Washington, who ordered his dispatch on *The American Crisis* read aloud to troops in the frozen dark before the Battle of Trenton in December 1776. The opening lines still resonate: "These are the times that try men's souls: The summer soldier and the sunshine patriot will, in this crisis, shrink from the service of his country; but he that stands by it now, deserves the love and thanks of man and woman. . . . The harder the conflict, the more glorious the triumph." Paine had returned the favor by dedicating his book *The Rights of Man* to Washington, writing, "Sir, I present you with a small treatise in defense of those principles of freedom which your exemplary virtue hath so eminently contributed to establishing. That the rights of man may become as universal as your benevolence can wish, and that you may enjoy the happiness of seeing the new world regenerate the old."

Their mutual admiration society did not survive the French Revolution. Paine was insulted by Washington's decision to keep America neutral in the broader European conflict he characterized as liberty versus monarchy. When the erratic and imperious revolutionary leader Maximilien Robespierre inevitably turned on him, Paine somehow blamed Washington for his lengthy imprisonment.

Paine's open letter to Washington, released in July 1796, summed up the sense of personal betrayal Democratic-Republicans felt toward their onetime hero, accusing him of selling out the revolution. "The lands obtained by the revolution were lavished upon partisans; the interest of the disbanded soldier was sold to the speculator; injustice was acted under the pretense of faith; and the chief of the army became the patron of the fraud," Paine wrote. "The world will be troubled to decide whether you are an APOSTATE or an IMPOSTOR—whether you have abandoned good principles, or whether you ever had any."

Paine eventually broke ties with France and died in America, in obscurity. But his fall from grace in what he called "the age of reason" does not look any better in the light of hindsight. As Christopher Hitchens wrote of Paine's attack on Washington, more than two centuries later, "The stuff was poor and it missed its mark by a mile and this is all that needs to be said."

Though Washington steeled himself for the constant onslaught, it took a toll. "He is also extremely affected by the attacks made and kept up on him in the public papers. I think he feels those things more than any person I ever yet met with," Jefferson wrote Madison after they secretly launched the *National Gazette*, "I am sincerely sorry to see them." But Jefferson was not so sorry that he would have deprived Washington of the experience: "inveloped in the rags of royalty, they can hardly be torn off without laceration."

By the end of his second term, Washington privately railed against his partisan newspaper persecutors, bitterly complaining in a final letter to Jefferson that he was "accused of being the enemy of one Nation, and subject to the influence of another" with every administration action twisted by "the grossest, most insidious mis-representations . . . in such exaggerated and indecent terms as could scarcely be applied to a Nero; a notorious defaulter; or even to a common pickpocket."

Through it all, Washington struggled to keep a sense of perspective, writing Gouverneur Morris to express concern that "[f]rom the complexion of some of our News-papers Foreigners would be led to believe that inveterate political dissentions existed among us, and that we are on the very verge of disunion; but the fact is otherwise . . . but this kind of representations is an evil which must be placed in opposition to the infinite benefits resulting from a free Press."

On a personal level, Washington tried to view the slings and arrows in the calm light of mild philosophy, seeking comfort from his honorable intentions, confessing to David Humphreys, "I have a consolation within that no earthly efforts can deprive me of, and that is, that neither ambitious nor interested motives have influenced my conduct. The arrows of malevolence, therefore, however barbed and well pointed, never can reach the most vulnerable part of me." Faced with the hair trigger critics that come with democracy, Washington understood that the value of a clear conscience was second to none.

A Time of Riots and Insurrection

★

Washington's deepest concerns were about disunion and the danger of foreign influence on our democracy. In his second term, he confronted both directly, as riots and insurrections erupted in the republic.

The veneer of national unity fell away with the proliferation of political clubs known as Democratic-Republican Societies, dedicated to the French revolutionary cause. Populist opposition to the administration came with divided loyalties, often expressed in dueling languages. Washington railed against them as "self-created societies," expressing some discomfort with democratic dissent. As their numbers increased to thirty-five organizations across the country, they rallied around the cause of the rakish new French ambassador, Edmond-Charles Genêt.

Representing the new revolutionary government, the red-haired and silver-tongued envoy claimed to have arrived solely to deepen the sense of solidarity between the two nations. But as he began a triumphal tour up the coast, it became apparent that the self-styled "Citizen Genêt" had less than honorable intentions.

His goal was not just to see that the United States took up France's side against England instead of following Washington's policy of neutrality, but also to foment a popular uprising against the president if he would not change course. Genêt carried with him secret instructions "to assist in every way the extension of the Kingdom of Liberty." As historian Harlow Giles Unger explained, "If Washington's government refused to cooperate, he was to exploit the Jeffersonian pro-French ferment in America to foment revolution, topple the American government, and convert the United States into a French puppet state. Once under French control, the United States would become part of a French-dominated American federation of Canada, Florida, Louisiana, and the French West Indies."

The throngs who celebrated Monsieur Genêt's arrival on our shores did not know his real ambitions. Genêt began his tour in Charleston, South Carolina, where he appealed to the living memory of blood spilled by the British. With crowds whipped into a frenzy, aided by French agents doing advance work with a local Jacobin Club, he benefited from ecstatic expressions of solidarity that included assistance from South Carolina governor William Moultrie to bypass federal law and help Genêt commission four privateer ships that promptly set out to attack British vessels. Genêt also commissioned a Revolutionary War hero, George Rogers Clark, as a French major general to lead a "legion of revolution" to attack Spanish holdings along the Gulf of Mexico, a deal sweetened by the promise of 1,000-acre land grants for soldiers fighting in the legion.

By spring of 1793, Genêt could report back to the French foreign minister "I have prepared the revolution of New Orleans and Canada." His stated next step was to lead a popular uprising that would force Washington to abandon neutrality or resign in favor of Jefferson.

When Genêt arrived in Philadelphia, thousands of supporters rallied outside his hotel. Vice President John Adams recalled "the terrorism excited by Genêt in 1793, when ten thousand people in the streets of Philadelphia, day after day, threatened to drag Washington out of his house and effect a revolution in the government, or compel it to declare war in favor of the French Revolution and against England." Adams ordered a cache of weapons from the War Department to protect his home.

As the crowds called for Washington's head, Jefferson was backing away from the French ambassador, who had predictably overplayed his hand. Genêt's recruitment efforts met the buzz saw of federal law when two American sailors were arrested disembarking from the modestly named, makeshift warship *Citizen Genêt*. Correspondence between Jefferson and an aide of Genêt's was discovered in which the secretary of state provided letters of introduction to the Kentucky governor, with implied endorsement of western vigilantes trying to take land from Spain. Jefferson denied the charges, but he knew Genêt was no longer defensible and, in a rare occurrence, he joined with Hamilton to recommend that Washington officially demand Genêt's recall.

The French minister found his papers revoked and Jefferson resigned as secretary of state soon after. Genêt was left begging Washington's administration for asylum, because the new cadre of Jacobins in Paris had called for his arrest and execution.

In a stunning show of magnanimity, Washington granted Genêt asylum, and the Frenchman who had been willing to overthrow the first government of the United States declared his allegiance to the American flag, renounced his French citizenship, married the daughter of New York governor George Clinton, and retired to a farm in Jamaica, Long Island. He died a high-living hypocrite who came to love the land he had sought to undermine as an arrogant youth. In another country he would have been hanged.

★

THE RAGE FOR INSURRECTION HIT its most violent note in 1794's Whiskey Rebellion. In the western hinterlands near Pittsburgh, the locals had not taken kindly to the Washington administration's 25 percent tax on their beloved Monongahela Rye Whiskey.

Washington had predicted the sin tax could stir up trouble. "It is possible," he wrote, "perhaps not improbable, that some demagogue may start up." In Lexington, Kentucky, an effigy of tax collector Thomas Marshall was dragged through the streets and then hanged. Alleghany tax collector Robert Johnson was tarred and feathered and left tied to a tree. A Revolutionary War veteran from western Pennsylvania, Major James McFarlane, led an attack on the home of Governor John Neville, a hero of the revolution, now in charge of the frontier district. On July 15, 1794, Neville's estate was burned to the ground. McFarlane was shot and killed in a skirmish with soldiers.

Nothing fuels an uprising like a martyr and McFarlane's funeral served as a recruitment drive for the Whiskey Rebellion. An ambitious local attorney named David Bradford assumed the role of ringleader of the resistance, proclaiming to the Mingo Creek Democratic Society, "We are ready for a state of revolution and the guillotine of France. . . . We are ready to inflict punishments on the miscreants that enervate and disgrace our government." Unfounded rumors enflamed the passions, with talk of an excise tax imposed on every farmer's plow and every child born.

Bradford dreamed of making himself ruler of an independent western state. He got himself elected a major general by the assembled citizens and arranged an assault on a Philadelphia-bound mail coach to determine which Pittsburgh citizens were in cahoots with the feds. He called on militia troops from four counties to make an assault on Pittsburgh, threatening to burn down the town of 376 residents that some of the more religious-minded rebels were already calling a "second Sodom."

On August 1, some 1,500 militiamen marched on Pittsburgh. Instead of being met with armed resistance, a canny reception committee of local leaders and tavern owners greeted the marchers with bear meat, ham, and venison, all to be washed down with plenty of whiskey, beer, and water. There were speeches galore, but by satiating their appetites and diverting their anger, the "only" violence done that day came in the way of drunken harassment and one home burned down.

Tales of unrest had already made their way to Washington at the other end of Pennsylvania, in the capital city of Philadelphia. An alarmed Hamilton opined "there is no road to despotism more sure or more to be dreaded than that which begins at anarchy."

The unity of the nation and the authority of the federal government seemed at stake. Washington put on his old uniform and climbed up on horseback to lead 12,000 militia troops. Washington's warrior days were long past, and by the time his advance soldiers reached western Pennsylvania, the rebels had dispersed and Bradford had fled south down the Mississippi River to Louisiana. Washington pardoned two captured leaders of the Whiskey Rebellion who had been sentenced to death. Another precedent was set amid discord and disorder: the president of the United States was unambiguously the commander in chief.

★

AGAINST THE BACKDROP OF AGITATION from revolutionary France, Washington was fighting a cold war with Britain. The English still held redcoat-occupied forts in the western territories and maintained an embargo on American imports. Washington was furious to find that British ships were boarding American boats on the high seas, confiscating goods and humiliating their crews.

But America wasn't in a position of sufficient strength to risk a return to war. So Washington sent Supreme Court chief justice John Jay on a mission to negotiate a treaty with Britain. Jay was one of the most experienced diplomats among the founding brothers, having helped seal the Paris peace deal that closed the Revolutionary War.

Washington's decision to send Jay raised concerns about the separation of powers. After all, the Supreme Court was supposed to check and balance the president as a coequal branch of government. Washington's eagerness to negotiate with England also fit the script pushed by political opponents who accused his administration of harboring a pro-British bias.

The treaty Jay returned home with after six months was far from perfect. Even Washington was initially disappointed, seeing that it did not afford America the respect of an equal independent nation. One concession was particularly odious, imposing British limits on what crops American ships could export. But despite its deficiencies, the treaty cracked open British ports and compelled them to abandon western forts. Most important, it seemed to secure peace at a time when America could not afford war.

In the summer of 1795, Washington submitted the Jay Treaty for Senate ratification, provoking a new constitutional crisis. Madison's Democratic-Republicans formally caucused as a party for the first time, constituting a majority. They demanded to see executive papers detailing the treaty negotiations. Furious, Washington refused to hand them over in the first invocation of national security to protect presidential prerogative, and he waded into partisan politics to prove his point, releasing secret minutes of the Constitutional Convention which showed Madison had once opposed giving Congress the power he now invoked. This clash caused Washington to break with Madison, effectively ending their founding friendship.

The political crisis intensified when the terms of the treaty, viewed as too lenient to the old enemy, were leaked to the *Aurora* by congressmen loyal to Jefferson. Newspapers raged that the Jay Treaty "originated in submission, progressed in secrecy, and is at last established by *fear*." At a Philadelphia town hall in July, Representative Blair McClenachan declared that it was the duty of every citizen to "kick the damned treaty to hell."

Jay was burned in effigy in city streets from Charleston to New York, and Washington was denounced as a puppet of the British monarchy. Hamilton was stoned by an angry mob when he tried to defend the treaty near his home on Wall Street, reportedly replying, "If you use such knock-down arguments, I must retire." Southern States threatened secession. Washington's executive mansion in Philadelphia was besieged, "surrounded by an innumerable multitude from day to day, buzzing, demanding war against England, cursing Washington, and crying success to the French patriots and virtuous Republicans."

In France, Ambassador James Monroe told salons that the president had become a British ally and sent anti-administration dispatches to the *Aurora*; when a dinner party host proposed a toast to Washington, Monroe suggested they toast "the Executive" instead. It's no surprise that Monroe was soon called back to the United States.

Washington nonetheless guided the treaty to a narrow victory in

Congress by biding his time, pairing the Jay Treaty with a more popular
Spanish treaty to open up the entire Mississippi River for trade and leveraging his still considerable national popularity.

"Firm as a majestic rock in the ocean," wrote one newspaper, "he
braves the tempest of popular clamor and the attacks of usurpations."
"One man outweighs them all in influence over the people," Jefferson
sighed.

However imperfect, the Jay Treaty proved a success. The terms of the
treaty served Washington's aims of increasing trade by reopening Brit-
ish-controlled West Indian ports to American goods. Aided by the innovation of Eli Whitney's cotton gin and war in Europe, American exports
increased 50 percent and import prices declined. But perhaps the supreme
achievement of the treaty was simply the time it bought for the United
States to grow in economic and military strength. The following two decades of prosperity were abruptly ended by the War of 1812 with the British, but the war's result, the preservation of American independence, might
well have been different without the treaty's breathing space.

None of that could be seen at the time of the treaty's passage. In political terms, the fallout was disastrous. Backlash to the Jay Treaty invigorated
the Democratic-Republican Party, permanently tarnished the Federalists
with pro-British associations, and caused Washington to once more de-
spair about the fragile state of the national union. But his commitment to
increased trade as a cornerstone of American foreign policy would fundamentally inform his Farewell Address. Washington succeeded in strengthening the nation while defying popular opinion.

Washington's Squabbling
Surrogate Sons

★

Historian James Thomas Flexner neatly captured the almost animal distrust between Washington's two most talented surrogate sons: "Jefferson considered Hamilton a vulgar upstart and Hamilton considered Jefferson a snob who railed about equality."

Hamilton was an ambitious young immigrant, drawn to New York City's interplay of commerce and art. He was brilliant, witty and prolific, but also stubborn, impetuous and quick to take offense. One critic called him a "political porcupine, armed at all points, [who] brandishes a shaft to every opposer."

Hamilton's penchant for peacocking, wearing brightly colored clothes and parading his intellect with cascades of rapid-fire speech, did little to endear him to colleagues. His flirtatious style led Martha Washington to name a feral cat "Hamilton" during the war. Even his sometime Federalist ally John Adams called Hamilton "the bastard brat of a Scotch peddler."

Gallons of ink have been spilled detailing how the orphaned Caribbean boy and the childless father of the nation helped forge the United States in war and peace. But Washington and Hamilton's relationship was far more than mentor and protégé.

Their mutual dependence began during the war, with the twenty-two-year-old aide-de-camp overseeing the forty-five-year-old General's correspondence. The opportunity to serve on Washington's wartime staff saved Alexander Hamilton from obscurity, and he transformed himself into an indispensable assistant. He channeled the older man's voice and reflected his vision and opinions. Both men were known in private for fiery tempers, but their strengths and weaknesses balanced each other, and for all their occasionally prickly differences, Washington grew to trust Hamilton's judgment more than any other member of his inner circle. The relationship was reinforced by philosophical agreement born of shared experience. Their wartime struggles with a weak and often incompetent Continental Congress drove both to believe in the need for national unity and a strong central government.

In the transition from revolution to governing, Hamilton assumed the role of Treasury secretary but he never entirely abandoned his role as speechwriter, dashing off congressional missives and diplomatic dispatches. He played a more integrated role in the Washington administration than any current cabinet official could imagine, functionally serving as chief of staff in addition to his other duties. He was perhaps the most powerful unelected man ever to serve in a president's administration.

*

HIS CHIEF CABINET RIVAL DID not have to climb as far or as fast. Thomas Jefferson's first memory was being carried on a pillow by a slave riding on horseback through his father's Virginia farm. The tall, thin, redhead was educated and elegant, imbued with a relaxed air of authority, but he contained a host of contradictions. Jefferson was a self-styled populist born into wealth but constantly in debt due to expensive tastes; insatiably curious about the wider world while cultivating a certain cerebral detachment in society. He was omnivorously intelligent but an uncomfortable orator. His political brilliance was self-evident but he publicly denied all ambition and disliked direct conflict, preferring to pull strings from behind the scenes, dispatching friends to fight on his behalf.

Jefferson's literary genius, evident in the Declaration of Independence, which he wrote at age thirty-three, still makes him the most romantic of the founding fathers. He was admirably consistent in his belief that democracy depended on dissent, and he did not sanction censure. But his idealistic nature and penchant for broad pronouncements could make him morally careless and often naïve. He fetishized the French Revolution long after it was revealed to be a monstrous new type of tyranny, and he didn't hesitate to actively undermine Washington's government while seeking to establish his own political party. "To remain a member of Washington's Cabinet, privy to all transactions, while secretly undermining it," wrote Conor Cruise O'Brien, "was an advantageous position, and one well suited to Jefferson's devious temperament."

Motivated by his personal dislike of Hamilton and their very different view of fiscal policy and the French revolution, Jefferson fanned the flames, writing Washington that Hamilton's economic plan "flowed from principles adverse to liberty, and was calculated to undermine and demolish the republic."

Soon they were, in Jefferson's words, "daily pitted in the cabinet like two cocks."

As the surrogate father of these squabbling sons, Washington tried mightily to reconcile Jefferson and Hamilton. During the summer of 1792, toward the end of his first term, he wrote urgently to each, appealing to their reason and goodwill, warning them of the consequences if their political disagreements festered into personal hatred.

To Jefferson, he wrote:

How unfortunate, and how much to be regretted then, that whilst we are encompassed on all sides with avowed enemies and insidious friends, that internal dissensions should be harrowing and tearing our vitals. . . . My earnest wish, and my fondest hope therefore is that instead of wounding suspicions and irritable charges, there may be liberal allowances, mutual forbearances, and temporizing yieldings on *all sides*. . . . Without them everything must rub, the wheels of Government will clog; our enemies will triumph; and by throwing their weight into the disaffected scale, may accomplish the ruin of the goodly fabric we have been erecting.

And to Hamilton, three days later:

> Differences in political opinions are as unavoidable as, to a certain
> point, they may perhaps be necessary; but it is to be regretted
> exceedingly that subjects cannot be discussed with temper on the
> one hand, or decisions submitted to without having the motives
> which led to them improperly implicated on the other: and this
> regret borders on chagrin when we find that men of abilities—
> zealous patriots—having the same *general* objects in view, and the
> same upright intentions to prosecute them, will not exercise more
> charity in deciding on the opinions and actions of one another.

Washington understood that democracies depend on an assumption of goodwill between fellow citizens. But the relationship between his two most talented cabinet secretaries seemed beyond repair.

Jefferson's perception that Washington was falling into the Hamiltonian camp was exaggerated. Washington pointed out that there were many examples of "my having decided against, as in favor" of Hamilton within cabinet debates. While Hamilton was pushing his polarizing plan to create a national bank, Washington was not sold on the idea even after its hard-won passage by Congress, requesting written arguments both pro and con from members of his cabinet as to whether it was constitutional. Attorney General Randolph and Jefferson were firmly opposed, arguing strict construction of the Constitution that limited powers. They proved so persuasive that Washington requested a veto message be drafted. But Hamilton responded with a 13,000-word defense of the bank bill, arguing that the Constitution gave Congress the power to pass laws that were "necessary and proper" to achieve governing goals, unless the means were explicitly forbidden. The expansive argument won the day, and Washington ended his delay by signing the bank bill right at the ten-day deadline.

This deliberative process indicated the extent to which Washington was determined to think and act independently, above factions, even within his own administration. As Jefferson and Hamilton increasingly represented opposing visions of America's economy, Washington tried to triangulate between the two, recognizing the agrarian present of the United States while anticipating and encouraging the industrial future.

But the view of Washington as Federalist with pro-British sympathies hardened in part because of Jefferson's insistence that if you were not with him you were against him. "Were parties here divided merely by a greediness for office, as in England, to take part in either would be unworthy of a reasonable and moral man," he conceded. "But where the principle of difference is as substantial and as strongly pronounced as between the republicans and the monocrats of our country, I hold it as honorable to take a firm and decided part, and as immoral to pursue a middle line, as between the parties of honest men and rogues."

For Jefferson, the choice was simply between right and wrong, good and evil. It was a belief that contained the fingerprints of fanaticism.

Yet Jefferson correctly observed the president's growing closeness to Hamilton. When Jefferson finally left the cabinet, Washington registered perfunctory disappointment, but he greeted Hamilton's resignation, thirteen months later, with real reluctance.

For the Treasury Secretary, leaving government was a matter of economic necessity. He was still a young man of modest means with a growing family. And so in 1795 Hamilton happily decamped to his adopted hometown of New York and established his law offices at 26 Broadway, a half block from the second executive mansion Washington had briefly occupied. He soon counted businesses and state governments as his clients, arguing foundational constitutional cases before the Supreme Court to rapt audiences, becoming wealthy though he famously undercharged for his services.

Unlike Jefferson, Hamilton remained close to Washington after his cabinet departure. "In every relation which you have borne to me, I have found that my confidence in your talents, exertions, and integrity has been well placed," Washington wrote after accepting his resignation. Correspondence with Jefferson ceased after July 1796. The contrast was clear.

As Washington's second term drew to a close, he became more liable to rely on Hamilton's suggestions wholesale. His penultimate message to Congress in December 1795 was written by Hamilton from New York. It was not a surprise that Washington would look to Hamilton when the time came for his Farewell Address.

★

BY EARLY 1796, RUMORS THAT Washington would leave office were percolating among the most influential members of Congress.

On a trip to Philadelphia that February, Hamilton let the news slip to Kentucky senator John Brown over a meal at Francis' Hotel, where Vice President Adams was living, a block from the executive mansion. The secret was effectively out among the governing class. Madison informed James Monroe of the news via a coded message transmitted in cipher, "It is now generally understood that the President will retire and Jefferson is the object on one side and Adams apparently on the other."

On March 24, Washington gave the nod to John Adams, hinting during a rare dinner between the two that his remaining "reign would be very short," as Adams recounted to his beloved wife, Abigail. "He repeated it three times at least, that this and that was of no consequence to him personally, as he had but a very little while to stay in his present situation."

Adams and Washington had never been close, but this after-dinner passing of the baton was vastly illuminating to the vice president: "He detained me there till nine o'clock, and was never more frank and open upon politics. I find his opinions and sentiments are more exactly like mine than I ever knew before, respecting England and France and our American parties."

By June, the clerk of the House, John Beckley, a burly Democratic-Republican partisan who loved playing hardball politics, wrote to Madison to confirm the rumors: "The president does not mean to resign, but merely to decline a reelection, and that to make known this intention, he designs about the month of August to publish an address to the people." Beckley's political intelligence was inevitably delivered with partisan barbs. "We may presume whose pen will indite it, and what views and principles it will be designed to propagate," he dished, calling Hamilton "the American Catiline," referring to the ruthless Roman senator who tried to seize power in a coup d'état that was stopped by Cicero.

Political intrigues were thick that summer in Philadelphia, but this time Washington would not change his mind. Not even an appeal from John Jay—"remain with us at least while the storm lasts, and until you can retire like the sun in a calm unclouded evening"—could talk him out of his long-desired retirement.

A Farewell "Importantly
and Lastingly Useful"

★

In the spring of 1796, Washington began a five-month correspondence
with Hamilton crafting the Farewell Address. The two sent back and
forth multiple drafts by mail in a time when it took two days to travel at a
gallop between Philadelphia and New York. There were fears of lost correspondence and cross talk in letters that passed each other on the Post
Road. Washington was concerned, with some justification, that his mail
was being intercepted.

Much of the language in the final Farewell Address was drafted by
Hamilton, but it was all subject to Washington's precise edits, often paring
back rhetorical excesses, removing flourishes or sentences that smacked of
false modesty.

The president was not a mouthpiece for Hamilton's ideas, as partisan opponents later charged. The ideas were all Washington's, developed
and articulated over decades in letters and speeches. Having kept Madison's draft of the first Farewell hidden for safekeeping for four years,
he dusted off the old document and updated it to reflect the momentous
events of his second term.

In the cold early months of 1796, Hamilton was traveling back and
forth from New York to Philadelphia on business. His law practice put
him in the singular position of defending the constitutionality of decisions
he had made as Treasury secretary in front of the Supreme Court. This
included one celebrated case, *Hylton v. United States*, in which Hamilton

successfully argued for three hours before a packed house, while desperately ill, to establish the government's right to levy annual taxes on luxury items like carriages.

It was during this visit, from February 17 through 24, that Hamilton apparently met with the president. History does not record exactly when they met or what was said, but it's perhaps not coincidental that the trip overlapped with the celebration of Washington's birthday. The day's parades and official greetings at the executive mansion were capped by a ball at Ricketts' amphitheater, which sometimes housed a circus. It is unlikely in the extreme that Hamilton would not have attended the festivities. What we do know is that sometime during this trip, the president asked Hamilton's assistance in preparing a farewell address that built off the now-distant Madison draft.

Perhaps giving Washington time to complete updating the address, Hamilton waited to follow up on their conversation until May, beginning the formal correspondence that created the Farewell Address: "When last in Philadelphia, you mentioned to me your wish that I should re-dress a certain paper which you had prepared."

Hamilton was being coy, but he pressed the president to ensure enough time to craft the address: "As it is important that a thing of this kind be done with great care, and much at leisure touched and re-touched, I submit a wish that as soon as you have given it the body you mean it to have that it may be sent to me."

Five days later, Washington mailed Hamilton his first draft—rearranging the key paragraphs from Madison's effort between his own extended additions, written in his own hand. He acknowledged his debt by urging discretion, mentioning that the existence of the early draft was "known also to one or two of those characters who are now strongest and foremost in the opposition to the government," clearly meaning Madison and Jefferson.

The theme of the Farewell was now expanded from its core warning to preserve national unity. Paragraphs on the dangers of partisan factions, excessive debt and especially the hidden intrigues that could draw us into foreign wars now occupied the text in uncharacteristically passionate prose.

Washington told Hamilton that the address should be "curtailed, if too verbose; and relieved of all tautology, not necessary to enforce the ideas in the original or quoted part. My wish is that the whole may appear in a plain style, and be handed to the public in an honest, unaffected, simple garb." The goal was to keep the tone and language of the Farewell Address comprehensible to people in every corner of the country. He instructed Hamilton that the speech should be written so that it would resonate with the "yeomanry of the country"—middle-class farmers, the independent-minded backbone of the young nation. These were the people who formed the balance of power and opinion. You couldn't talk down to them—you had to meet them eye to eye.

Washington also worried about the length. "All the columns of a large Gazette would scarcely, I conceive, contain the present draft. But having made no accurate calculation of this matter I may be much mistaken," he wrote Hamilton.

Reviewing the draft in his home on 56 Pine Street and his law office at 26 Broadway, a half mile apart in lower Manhattan, Hamilton reduced the president's ruminations into an outline of twenty-three roman-numeraled points.

It was a busy summer in the city and Hamilton balanced work on Washington's Farewell with his law practice, while also responding to regular requests for advice from his successors in the administration. He found time to suggest means for securing loans to the federal bank, counseled the completion of navy frigates and passed on intelligence regarding French plots to seize American ships, while advising on a replacement for James Monroe as ambassador to France. He proposed quarantine policy for a ship full of 450 Irish immigrants in New York Harbor afflicted with yellow fever, wrote flirtatious letters to his sister-in-law Angelica and advised clients on business matters. He also suffered from seasonal ailments, likely related to malarial infection during his youth in the Caribbean, and a digestive disorder that forced him to give up champagne. For all the crowded hours, Hamilton found time to glory in the passage of the Jay Treaty ("Our own Jacobins have made a violent effort against me, but a complete victory has been gained to their utter confusion") while telling a fellow Federalist, "Our affairs are critical, and *we* must be dispassionate and wise."

Hamilton wrote quickly, combining massive output and clarity of thought, needing minimal revisions. He allowed his ideas to marinate while walking outdoors or pacing the floor, took a brief nap when possible, then wrote for hours straight, fortified by cups of coffee.

Years later, Eliza Hamilton cherished the memory of her husband writing the Farewell Address during those summer months, "principally at such times as his office was seldom frequented by his clients and visitors, and during the absence of his students to avoid interruption; at which times he was in the habit of calling me to sit with him, that he might read to me as he wrote, in order, as he said, to discover how it sounded upon the ear, and making the remark, 'my dear Eliza, you must be to me what Moliere's old nurse was to him.' "

By reading the text out loud to an affectionate audience, Hamilton was applying the old speechwriter's trick of writing for the ear as well as the eye, despite the fact that he knew the speech would be printed in a newspaper and not spoken. He was writing for a larger audience: posterity rather than simply this president.

Hamilton attracted jealous attention because of what his partisan enemies characterized as his incautious attitude toward his ghostwriting for the president. "He has often compared his influence over the President to that of the wind upon a weathercock, or of that over an automaton moved only by the hand which directs it," sneered Jeffersonian journalist James Callender, in his annual partisan publication. "This style was both imprudent and ungrateful. His power was very great, but not entirely unbounded."

But Washington was in need of a confident editor. This most self-monitoring man paraded his hurts on the pages of the first draft of the Farewell Address. He wanted to settle scores. Venting about the unfairness of the partisan press must have been emotionally satisfying, but it was unpresidential. "Some of the gazettes of the United States have teemed with all the invective that disappointment, ignorance of facts, and malicious falsehoods could invent to misrepresent my politics and affections; to wound my reputation and feelings; and to weaken, if not entirely to destroy, the confidence that you have pleased to repose in me. It might be expected at the parting scene of my public life that I should take some notice of such virulent abuse. But, as heretofore, I shall pass them over in utter silence, never having myself, nor by any other with my participation or knowledge, written or published a scrap in answer to any of them." Hamilton tactfully recommended eliminating this litany of complaints.

Hamilton also dialed back Washington's self-pitying flourishes. He deleted the president's description of "the gray hairs" he'd gained in the service of his country, asking that his "errors, however numerous, if they are not criminal, may be consigned to the tomb of oblivion."

Washington wanted a second editor involved so he instructed Hamilton to reach out to John Jay, newly elected governor of New York, to serve as adult supervision for the sometimes headstrong Hamilton. "Having no other wish than to promote the true and permanent interests of this country," Washington wrote, "I am anxious, always, to compare the opinions of those who in whom I confide with one another; and these again (without being bound by them) with my own, that I may extract all the good I can." He expressed confidence "in the abilities, and purity of Mr. Jay's views as well as his experience." At the president's request, two authors of the Federalist Papers were reunited on the southern tip of Manhattan.

They met in secret at the governor's residence, the stone mansion dubbed "The Government House," plopped on the plum real estate of the southern end of Bowling Green. Enjoying the breeze off the bay one summer day, Hamilton read his draft aloud (avoiding Washington's first draft entirely) and then the two men pored over it "deliberately to discuss and consider, paragraph by paragraph," until they came to final agreement on the contents and their expression.

Jay suggested that they reach out to other wise eyes for wider consultation, but his idea was brushed aside by the possessive Hamilton, who believed the input of too many elder statesmen was liable to ruin an inspired idea.

On July 5, the day after the twentieth anniversary of the Declaration of Independence, Hamilton wrote Washington, informing him that he should expect not one but two drafts for his consideration: "I have completed the first draft of a certain paper and shall shortly transcribe, correct, and forward it. I will then also prepare and send forward without delay the original paper corrected upon the general plan of it, so that you may have both before you for a choice in full time and for alternation if necessary."

Twenty-five days later, Hamilton sent Washington his version of the address, reordering the essential points and combining Washington's core sentiments with his style: "I have endeavored," he wrote, "to make [it] as perfect as my time and engagements would permit. It has been my object to render this act *importantly and lastingly* useful . . . to embrace such reflections and sentiments as will wear well, progress in approbation with time, and redound to future reputation."

He then downplayed expectations for the second version, rooted more closely in Washington's first-pass draft, with its dependence on Madison's 1792 effort: "I confess the more I have considered the matter the less eligible this plan has appeared to me—there seems to be a certain awkwardness in the thing."

He then followed through with the second version, well after Washington had time to digest his preferred draft. His tactics displayed more than a passing proficiency with office politics: Hamilton was framing the choice weighted to his desired direction. But lest he be accused of putting a finger on the scales of Washington's judgment, Hamilton made it clear that "[i]f there be any part you wish to transfer from one to another, any part to be changed, or if there be any material idea in your own draft which has happened to be omitted and which you wished introduced—in short if there be anything further in the matter in which I can be of any [service], I will with great pleasure obey your commands."

Washington surveyed the results over "several serious and attentive readings" from a summer respite at Mount Vernon and concluded that he greatly preferred Hamilton's version, pronouncing it "more copious on material points; more dignified on the whole; and with less egotism." And so Hamilton's draft became the basis of the final Farewell.

There was one major point of disagreement between the president and his speechwriter: how much detail to include on Washington's proposal for a national college. Washington wrote Hamilton that he wished to include "as one of the surest means enlightening . . . our citizens . . . the establishment of a university; where the youth from *all parts* of the United States might receive the polish of erudition in the arts, sciences, and belle lettres."

Hamilton counseled the president that this high-minded idea was better suited for the president's final address to Congress in December 1796, making that speech focused on policy while the Farewell would be focused on enduring principles. But Washington was insistent and a compromise was reached in which Hamilton agreed to add a paragraph on the plan in the speech itself, though more detailed explications conveniently were left off later drafts of the address. Ultimately a short paragraph regarding the creation of "institutions for the general diffusion of knowledge" was literally cut and pasted into the document by Washington himself.

When Hamilton sent the president his final draft on September 6, he apologized for not having the time to send a clean, rewritten version, blaming ill health: "Had I *health* enough, it was my intention to have written it over, in which case I could have both improved and abridged," Hamilton wrote. "But this is not the case. I seem now to have regularly a period of ill health every summer." His elegant prose had fleshed out the Farewell. Now it needed to be pared back by its principal.

★

IN SEPTEMBER, WASHINGTON TOOK THE reins, working on the Farewell Address in the three-story red-brick Philadelphia home that served as the executive mansion. Leased for $500 a year from Washington's friend, the "financier of the Revolution," Robert Morris, it stood on a forty-five-foot-wide double lot, with its gardens, ice house and stables contained by a brick wall that extended beyond the structure. At the time it was the largest house in Philadelphia, then the largest city in the United States.

There was no exterior heraldry indicating it was the president's house. It was not set apart from the bustle of daily city life: next door was a hairdresser's salon and a wine shop stood nearby. A block down the street stood the brick house where Jefferson had drafted the Declaration of Independence twenty years earlier.

A visitor to the makeshift executive mansion would find the front parlor unattended. The state and family dining rooms opened up immediately to a visitor's left, and a formal drawing room to the right, on the same floor as the expansive kitchen toward the back. A grand wooden staircase led to the second floor, containing two drawing rooms with sofas sitting upon rugs facing a fireplace. At the top of a steep back staircase stood the president's private office. It overlooked a low rooftop and a narrow privy yard—a fancy term for an outhouse. In the distance, slave quarters and stables were framed by the spire of Independence Hall, less than a block away on Chestnut Street.

The president's desk was an ornate 350-pound mahogany and pine rolltop purchased and built in 1789 from the New York cabinetmaker Thomas Burling. Washington often worked by candlelight, placing two candles in a brass stand that magnified the light off a reflective brass backboard lined with green silk to reduce glare. He sharpened his own quills with a knife and was a methodical draftsman.

His beloved step-granddaughter Nelly Custis, then a bright-eyed teenager living in the president's house, later recalled watching him write the Farewell Address:

> I did see the President Washington repeatedly in the act of writing
> the "Farewell Address," in the day time, and also at night by the

candlestick you have seen at Audley,* of two lights and a shade for the eyes whilst the light was thrown on the paper. I always passed the door of his office in my way to my grandmother's chamber at the head of the steep stairs, which landed close to his door. That door was generally open, and I have been sent to his room with messages, and at night have passed the door and seen him writing as I passed to ascend the stairs with grandmama.

This letter is the only surviving eyewitness account of Washington writing the Farewell Address.

Affectionately described by her grandmother Martha as "a wild little creature," whom she tried to tame with interminable harpsichord lessons, Nelly kept a green parrot as a pet in the president's mansion. And though the note, written to her nephew Lewis Washington in 1852, contains more than a trace of defensiveness about the nineteenth-century buzz that Washington was not the author of his own Farewell Address, her facts stack up. The layout of the house is accurate, and her account of the writing and editing gives us a hint of the hard work behind its creation.

By mid-September, Washington had rewritten the draft in longhand. In the final written copy, he struck through 174 out of 1,086 lines with tight circular script designed to obscure the underlying text. His deletions as well as additions remain as evidence of his thought process. He crossed out a public mea culpa for the "involuntary errors I have probably committed have been the sources of no serious or lasting mischief to our country," with the margin note that it was "obliterated to avoid the imputation of affected modesty."

He dismissed a pointed riff on the dangers of luxury ("Cultivate industry and frugality, as auxiliaries to good morals and source of private and public prosperity. . . . Is there not more luxury among us, and more

---

* Audley was the name of the rural Virginia estate where Nelly lived at toward the end of her life, when the letter was written in 1852.

diffusively, than suits the actual stage of our national progress?") despite having hit this theme in previous letters in which he pondered "whether the luxury, effeminacy, and corruptions which are introduced by [foreign trade] are counterbalanced by the convenience and wealth of which it is productive." This intriguing idea was swiftly dispatched, with "not sufficiently important" written in the margins.

He was also aware of shades of meaning in word choices that might inspire future misinterpretation. For example, where Hamilton wrote about the importance of preserving public credit, Washington changed the advice to "use it as little as possible" to "use it as sparingly as possible" and changed his maxim of "avoiding occasions of expense" to "shunning occasions of expense." In both cases, the surgical word changes suggested a limited use of debt rather than a prohibition against it.

Washington also tamped down several sentences that might be seen as too full-throated an endorsement of Hamilton's Federalist perspective: "I shall not conceal from you the belief I entertain that your government as at present constituted is far more likely to prove too feeble than too powerful."

These edits not only establish Washington as the final arbiter of his address; they show his mind at work, thinking through not only the precision of the language but anticipating the ways articulations might be attacked by contemporary critics or misinterpreted by future generations.

When Washington's work was done, Nelly recalled that the president called her from Martha's bedchamber "and requested me to bring him a needle with silk to sew the leaves together. The Address was in his hand when I gave him the needle, and I saw him sew them in the form of a book; the only circumstance I could not take an oath on is the color of the silk. It was a spool of tambouring silk, light blue or light lead color."

Washington had asked for Hamilton's input on which publisher he thought might be most appropriate to debut the address, though it's possible that he knew the names of his enemies in the press—those "infamous scribblers"—better than his administration's allies.

Hamilton recommended John Dunlap of the *American Daily Advertiser* in Philadelphia—whose presses had first printed the Declaration of Independence in 1776. But Hamilton was apparently unaware that Dunlap had recently sold his share of the business to his onetime apprentice David Claypoole, who had renamed the gazette at the start of the year to *Claypoole's American Daily Advertiser.*

The publisher had a history of fidelity to the revolution. Claypoole was a cousin by marriage to Betsy Ross, who is credited with sewing the first American flag. At nineteen, he volunteered for the local infantry as a private and rose to the level of lieutenant, though he saw little combat. Dunlap and he were selected as the printer of official documents from the Articles of Confederation to the Constitutional Convention. Claypoole also served in the cavalry dispatched during the Whiskey Rebellion. He sired thirteen children with three wives, all of whom he outlived.

Even if their paper had never published the Farewell Address, Claypoole and Dunlap would still earn a minor spot in the journalists' hall of fame for publishing one of the first successful daily newspapers in the United States. Washington was a longtime, and sometimes long-suffering, subscriber, writing to complain from Mount Vernon that he had not been receiving his paper delivery regularly. ("I do not get one paper in five of them—was I to say one in ten, I should be nearer to the mark.")

So why would Washington and Hamilton not have given the scoop to a long-standing partisan ally like John Fenno of the dependably Federalist *Gazette of the United States?* The answer may be that pro-administration newspapers were tainted with political favoritism at a time when Washington wanted to appeal to all Americans. Claypoole and Dunlap had avoided the fashionable trap of becoming a viciously partisan press, perhaps because of their broader congressional printing contracts.

The *American Daily Advertiser* was later characterized as "never flaunting in the gaudy glare of party allurements; never stained with the ribaldry and virulence of party recrimination. It is patriarchal, looking alike to the wants and benefits of all our citizens, as common children of the same city family."

In other words, its editorial view was independent and reflected the virtues of national unity that Washington championed in his Farewell Address.

Washington presented his cabinet with a full draft of the address on Thursday morning, September 15, giving them the courtesy of a few days' advance notice, too late to make any major revisions, let alone to change course.

That same afternoon, Washington sent a message—hand-delivered by his personal secretary Tobias Lear—to David Claypoole, requesting the pleasure of his presence.

Years later, when Claypoole was living in genteel poverty after blowing his newspaper fortune, he recalled finding the president "sitting alone in the drawing room" of the executive mansion. Washington asked Claypoole to take a seat beside him on a couch angled to the left of the fireplace and told him of his intention to retire from the presidency, confiding "that he had some thoughts and reflections on the occasion, which he deemed proper to communicate to the people of the United States, in the form of an address, and which he wished to appear in the Daily Advertiser."

The president asked what was the earliest and most auspicious moment to publish his message and Claypoole—presumably thinking of increased circulation and the fact that the *Advertiser* did not publish on Sunday—suggested the following Monday, September 19.

On Friday morning, September 16, Tobias Lear carried a copy of the Farewell Address on the six-minute march from the executive mansion on what is now Sixth and Market Streets to Claypoole's offices on the corner of Market and First. Subsequent drafts were exchanged, with two different versions personally "examined by the President," who gave specific instructions as to how the address should be presented on the page. Claypoole later remembered that Washington "made but few alterations from the original, except in the punctuation, in which he was very minute." Perhaps inspired by symbolic symmetry, the letter to the American people was dated September 17—nine years to the day since the Constitution had been approved by the closed convention at Independence Hall.

Claypoole returned the final manuscript to the president in person. It consisted, Nelly remembered, of "thirty-two quarto pages of letter paper sewn together as a book, with many alterations and interlineations. Words, sentences, and even paragraphs had been erased or replaced, and several pages were almost entirely expunged."

When Claypoole expressed reluctance to part with the seven-inch by nine-inch document, Washington made the uncharacteristically impetuous decision to offer the original manuscript to the covetous publisher.

As the *American Daily Advertiser* hit the streets on Monday afternoon, Washington was already rolling toward Mount Vernon in a carriage with Martha beside him. A cold wind had begun to come from the north, and a soaking rainstorm pelted the people of Philadelphia.

Washington's diary recorded the day with typical understatement: "Address to the people of the United States was this day published in Claypoole's paper notifying my intention of declining being considered a candidate for the Presidency of the United States of America. . . . Left the city this morning on my way to Mount Vernon."

News of his decision to leave the presidency spread quickly. On the same day, it was reprinted in three Philadelphia papers, including the stridently pro-Federalist *Gazette of the United States*. Even the *Aurora*, Washington's most rabid opponent, published the address in two installments on September 20 and 21. The first paper outside of Philadelphia to reprint the address was New York's *Minerva and Mercantile Evening Advertiser*, which published the news on Tuesday, September 20, telling its readers, "This address, whether considered as departing advice of an old friend, or as a political lecture of a great patriot and statesman, is entitled to our admiration and respect. It is like a rich entertainment, on taking leave of a dear friend, which we enjoy with mingled emotions of pleasure, sensibility and regret."

It took until the end of October for readers in the western outposts of Cincinnati or Lexington to get the news. London found out only in early November; where one paper described it as being "replete with wisdom, and is applicable in many points of view to our own circumstances as well as those of America. Coming from an authority so pure and so grave, and so entirely disinterested, his opinion may be respected" as a voice against "the force of foreign corruption and foreign treasons, and of domestic violence and the tyranny of factions." After reading the address, a famed Scottish preacher and author named Archibald Alison called it "unequaled by any composition of uninspired wisdom" and declared Washington "a Cromwell without his ambitions. . . . [A]fter having raised his country, by his exertions, to the rank of an independent state, he closed his career by a voluntary relinquishment of the power which a grateful people had bestowed."

Curiously, Washington's announcement was not formally called a "Farewell Address" until it was published under that name by the *Courier of New Hampshire* on October 11. Its publisher, George Hough, attached an editorial to the publication saying, "We recommend to our customers a careful preservation of this week's paper, and the frequent perusal of its contents. . . . Let the address from the man in whom we have long confided, be treasured up, as a choice legacy of experience, wisdom, and patriotism—and transmitted as an inheritance to our children."

Over the next twenty years, more than 100 different editions of the Farewell Address were published by printing houses and civic societies, dwarfing republication of the Declaration of Independence. Interest peaked particularly in times of national crisis, with forty-five editions pushed out during the War of 1812 alone.

Americans did not have Washington to lead them, but they still had his advice to guide them.

WASHINGTON'S PILLARS OF LIBERTY

The speech was sprawling: 6,000 words that summed up the wisdom and warnings of the most famous man in America.

Washington's Farewell offered a road map for the republic's future, rooted in the lessons of the shared past. It diagnosed problems that had afflicted democratic republics throughout history and presented policy prescriptions that reflected first principles. In a changing world, it offered the promise of durable wisdom that could stand the test of time. What it lacked was an easily decipherable index.

The Farewell Address can be distilled into six broad themes, pillars of liberty upon which the American republic could stand. Washington often described core principles as "pillars." In his first farewell, the 1783 Circular Letter to the States, Washington outlined "the pillars on which the glorious fabric of our independency and national character must be supported." Before his inauguration in 1789, he called "Harmony, Honesty, Industry and Frugality" the "four great and essential pillars of public felicity."

Informed by eight years as president, Washington refined his ideas into new pillars of liberty: National Unity, Political Moderation, Fiscal Discipline, Virtue and Religion, Education and Foreign Policy.

His overriding focus was turning the fact of independence into enduring liberty. This is not an incidental distinction: While freedom can be a state of nature, liberty requires a degree of self-discipline. It is the essence of self-governance.

During the writing of the Farewell Address, Washington and his speechwriters, Madison and Hamilton, inevitably responded to current events, filtering controversies through their political prisms. But the ideas were all decidedly Washington's, reflecting hard-won lessons learned in different chapters of his life as a surveyor, soldier, politician, entrepreneur, citizen and statesman. The stories of how he arrived at these conclusions constitute an autobiography of ideas.

Washington hoped his life could be seen as a testament to the idea that character is the architect of achievement. A close reading of the Farewell Address offers a rare window into the process by which Washington tried to reveal his character and the character of our nation at the same time.

National Unity
JOIN OR DIE

★

The unity of government which constitutes you one people is also now dear to you. It is justly so, for it is a main pillar in the edifice of your real independence, the support of your tranquility at home, your peace abroad; of your safety; of your prosperity; of that very liberty which you so highly prize .... Citizens, by birth or choice, of a common country, that country has a right to concentrate your affections. The name of American, which belongs to you in your national capacity, must always exalt the just pride of patriotism more than any appellation derived from local discriminations. With slight shades of difference, you have the same religion, manners, habits, and political principles. You have in a common cause fought and triumphed together; the independence and liberty you possess are the work of joint counsels, and joint efforts of common dangers, sufferings, and successes.

As a young man, Washington explored the western frontier. Trusted at sixteen to lead an expedition for the Ohio Company as a surveyor, Washington enjoyed wilderness work, tromping through hills and valleys. Surveying required a love of the outdoors, a mathematical mind and an artist's touch for hand-drawing detailed maps, using his compass, chain and brain. The Virginia gentry funding the expedition were looking for land deals that could turn a quick profit, but young Washington had a more expansive vision, seeing future towns and cities in the untamed spaces of the Shenandoah Valley, what he would later call "the rising Empire" in the New World.

This took imagination at a time when the population of the entire eastern seaboard was fewer than 1 million people and the frontier began just a few miles inland from the coast, a vast wilderness controlled by Native American tribes dotted with remote military outposts. But Washington believed that rivers could be vital arteries for future trade. As a planter's son, he appreciated that the richness of the soil and the vastness of the land could allow America to not only become self-sufficient but also quickly outpace the growth of the Old World.

As Washington grew older, he embarked on other excursions into the wilderness, sometimes as a soldier and other times as a speculator. His first land purchase occurred when he was barely out of his teenage years, snatching up 1,500 acres surrounding Bullskin Creek in the wilderness of Frederick County, Virginia. He eventually accumulated 10,000 acres on the Ohio River and forty continuous miles along the northwest-flowing Great Kanawha River in present-day West Virginia.

At the intersection of those rivers he saw the chance to build a great city; he proclaimed "for fertility of soil, pleasantness of clime, and other natural advantages, [it] is equal to any known tract of the universe of the same extent."

This was unusual enthusiasm from the always understated Washington, but the prospect of profits from agriculture and canal trade could do that to him. Over the years, he variously schemed to attract tenant farmers with three-generation leases and to raise domesticated buffalo herds. Today, the intersection of the two rivers that he believed would sprout a great city is the site of Point Pleasant, West Virginia, population 4,350.

Washington was a nationalist before there was a nation. He ventured off American soil only once, accompanying his beloved older half brother Lawrence on a trip to the lush and prosperous Caribbean trading island of Barbados. While visiting, he dined with the island's elite "Beefsteak and Tripe Club" and admired the rigorous grandeur of the British military so much that he resolved to become a soldier. He also contracted a serious case of smallpox—a brush with death that turned out to be a blessing because it inoculated him from the deadly illness during the Revolutionary War.

Despite his limited travels abroad, Washington was able to see further than most. He imagined the continent not as it was, but as it could be—an independent nation in the Americas.

While the size of the coastal colonies was a strategic and commercial asset, no one had ever cobbled together a unified republic on such a scale. Political thinkers from ancient times to the Enlightenment era believed that sustaining such a large republic was impossible. The French philosopher Montesquieu summed up this conventional wisdom, declaring, "It is in the nature of a republic to have only a small territory; otherwise, it can scarcely continue to exist. . . . In a large republic, the common good is sacrificed to a thousand considerations. . . . In a small one, the public good is better felt, better known, lies nearer to each citizen."

The regional differences within the colonies were vast. After independence, there were 4 million people spread out over 1,000 miles of coastline, and only 60 percent of the American population was of English descent. The former colonies did not even have a common currency of communication. Dutch was still spoken throughout much of upstate New York, and French was the lingua franca of Maine, Vermont and parts of New Hampshire. German dominated commerce in Germantown, outside of Philadelphia, and even into the western reaches of the state.

★

WHEN WASHINGTON TOOK COMMAND OF the rebellious Continental Army in 1775, he addressed these divisions directly: "It is hoped that all distinctions of Colonies will be laid aside, so that one and the same spirit may animate the whole, and the only contest be, who shall render, on this great and trying occasion, the most essential service to the great and common cause in which we are all engaged." Regional rivalries had to be overcome to create a new nation.

Even in 1776, Washington saw the fatal dangers of national disintegration, writing, "nothing but disunion can hurt our cause—this will ruin it, if great prudence, temper, and moderation is not mixed in our counsels and made the governing principles of the contending parties."

The urgency of this idea had been captured earlier by one of the first American political cartoons, symbolizing the need for American unity. Produced by Benjamin Franklin's *Philadelphia Gazette*, the wood carving showed a snake cut up into sections, representing the states from South Carolina to New England, above the slogan "Join or Die." An accompanying editorial by Franklin decried the "extreme difficulty of bringing so many different governments and assemblies to agree in any speedy and effectual measures for our common defense and security."

During the war, Washington battled the parochial interests of the Continental Congress almost as intensely as he battled the British. The state representatives could not even agree on steady funding for the troops who were fighting to win independence. Shortsighted self-interest drove the separatism that almost doomed the Union from its birth. But Washington constantly reminded his fellow citizens that the war had been won by the United States as a whole, not any single state.

His Circular Letter to the States viewed the opportunities of independence with a surveyor's eye, returning to the strategic and economic benefits of the peculiar position of the United States on the globe. We were isolated from the bloody conflicts of Europe by a mighty ocean; to our west lay vast and valuable expanses of land. The result was a perfect place to enact the American experiment:

"The citizens of America, placed in the most enviable condition, as the sole lords and proprietors of a vast tract of continent, comprehending all the various soils and climates of the world, and abounding with all the necessaries and conveniences of life, are now by the late satisfactory pacification, acknowledged to be possessed of absolute freedom and independency," Washington wrote. "They are, from this period, to be considered as the actors on a most conspicuous theater, which seems to be peculiarly designated by Providence for the display of human greatness and felicity."

Washington understood that the United States' independence was paradoxically inseparable from its interdependence. The individual and the community existed in concert. Success would come from leveraging its combined strength rather than re-creating a European-style landlocked competition of solely self-interested states.

"Whatever measures have a tendency to dissolve the Union," Washington wrote, "or contribute to violate or lessen sovereign authority, ought to be considered as hostile to the liberty and independency of America."

After the war, Washington watched the weakness of the Articles of Confederation with alarm, fearing that the lack of a strong, unified central government without a chief executive would doom our unruly infant nation to devolve into separate countries, either sparking civil war or inviting reconquest. Washington wrote James Madison, "Thirteen sovereignties pulling against each other, and all tugging at the federal head, will soon bring ruin on the whole; whereas a liberal and energetic Constitution, well guarded and closely watched . . . might restore us to that degree of respectability and consequence to which we had a fair claim, and the brightest prospect of attaining."

The specter of historic failure haunted the founders. In the summer of 1786, James Madison was already embarked on an ambitious inquiry at his family home in the Blue Ridge Mountains, known as Montpelier, studying ancient history to determine the mistakes that previous confederations had made so that America might avoid the same fate.

Madison asked Jefferson, still ensconced in Paris, to procure books for him. Jefferson responded by sending two trunks of classic texts from abroad, including Diderot, Voltaire, Plutarch, and Polybius. Madison went through the histories methodically, compiling his "Notes on Ancient and Modern Confederacies," which made such an impression on Washington that he copied the notes into his own hand.

Tracing the arcs of the ancient republics of Lycia and Athens to the comparatively modern case studies of the Swiss Confederation and the Treaty of Utrecht, Madison saw consistent themes: initial unity compelled by a common external enemy, later overcome by squabbles among regional special interests, often encouraged by foreign powers looking to undermine national sovereignty. Weakness invited violation. There were vultures everywhere.

The case of the ancient Lycian League, a confederation of twenty-six cities and towns along the southern Mediterranean coast of what is now Turkey, provided positive instruction as well as a cautionary tale. This civilization flourished in the fifth century BC, possessing its own language and alphabet. But for Madison's purposes, its innovation was proportional representation in the central governing council—larger cities received three and the smallest hamlets got one—with commensurate taxation based on the number of seats in the legislature. This example inspired Madison to repeatedly refer to the otherwise obscure ancient republic in the constitutional debates and in the Federalist Papers.

From Greek history, particularly the crumbling of the Amphictyonic League of city-states, Madison took the lesson that a too-decentralized confederation could be split apart by regional rivalries and foreign intrigues.

These Greek city-states had banded together to beat back a foreign invasion from Persia. But their citizens continued to place their loyalties in their cities. Athens and Sparta, Madison noted in Federalist 18, "became first rivals and then enemies; and did each other infinitely more mischief than they had suffered from Xerxes," the Persian king. "Hence, the weakness, the disorders, and finally the destruction of the confederacy," which occurred when King Philip of Macedon, father of Alexander the Great, infiltrated select cities with bribes masquerading as foreign aid and splintered the alliance in order to ultimately conquer it. As Hamilton later explained, "ambitious Philip, under the mask of an ally to one, invaded the liberties of each, and finally subverted the whole." Foreign influence in domestic politics could be deadly to a democracy.

Edward Gibbon's *The History of the Decline and Fall of the Roman Empire* was a bestseller with multiple printings accompanying successive volumes issued from the 1780s through the 1790s. Washington owned a copy and it was one of the most popular tomes in the local New York City library when the first Congress was in town. Gibbon's popular history reflected contemporary anxieties about the dissolution of the British Empire, which had, of course, lost its American colonies. His four key causes of Roman decline resonated with his contemporaries. The "injuries of time and nature" were beyond any man's reach, and Gibbon's attacks on Christianity were notoriously controversial. But his warnings on the "domestic quarrels" driven by the ambitions of unscrupulous men—as well as on the destabilizing impact of excessive debt, along with a lazy and licentious elite culture—found an attentive audience across the Atlantic.

Madison's study of past civilizations led directly to an analysis of America's vulnerabilities under the Articles of Confederation, titled "Vices of the Political System of the United States."

Madison presented a new vision of America's vast geography. Instead of being considered a fatal weakness for a republic, Madison argued that size and scope could be a source of strength. His study of the past was prologue for the U.S. Constitution. He recorded the accumulated lessons in a forty-one-page pocket-sized booklet, which he referred to during the Constitutional Convention. These themes flowed throughout the Federalist Papers' rapid-response arguments for ratification, with Madison borrowing some of his earlier paragraphs wholesale.

The Anti-Federalists arguing against the Constitution cited Montesquieu's belief that "it is in the nature of a republic to have only a small territory; otherwise, it can scarcely continue to exist."

Madison's response is famously expressed in Federalist 10, "The Utility of the Union as a Safeguard against Domestic Faction and Insurrection"—arguing that tyranny of the majority was most likely to occur in small republics. When a republic holds a critical mass of diverse interests, no single group is likely to hold the upper hand for long. The combination of diversity and size serves as a cooling mechanism on more heated local passions and prejudices. In a large republic, the necessity of cobbling together broad governing coalitions means that narrow self-interest is forced to give way to a more enlightened self-interest, in the recognition that pursuing the common good can bring about mutual benefits.*

Hamilton also cited Madison's research in the Federalist Papers, arguing: "A firm Union will be of the utmost moment to the peace and liberty of the States, as a barrier against domestic faction and insurrection. It is impossible to read the history of the petty republics of Greece and Italy without feeling sensations of horror and disgust at the distractions with which they were continually agitated, and at the rapid succession of revolutions by which they were kept in a state of perpetual vibration between the extremes of tyranny and anarchy."

After its revolution, France was soon providing a contemporary example of this "perpetual vibration between the extremes."

Jefferson's Jacobin sympathies were widely shared at the time. The forces urging an international expansion of liberty were naturally at odds with more practical-minded men who believed that America's gains were still fragile.

Washington was in the civilization-building business. At the outset of his administration, he told Madison, "As the first of everything in our situation will serve to establish a precedent, it is devoutly wished on my part that these precedents may be fixed on true principles." He wanted to secure a solid foundation for the American experiment, securing enough time to gain economic and military strength while establishing a national character that could solidify the Union. And he reluctantly understood that he could best strengthen our national Union through the strength of his own example.

Washington embarked on three extensive trips throughout the thirteen states in his first term—first to New England (sidestepping Rhode Island

---

* Madison's missive contained aphorisms that would later find their way into Washington's Farewell Address, such as "It is too often forgotten, by nations as well as by individuals that honesty is the best policy."

and Vermont, which hadn't yet joined the Union), then Long Island, and finally to the southern states.

What he learned on his listening tour pleased him: "The country appears to be in a very improving state, and industry and frugality are becoming much more fashionable than they have hitherto been there. Tranquility reigns among the people, with the disposition towards general government which is likely to preserve it. They begin to feel the good effects of equal laws and equal protection."

For Washington, the prime benefits of union were protection and prosperity. He understood the need to root attachments to rational self-interest but then flipped the script by emphasizing the larger responsibilities that came with individual rights: "Every citizen who enjoys the protection of a free government owes not only a portion of his property, but even of his personal services, to the defense of it."

The 1792 draft of the Farewell Address devoted much of its brief text to this argument for embracing the Union, rooted in the enlightened self-interest of each state and individual.

We may all be considered as the children of one common country.
We have all been embarked in one common cause. We have all
had our share in common sufferings and common successes.
The portion of the Earth allotted for the theater of our fortunes
fulfills our most sanguine desires. All its essential interests are
the same; whilst its diversities arising from climate from soil, and
from the other local and lesser peculiarities, will naturally form a
mutual relation of the parts, that may give the whole a more entire
independence than has perhaps fallen to the lot of any other nation.
To confirm these motives to an affectionate and permanent Union,
and to secure the great objects of it, we have established a common
government, which being free in its principles, being founded in
our own choice, being intended as the guardian of our common

rights and the patron of our common interests . . . seems to promise everything that can be expected from such an institution.

The sum of the United States was greater than its parts. And if we squandered this opportunity for happiness in a blessed portion of earth, it would be a permanent black mark in the pages of history. And it was for the sake of national unity—and to avoid risk of civil war—that Washington agreed to stay in office.

While the bitter fights of his second term expanded the focus of the final Farewell Address to include warnings about the dangers of extremism, debt and foreign alliances, Washington still chose to open with the importance of national unity.

He was trying to establish the idea of the American "citizen"—using the word eight times in the Farewell Address and more than 1,000 times in his correspondence. This was exceeded only by Washington's invocation of the word "Union"—used more than twenty times in the Farewell Address and more than 3,000 times in his letters.

A strong sense of citizenship—a new concept in a new nation—was essential to securing the Union. And when he used the word *American* in this section of the manuscript, he underlined the term twice for emphasis.

*

WASHINGTON'S PASSION FOR NATIONAL UNITY did not provoke much self-examination as far as Native Americans were concerned. He'd surveyed their territory, fighting alongside and against them. He knew that American expansion would displace the tribes. But this had been the case since European settlers arrived in what they called "the New World" and it did not drive the first president to distraction. Instead, he busied himself negotiating treaties and peace between warring tribes, meeting with representatives of the Creeks and the Chickasaws—and exhorting the Cherokee to achieve economic independence through cattle ranching and corn and cotton production—all in the August during which he was drafting the Farewell Address. He detailed negotiations in his subsequent speech to Congress and dined with "four sets of Indians on four several days" in early December, according to Vice President John Adams, including "the widow and children of Hanging Maw, a famous friend of ours who was basely murdered by some white people."

These concerns were a fact of life on the frontier. "Next to the case of the black race within our bosom," attested Madison, "that of the red on our borders is the problem most baffling to the policy of our country."

Washington's focus on national unity also skipped over the slaves who surrounded him at home. When his wife's personal attendant Oney Judge and their celebrated chef Hercules separately fled to freedom from Philadelphia, Washington was furious, placing ads for their capture in local newspapers. Judge, who was scheduled to be given away as a wedding present, escaped during dinner one night to live for four decades in New Hampshire as a free woman; Hercules was never heard from again.

★

WASHINGTON UNABASHEDLY ENCOURAGED IMMIGRATION TO America's vast lands, but he also championed assimilation as a means of establishing a national character. Before assuming the presidency, he presented a vision of America as a beacon of freedom that could create economic benefits for everyone. Rendering our nation "the asylum of pacific and industrious characters from all parts of Europe would encourage the cultivation of the Earth by the high price which its products would command—and would draw the wealth, and wealthy men, of other Nations into our bosom, by giving security to prosperity and liberty to its holders."

After six years in office, he shifted his emphasis slightly, placing primacy in a letter to Vice President Adams on the integration of immigrant cultures: "by an intermixture with our people, they, or their descendants, get assimilated to our customs, measures, and laws: in a word, soon become one people." This was partially informed by the insurrections seeded by the agents of France, raising the prospect of new residents who did not feel America was their first loyalty. An emphasis on assimilation could ease those concerns while keeping America's population ascendant.

These perspectives foreshadowed what Washington would write in the Farewell Address: "Citizens, by birth or choice, of a common country, that country has a right to concentrate your affections. The name of American, which belongs to you in your national capacity, must always exalt the just pride of patriotism more than any appellation derived from local discriminations. With slight shades of difference, you have the same religion, manners, habits, and political principles."

★

IN HIS FAREWELL, WASHINGTON OFFERED an extended tour of the beneficial economic interdependence underlying our newly independent nation.

> The North, in an unrestrained intercourse with the South,
> protected by the equal laws of a common government, finds
> in the productions of the latter great additional resources of
> maritime and commercial enterprise and precious materials of
> manufacturing industry.
>   The South, in the same intercourse, benefiting by the agency
> of the North, sees its agriculture grow and its commerce expand.
> Turning partly into its own channels the seamen of the North, it
> finds its particular navigation invigorated; and, while it contributes,
> in different ways, to nourish and increase the general mass of the
> national navigation, it looks forward to the protection of a maritime
> strength, to which itself is unequally adapted.
>   The East, in a like intercourse with the West, already finds,
> and in the progressive improvement of interior communications
> by land and water, will more and more find a valuable vent for the
> commodities which it brings from abroad, or manufactures at home.
>   The West derives from the East supplies requisite to its growth

and comfort, and, what is perhaps of still greater consequence, it must of necessity owe the secure enjoyment of indispensable outlets for its own productions to the weight, influence, and the future maritime strength of the Atlantic side of the Union, directed by an indissoluble community of interest as one nation. Any other tenure by which the West can hold this essential advantage, whether derived from its own separate strength, or from an apostate and unnatural connection with any foreign power, must be intrinsically precarious.

Washington's argument for national unity was rooted in the most elemental considerations of civilization—personal safety and increased prosperity. He was careful to harness realistic appeals to regional self-interest.

While the divisions between North and South, and urban and rural economies, still resonate today, Washington's appeal to western citizens is a bit harder to appreciate. The western frontier then was the Appalachian region, bounded by the Mississippi River, where there were competing claims for trade and association, particularly from the colonial outposts of France and Spain, which stretched along the Gulf Coast. Washington argued that these foreign powers could not be dependable local allies on our continent.

American unity could offer military protection while helping states "avoid the necessity of those overgrown military establishments which, under any form of government, are inauspicious to liberty, and which are to be regarded as particularly hostile to republican liberty." With the federal government responsible for national defense, states could invest in civic improvements rather than competing armies, keeping local government small and responsive.

To those who argued that history showed no democratic republic could be sustained on such a large geographic scale, Washington had a practical answer: "Let experience solve it. To listen to mere speculation in such a case were criminal. . . . It is well worth a fair and full experiment."

After the sacrifices of war and the struggles to find the right form of government, Washington counseled patience: give our young nation time to strengthen our economic, military, and civic bonds. Don't let theory overwhelm the accumulation of experience.

The subject of national unity could inspire Washington to rare rhetorical heights: it was nothing less than "the palladium of your political safety and prosperity" and "a main pillar in the edifice of your real independence, the support of your tranquility at home, your peace abroad; of your safety; of your prosperity; of that very liberty which you so highly prize."

The dangers presented by unscrupulous men and foreign nations was never far from Washington's mind, and he cautioned citizens against those conniving dividers. Independence depended on unity.

"It is easy to foresee that, from different causes and from different quarters, much pains will be taken, many artifices employed to weaken in your minds the conviction of this truth," he wrote. The Union must be guarded with "jealous anxiety" against these "internal and external enemies." Citizens should get in the habit of "indignantly frowning upon the first dawning of every attempt to alienate any portion of our country from the rest, or to enfeeble the sacred ties which now link together the various parts."

In Washington's view, we must transcend our tribalism to survive.

Political Moderation
THE FIGHT AGAINST FACTIONS

★

The alternate domination of one faction over another, sharpened by the spirit of revenge, natural to party dissension, which in different ages and countries has perpetrated the most horrid enormities, is itself a frightful despotism. . . . It serves always to distract the public councils and enfeeble the public administration. It agitates the community with ill-founded jealousies and false alarms, kindles the animosity of one part against another, foments occasionally riot and insurrection. . . . There being constant danger of excess, the effort ought to be by force of public opinion, to mitigate and assuage it.

"I was no party man myself," Washington wrote Thomas Jefferson, "and the first wish of my heart was, if parties did exist, to reconcile them."

As our first and only independent president, Washington's independence was a function not only of his pioneering place in American history but also of political principles he developed over a lifetime.

To Washington, moderation was a source of strength. He viewed its essential judiciousness as a guiding principle of good government, rooted in ancient wisdom as well as Enlightenment-era liberalism. Much could be achieved "by *prudence*, much by *conciliation*, and much by *firmness*." A stable, civil society depends on resisting intolerant extremes.

The Constitution did not mention political parties and during the debate over ratification, Madison and Hamilton praised the Constitution's "spirit of moderation" in contrast to the "intolerant spirit" of "those who are ever so much persuaded of their being in the right in any controversy."

Washington was non-partisan but he was not neutral. He was decisive after consulting differing opinions. "He seeks information from all quarters, and judges more independently than any man I ever knew," attested Vice President Adams. "It is of so much importance to the public that he should preserve this superiority." Independence ensured superior perspective in the executive.

In the tempestuous early days of the republic, only Washington had the stature to appear above politics, with the ability to transcend tribal loyalties. Even Jefferson recognized that Washington was "the only man in the U.S. who possessed the confidence of the whole . . . there was no other person thought anything more than the head of a party."

But Washington was an intuitive student of human nature, not naïve about the tendency of people to cluster into political factions, driven by self-interest. His understanding of history led him to believe that partisan impulses needed to be restrained by a wise and vigilant citizenry. In one of his deleted lines from the final draft of the Farewell Address, Washington asserted that "the conflicts of popular factions are the chief, if not the only, inlets of usurpation and tyranny."

Washington understood the danger of demagogues in a democracy. He was a passionate advocate of moderation as a means of calming partisan passions and creating problem-solving coalitions. John Adams also believed that "without the great political virtues of humility, patience, and moderation . . . every man in power becomes a ravenous beast of prey." And it was a source of personal pain for Washington to see his cabinet degenerate into exaggerated suspicions and vicious slanders. Most frustrating was to watch his motives twisted and attacked for partisan gain by "infamous scribblers" in the newspapers.

This was evidence of his earliest concerns. Even in the days after winning independence from Britain, Washington warned of the dangerous interplay between extremes. "There is a natural and necessary progression from the extreme of anarchy to the extreme of tyranny," he wrote in his Circular Letter to the States, and "arbitrary power is most easily established on the ruins of liberty abused to licentiousness." As liberty in France turned to anarchy and then tyranny during his administration, it confirmed his deepest instincts.

As a young man, Washington devoured the popular early-eighteenth-century essays of Joseph Addison in the *Spectator* of London. Addison was the author of his favorite play, *Cato,* and while reflecting on the sources of England's bloody civil war in the 1640s, he had written an influential essay on "the Malice of Parties":

> There cannot a greater judgment befall a country than a dreadful
> spirit of division as rends a government into two distinct
> people, and makes them greater strangers, and more averse to
> one another, than if they were actually two different nations.
> The effects of such a division are pernicious to the last degree,
> not only with regard to those advantages which they give the
> common enemy, but to those private evils which they produce in
> the heart of almost every particular person. This influence is very
> fatal both to men's morals and their understandings; it sinks the
> virtue of a nation, and not only so, but destroys even common
> sense. A furious party spirit, when it rages in its full violence,
> exerts itself in civil war and bloodshed; and when it is under its
> greatest restraints, naturally breaks out in falsehood, detraction,
> calumny, and a partial administration of justice. In a word, it fills
> a nation with spleen and rancor, and extinguishes all the seeds of
> good nature, compassion, and humanity.

Addison was not the only wise voice warning the revolutionary generation against the danger of hyper-partisanship.

The English poet Alexander Pope declared that party spirit "is but the madness of many for the gain of a few." The early-eighteenth-century

British opposition leader Bolingbroke reflected on the evils of parties from experience, "Party is a political evil, and faction is the worst of all parties." Informed by both journalism and politics, Bolingbroke wrote that "a man who has not seen the inside of parties, nor had opportunities to examine nearly their secret motives, can hardly conceive how little share principle of any sort, though principle of some sort or other be always pretended, has in the determination of their conduct."

Montesquieu, the philosopher most cited by the founders, was a passionate moderate. He believed "political liberty is found only in moderate governments," and argued that "the spirit of moderation should be that of the legislator. The political good, like the moral good always is found between two limits." He was careful, however, to explain that "I mean the moderation founded on virtue, not the one that comes from faintheartedness and from laziness of soul."

Madison's favorite political philosopher, David Hume, the champion of checks and balances, argued that "factions subvert government, render laws impotent, and beget the fiercest animosities among men of the same nation who ought to give mutual assistance to each other." "Moderation," Hume continued, "is of advantage to every establishment."

This Enlightenment-era distrust of faction had its roots in classical wisdom. Plato listed moderation among the four cardinal virtues in his *Republic*, alongside wisdom, courage and justice. Socrates taught his students to "avoid extremes on either side," while Aristotle advocated the so-called golden mean between extremes as the key to virtue and happiness. It is the soul of reason against ravenous self-interest.

In *The History of the Peloponnesian War*, the historian Thucydides wrote of how the city Corcyra was destroyed by internal factions: "Both ventured on most horrible outrages, and prosecuted their revenges still farther, without any regard of justice or the public good. . . . The neutrals of the city were destroyed by both factions; partly because they would not side with them, and partly for envy that they should so escape."

In *On Duties*, Cicero warned that those "who propose to take charge of the affairs of government should not fail to remember . . . [that] those who care for the interests of a part of the citizens and neglect another part, introduce into the civil service a dangerous element—dissension and party strife."

In *The History of the Decline and Fall of the Roman Empire,* Edward Gibbon warned of the factional fighting that eroded civilization, cautioning that only fidelity to the calm perspective that comes from philosophy "is able to eradicate from the human mind the latent and deadly principle of fanaticism."

Centuries of wisdom lay behind Madison's denunciation of "factions" in the Federalist Papers. "By a faction," he explained, "I understand a number of citizens, whether amounting to a majority or a minority of the whole, who are united and actuated by some common impulse of passion, or of interest, adversed to the rights of other citizens, or to the permanent and aggregate interests of the community."

The founding fathers' suspicion of faction was rooted in the classical tradition that celebrated the virtue of moderation—and the subsequent independence of thought and action that moderation can create. "According to the classical doctrine, membership in a political party inevitably involved defending the indefensible vices of one's allies and attempting to dominate one's fellow citizens in order to satisfy a narrow self-interest," wrote Carl J. Richard in *The Founders and the Classics.* "In the eighteenth century the greatest compliment one man could pay another was to call him 'disinterested.' To be disinterested was to place justice above all considerations, including one's own interests and those of one's family, friends, and political allies."

*

WASHINGTON WAS A DECIDEDLY DISINTERESTED man, but he was not an accidental politician. His ambition was vast, though he was reluctant to parade it too plainly. He understood that the seeker is never as valued as the sought.

At twenty-three, Washington aimed for election to Virginia's House of Burgesses and lost. He tried again three years later and won, aided by a newfound willingness to campaign, colonial-style: he analyzed the local voter rolls alphabetically and then plied the local electorate with booze on Election Day. Grateful citizens returned the favor.

Washington was not the loudest member of the colonial legislature. He cultivated a reputation as a steadying force in tumultuous times. "That dispassionate voice also would help persuade Americans of his trustworthiness with power," explained Paul K. Longmore in *The Invention of George Washington*. "They praised patriotic zeal, but they feared fierce passions once unleashed. Emotional anarchy might end in political tyranny. Washington would prove his fitness to lead a revolution by his mastery of himself."

As the British Crown sowed seeds of colonial dissension with its tax schemes, Washington worked with his legislative colleague George Mason on a form of economic civil resistance known as nonimportation, which sought to reduce taxes paid to Parliament by increasing local self-sufficiency, the first "Buy American" campaign.

The House of Burgesses was divided between moderates and militants in their resistance to the British royals, and Washington played a pivotal role by bridging the divides with personal diplomacy, dining with leaders of the different factions. Washington's role as a convener on common ground reinforced his reputation as a man of the center, able to wield the balance of power.

Washington's carefully cultivated political profile, along with his military experience in the French and Indian War and his imposing physical stature, led to his selection as the leader of the Continental Army in 1776. His moderate temperament was praised by contemporaries: "he seems discrete and virtuous," offered Connecticut delegate Eliphalet Dyer, "no harum-scarum, ranting, swearing fellow, but sober, steady, and calm." A final added inducement was the virtue of geographic balance: a Virginian could unite the nation by leading an army that was then based in Boston.

Politics, of course, did not end during wartime. Even in a time of existential threat, when the presence of a common enemy should have produced a sustained unity of purpose, the individual states' self-interest repeatedly trumped the national interest. There was no political will to raise revenue to pay the soldiers. Washington's frustration with the weak and fractured Congress helped form his belief that a strong central government led by an honest, energetic executive was essential to a successful democracy.

As the war persisted, public enthusiasm waned. In April 1778, Washington complained to a congressional delegate that people "may talk of patriotism—they may draw a few examples from ancient story of great achievements performed by its influence; but whoever builds upon it, as a sufficient basis for conducting a long and bloody war, will find themselves deceived in the end. We must take the passions of men as nature has given them."

While appeals to patriotism could be a powerful short-term motivator, Washington wrote, "a great and lasting war can never be supported on this principle alone. It must be aided by a prospect of interest or some reward. For a time it may, of itself, push men to action—to bear much—to encounter difficulties; but it will not endure unassisted by interest." Washington's frustration hardened over time into one of his favorite maxims: "Democratical states must always *feel* before they can *see:* it is this that makes their governments slow—but the people will be right at last."

During these dark days, amid "the want of harmony in our councils—the declining zeal of the people," Washington wrote his friend Gouverneur Morris, "it is well worth the ambition of a patriot statesman at this juncture to endeavor to pacify party differences—to give fresh vigor to the springs of government—to inspire the people with confidence."

Washington's call for a "patriot statesman" echoed Bolingbroke's call for a "Patriot King" in a widely read 1749 pamphlet that articulated an antidote to the corruption and fanaticism of parties that led to England's civil war. For Bolingbroke, the ideal was a benign monarch who could "defeat the designs, and break the spirit of faction" in a parliamentary democracy, toward the goal of delivering "true principles of government independent of all." Washington's substitution of "statesman" for "king" reframed the concept for an American audience. The ideal of a strong leader who operated beyond partisanship retained its attractiveness.

★

WHEN THE WAR ENDED, WASHINGTON was again forced to confront faction, this time in his own officer corps as frustration over the failure of Congress threatened mutiny.

As Washington's soldiers decamped, the standing army decreased to just over 500 soldiers. Those who remained griped with good reason that the impotent Continental Congress seemed both unable and unwilling to pay their wartime salaries or offer pensions, especially for those wounded or maimed. In the vacuum created by the cessation of hostilities, the grumbling erupted into seditious scheming.

On March 10, 1783, an anonymous letter circulated among the soldiers and generals who remained at Washington's headquarters in Newburgh. It argued for "a bolder tone" in demanding back pay while mocking "the man who would advise to more moderation and longer forbearance." The letter called for an impromptu meeting in the absence of General Washington to discuss taking matters into their own hands.

Whether this was a bluff or an outright threat against the Continental Congress, it represented a dangerous step for the newly independent nation: it looked like the beginning of a coup d'état. Some officers floated the idea of Washington assuming the mantle of monarch. English history seemed to be repeating itself, as with Cromwell: once again, a revolution against a king looked set to devolve into discord and propel the rise of a military dictator.

Washington responded by crashing the plotters' meeting and confronting the officers by surprise. He aimed to address their concerns, but also to calm passions and turn the army toward a more constructive path. In remarks that he wrote himself, Washington acknowledged their frustrations and temptations but slammed the plotters' argument that a path of patience and moderation was weak and indeterminate. "To suspect the man who shall recommend moderate measures and longer forbearance—I spurn it—as every man who regards that liberty, and reveres that Justice for which we contend, ultimately must. For if men are to be precluded from offering their sentiments on a matter, which may involve the most serious and alarming consequences that can invite the consideration of mankind, reason is of no use to us—the freedom of speech may be taken away—and, dumb and silent, we may be led, like sheep, to the slaughter." This was a full-throated defense of the wisdom that comes from walking a middle path, attacking the disastrous consequences that could come from falling for demagogues.

"Let me entreat you, gentlemen, on your part, not to take any measures, which, viewed in the calm light of reason, will lessen the dignity and sully the glory you have hitherto maintained. . . . And let me conjure you, in the name of our common country—as you value your own sacred honor," Washington said, gravely echoing the closing sentence of the Declaration of Independence, "as you respect the rights of humanity, and as you regard the military and national character of America, to express your utmost horror and detestation of the man who wishes, under any specious pretenses, to overturn the liberties of our country, and who wickedly attempts to open the floodgates of civil discord and deluge our rising empire in blood."

Washington's uncharacteristically passionate speech began to calm the anger of his officers, but it was a bit of theater at the end of his remarks that truly turned the tide. Preparing to read a letter he had written to the Continental Congress on their behalf, he took a pair of spectacles out of their case in his breast pocket. "Gentlemen, you must pardon me," he explained. "I have not only grown gray, but almost blind, in the service of my country."

With that simple aside, revealing vulnerability in the man they had regarded as almost invulnerable, several plotting officers began to weep. By taking the risk of intimacy, Washington managed to stop infamous history from repeating.

★

FOUR YEARS LATER, AS PRESIDENT of the Constitutional Convention in Philadelphia, Washington also sought to forge constructive coalitions to contain the forces of faction.

Compromise and moderation were the means by which the Constitution was achieved. Small states and large states fitfully worked out their concerns over representation, and the abolition of slavery was unfortunately tabled as too divisive to tackle while maintaining the Union at the time. As Washington biographer James Thomas Flexner wrote, "It certainly was a blessing that the political parties which were to become inherent in the American governmental system had not yet evolved. Two or more teams pulling against each other for political advantage would have wrecked the Constitutional Convention."

Washington tried to appear nonpartisan and serve as an honest broker, but he was not an aloof leader. As he had during his time in the House of Burgesses, he took the time to lobby members over tea and at taverns like the Indian Queen and City Tavern. Privately, he railed against "narrow-minded politicians . . . under the influence of local views." Even in session, where he refrained from speaking to avoid compromising his independent authority, his eyes betrayed his judgments, and delegates sought his approval.

The other player with maximum moral sway was the aging Benjamin Franklin. Too sick to speak in the final days of the convention, he handed his final remarks to a colleague to read as he sat in Independence Hall.

> I confess that there are several parts of this Constitution which I do not at present approve, but I am not sure I shall never approve them. . . . The older I grow, the more apt I am to doubt my own judgment, and to pay more respect to the judgment of others. . . . I doubt too whether any other Convention we can obtain may be able to make a better Constitution. For when you assemble a number of men to have the advantage of their joint

wisdom, you inevitably assemble with those men, all their prejudices, their passions, their errors of opinion, their local interests, and their selfish views. From such an Assembly can a perfect production be expected? It therefore astonishes me, Sir, to find this system approaching so near to perfection as it does; and I think it will astonish our enemies, who are waiting with confidence to hear that our councils are confounded like those of the builders of Babel, and that our States are on the point of separation, only to meet hereafter for the purpose of cutting one another's throats. Thus I consent, Sir, to this Constitution because I expect no better, and because I am not sure, that it is not the best. . . . On the whole, Sir, I cannot help expressing a wish that every member of the Convention who may still have objections to it would, with me, on this occasion doubt a little of his own infallibility.

Franklin's argument for not making the perfect the enemy of the good served as a powerful rebuke to the absolutism of those obstructionists who tried to derail the Constitution in the naïve belief they might achieve something more ideologically pure down the road. Moderation requires humility and the willingness, as Franklin said, to doubt a little in your own infallibility.

In the end, as Catherine Drinker Bowen wrote in *Miracle at Philadelphia,* "In the Constitutional Convention, the spirit of compromise reigned in grace and glory; as Washington presided, it sat on his shoulder like the dove."

Compromise was at the heart of the document. The Constitution's structural insight of checks and balances, dividing authority into three separate accountable branches of government, was intended to enshrine moderation. No one could rule without their reasoning resonating with the others. As Peter Berkowitz argues, "The framers' aim was to constitutionalize liberty by institutionalizing political moderation."

Compromise, of course, did not mean consensus: the Constitution passed with 39 votes of the 55 delegates present, after nearly 100 days of debate. Friendships were fractured and some of the remaining opposition lurched toward the apocalyptic, with the Anti-Federalist sheriff of New

York County, Marinus Willett, calling the new Constitution "a monster with open mouth and monstrous teeth ready to devour all before it."

In contrast, the Federalist Papers repeatedly extolled the virtue of the middle ground as a positive good, with Madison saluting "the spirit of moderation" that led to the compromises in the Constitution and Hamilton declaring that "these judicious reflections contain a lesson of moderation to all sincere lovers of the Union."

Hamilton harbored many of Washington's concerns about demagogues and the way they could connive to divide the nation: "There are seasons in every country when noise and impudence pass current for worth; and in popular commotions especially, the clamors of interested and factious men are often mistaken for patriotism." Hamilton even imagined how one could rise to power as a populist demagogue: "I would mount the hobbyhorse of popularity, I would cry out usurpation, danger to liberty etc. etc. I would endeavor to prostrate the national government, raise a ferment, and then ride the whirlwind and direct the storm."

Madison also wrestled with the question of "the violence of faction" and republics' "propensity to this dangerous vice." He devised an ingenious argument that harnessed competing self-interests without sacrificing the "public good." "The influence of factious leaders may kindle a flame within their particular States, but will be unable to spread a general conflagration through the other States."

Cobbling together a majority would require finding common ground, harnessing self-interest to achieve something greater: "Ambition must be made to counteract ambition." For Madison, pluralism was the cure for hyper-partisanship.

★

WHEN WASHINGTON BECAME PRESIDENT, HE intended to establish a government above faction and special interests. "No local prejudices or attachments; no separate views, nor party animosities," he promised in his first inaugural address, "will misdirect the comprehensive and equal eye which ought to watch over this great assemblage of communities and interests."

Washington did not want or expect unanimity of opinion in his cabinet, perhaps reflecting the idea that in a place where everyone thinks alike, no one is thinking very much.

He was aware of his limits on specific issues—especially law and finance. A competition of ideas and opinions was something to be celebrated, as he made clear in a letter to the governor of North Carolina two months after taking the oath of office: "A difference of opinion on political points is not to be imputed to freemen as a fault, since it is to be presumed that they are all actuated by an equally laudable and sacred regard for the liberties of their country."

People project their own perspectives onto the world around them and Washington imagined that his fellow citizens were equally disinterested. As he told the Pennsylvania legislature in a September 1789 letter, "It should be the highest ambition of every American to extend his views beyond himself, and to bear in mind that his conduct will not only affect himself, his country, and his immediate posterity, but that its influence may be co-extensive with the world and stamp political happiness or misery on ages yet unborn."

But as Washington preached an enlightened self-interest consistent with classical liberalism, dissension grew in his cabinet ranks, as political divisions hardened and suspicions drove onetime allies apart. He was always aware that these fault lines could rupture the fragile federal government.

"My greatest fear has been that the nation would not be sufficiently cool and moderate in making arrangements for the security of that liberty," he wrote after nine months in office. "If we mean to support the liberty and independence which it has cost us so much blood and treasure to establish," he wrote to Rhode Island governor Arthur Fenner, "we must drive far away the demon of party spirit and local reproach." But "the demon of party spirit" had only begun.

At first the divisions were subterranean, exacerbated by the partisan press. The establishment of what Washington unwisely criticized as "self-created" Democratic-Republican Societies, enthralled with the French Revolution, further enflamed the nation's passions. Protests over Washington's proclamation of neutrality between England and France soon turned to riots over the Jay Treaty. Each faction saw the other as a treasonous proxy for England or France, and each saw the other as a threat to the republican covenant created by the Constitution.

Hamilton accused Jefferson of harboring a "womanish attachment" to France and railed against Jacobin excesses, warning that "there is no stronger sign of combinations unfriendly to the general good than when partisans of those in power raise an indiscriminate cry against men of property."

For Jefferson, the rise of political parties simply reflected eternal debates between urban elites who favored a strong central government and self-sufficient rural citizens who backed states' rights—they were "nature's Tories and Whigs."* Washington feared that the increasing bitterness could destroy the American experiment.

In the early days of this discord, Washington did his best to bring Jefferson and Hamilton together, arguing that he "was no believer in the infallibility of the politics or measures of *any man living*." He urged an assumption of goodwill: "It is to be regretted exceedingly that subjects cannot be discussed with temper on the one hand, or decisions submitted to without having the motives which led to them improperly implicated on the other: and this regret borders on chagrin when we find that men of abilities—zealous patriots—having the same *general* objects in view, and the same upright intentions to prosecute them, will not exercise more charity in deciding on the opinions and actions of one another."

---

* Whether from conviction or for effect, Jefferson would later occasionally express regret for unleashing the forces of hyper-partisanship in the republic. "You and I have formerly seen warm debates and high political passions," he wrote Edward Rutledge in 1797. "But gentlemen of different politics would then speak to each other, and separate the business of the senate from that of society. It is not so now. Men who have been intimate all their lives, cross the streets to avoid meeting, and turn their heads another way, lest they should be obliged to touch their hats. This may do for young men, with whom passion is enjoyment," wrote Jefferson. "But it is afflicting to peaceable minds."

Washington might as well have been quoting his boyhood idol Addison: "How many honest minds are filled with uncharitable and barbarous notions, out of their zeal for the public good? What cruelties and outrages would they not commit against men of an adverse party, whom they would honor and esteem, if instead of considering them as they are represented, they knew them as they are? Thus are persons of the greatest probity seduced into shameful errors and prejudices, and made bad men even by that noblest of principles, the love of their country."

Washington's advice on how to manage the partisan passions offers evidence of his belief in moderation and modesty when "both sides have strained the cords beyond their bearing." At such times, he wrote, "a middle course would be found the best, until experience shall have pointed out the right mode—or, which is not to be expected, because it is denied to mortals—there shall be some *infallible* rule by which we could forejudge events."

Perfection is never on the political menu. Principled compromise is key, and in its absence, a middle course rooted in enduring values, adjusted by experience, is the best approach for an independent executive to pursue.

But in his attempts to govern above the partisan fray, Washington found himself increasingly alone. Frustrated, he wrote to his second secretary of war, Timothy Pickering, that the trials of "one, who is of no party, and whose sole wish is to pursue with undeviating steps a path which would lead this country to respectability, wealth, and happiness is exceedingly to be lamented." But that was "the turbulence of human passions in party disputes when victory, more than *truth*, is the palm contended for."

He continued this pained riff in a letter to John Jay in the spring of 1796: "I am sure the mass of citizens in the United States mean well; and I firmly believe they will always act well whenever they can obtain a right understanding of matters . . . [but] the inventors and abettors of pernicious measures use infinitely more industry in disseminating the poison, than the well-disposed part of the community do to furnish the antidote."

As Washington faced his Farewell Address, he needed to confront factions with enduring wisdom. "He wanted to carve out a middle course and do so in a moderate tone," explains historian Joseph Ellis; he pushed "his most ardent critics to the fringes of the ongoing debate, where their shrill accusations and throbbing moral certainty could languish in deserved obscurity."

And so when he picked back up Madison's first draft in the spring of 1796, Washington added new language, explaining to the public that given the "considerable changes . . . both at home and abroad, I shall ask your indulgence while I express with more lively sensibility the following most ardent wishes of my heart."

The next line in the draft drove right to the rise of faction: "That party disputes among all the friends and lovers of their country may subside, or, as the wisdom of Providence hath ordained that men, on the same subjects, shall not always think alike, that charity and benevolence, when they happen to differ, may so far shed their benign influence as to banish those invectives which proceed from illiberal prejudices and jealousy."

In a line he deleted from the final draft, Washington went even further, warning that in a large republic, a military coup was unlikely to undermine democracy, even if backed by the wealthy and powerful. The base of the country was too broad. "In such republics," he said, "it is safe to assert that the conflicts of popular factions are the chief, if not the only, inlets of usurpation and tyranny."

In the Farewell, Washington acknowledged that the spirit of party "unfortunately, is inseparable from our nature, having its root in the strongest passions of the human mind. It exists under different shapes in all governments." But he understood partisans' perspective, stating plainly, "there is an opinion that parties in free countries are useful checks upon the administration of the government and serve to keep alive the spirit of liberty. This within certain limits is probably true."

Beyond those wise limits, Washington warned, rampant factions were a "fatal tendency" in democracies. "They serve to organize faction, to give it an artificial and extraordinary force; to put, in the place of the delegated will of the nation the will of a party, often a small but artful and enter-prising minority of the community, according to the alternate triumphs of different parties, to make the public administration the mirror of the ill-concerted and incongruous projects of faction, rather than the organ of consistent and wholesome plans digested by common counsels and modi-fied by mutual interests."

The thin history of republics up to that point showed that partisan fac-tions led by "cunning, ambitious, and unprincipled men" distorted democ-racies by pursuing narrow agendas at the expense of the national interest.

Washington identified regional parties based on "geographical dis-criminations" as a particular danger, because they undermined national unity in pursuit of power. "Designing men may endeavor to excite a belief that there is a real difference of local interests and views" by misrepresent-ing the "opinions and aims" of people from other states and regions. "You cannot shield yourselves too much against the jealousies and heartburnings which spring from these misrepresentations," Washington warned. "They tend to render alien to each other those who ought to be bound together by fraternal affection."

But the greatest danger could spring from the chaos of a dysfunctional democracy, compounded by relentless party warfare, which, Washington warned, would erode faith in the effectiveness of self-governance and open the door to a demagogue with authoritarian ambitions. "The disorders and miseries which result gradually incline the minds of men to seek security and repose in the absolute power of an individual; and sooner or later the chief of some prevailing faction, more able or more fortunate than his com-petitors, turns this disposition to the purposes of his own elevation, on the ruins of public liberty."

History showed that the appeal of such a strong man was a well-trod path to the destruction of liberty. These figures were "enabled to subvert the power of the people and to usurp for themselves the reins of govern-ment, destroying afterwards the very engines which have lifted them to unjust dominion."

The specific circumstances of this degradation to democracy could change in different times, but the underlying dangers were eternal. Washington's description in the final draft of the Farewell Address of the destructive effects of faction was positively prophetic:

> The spirit of revenge, natural to party dissension, which in different
> ages and countries has perpetrated the most horrid enormities,
> is itself a frightful despotism. . . . It serves always to distract the
> public councils and enfeeble the public administration. It agitates
> the community with ill-founded jealousies and false alarms, kindles
> the animosity of one part against another, foments occasionally
> riot and insurrection. It opens the door to foreign influence and
> corruption, which finds a facilitated access to the government itself
> through the channels of party passions."

Washington's remedy was modest but comprehensive: partisanship could not be removed from democracy, but it could be constrained by vigilant citizens and the sober-minded separation of powers.

"The common and continual mischiefs of the spirit of party are sufficient to make it the interest and duty of a wise people to discourage and restrain it," Washington wrote. Doubling down for emphasis, he added that "there being constant danger of excess, the effort ought to be, by force of public opinion, to mitigate and assuage it."

The responsibility lay in citizens as well as civic leaders to preach the virtue of moderation and push back on professional polarizers with fact-based debates to cool overheated enthusiasms. It also depended on the example of an efficient and effective government led by an energetic executive determined to defend the national interest against special interests. "For the efficient management of your common interests, in a country so extensive as ours, a government of as much vigor as is consistent with the perfect security of liberty is indispensable. Liberty itself will find in such a government, with powers properly distributed and adjusted, its surest guardian.

It is, indeed, little else than a name, where the government is too feeble to withstand the enterprises of faction."

Washington reached back to the Federalist Papers for imagery to help readers feel before they could see. Almost a decade earlier, Madison had written of how "[l]iberty is to faction what air is to fire, an aliment without which it instantly expires. But it could not be less folly to abolish liberty, which is essential to political life, because it nourishes faction, than it would be to wish the annihilation of air, which is essential to animal life, because it imparts to fire its destructive agency."

Washington extended the metaphor to address partisan passions: "A fire not to be quenched, it demands a uniform vigilance to prevent its bursting into a flame, lest, instead of warming, it should consume." After all, harnessing fire was a hallmark of civilization, but it needed to be constructively contained or it could burn the whole house down. This is also the case with competing parties in the perpetual balancing act that is a free government.

For Washington, this wise balance was the prime pillar of our political liberty. By devoting so much of his Farewell Address to warning about the dangers of hyper-partisanship, Washington penned a manifesto for moderation, a guide for future leaders and citizens who would try to walk the line between the extremes, focused on the never-ending task of forming a more perfect union.

Fiscal Discipline
DEBT AND TAXES

★

As a very important source of strength and security, cherish public credit.
One method of preserving it is to use it as sparingly as possible, avoiding
occasions of expense by cultivating peace, but remembering also that timely
disbursements to prepare for danger frequently prevent much greater dis-
bursements to repel it, avoiding likewise the accumulation of debt, not only
by shunning occasions of expense, but by vigorous exertion in time of peace
to discharge the debts which unavoidable wars may have occasioned, not
ungenerously throwing upon posterity the burden which we ourselves ought to
bear. . . . It is essential that you should practically bear in mind that towards
the payment of debts there must be revenue; that to have revenue there must
be taxes; that no taxes can be devised which are not more or less inconve-
nient and unpleasant.

The specter of debt hung over George Washington's head all his life.
Even as he prepared to take the oath of office, the master of Mount Vernon
was looking for a £1,000 loan to pay off his debts. To his humiliation, the
president-elect found that his credit was not good enough to secure a sufficient loan. The sheriff of Fairfax County had to be turned away three times
before Washington could pay the local taxes on his land. He confessed to
his lifelong friend and neighbor, Dr. James Craik, "I never felt the want of
money so sensibly since I was a boy of 15 years old."

He hadn't grown up in great privilege. The Washington family was second-tier Virginia aristocracy, notably less wealthy than their neighbors, the Fairfaxes. The family home on a ridge overlooking the Rappahannock River burned down on Christmas Eve in 1740, when George was eight years old. His father died three years later, leaving the family at loose ends. At sixteen, George cut short his schooling and began working as a surveyor.

After marrying into wealth at age twenty-seven, he was free to pursue the life of a gentleman farmer. He resolved to succeed where his father and brothers had failed, building a profitable plantation and rising to the top rank of Virginia gentry.

This required investment and George set his eyes on growing tobacco, the most prestigious and profitable crop. At the time, easy credit was transforming the colonial upper classes, creating a rush to secure each family's social status with imported luxury goods. George showered his stepchildren with expensive toys from London and imported a six-horse chariot emblazoned with his family coat of arms, atop the motto *Exitus Acta Probat*—a quote from Ovid, "The outcome justifies the deed."

But tobacco was also a competitive crop, and Washington found it hard to break into the market with a high-quality product. His relationship with his chief sales agents in London, Robert Carey & Company, grew fraught as Washington became convinced they were gouging him while underselling his crops. From the seeds of this unhappy business arrangement grew Washington's resentment against the power of distant forces in England that could make or break a man without ever seeing his face.

He was land rich, but cash poor. Debts mounted as Washington doubled down on investment in Mount Vernon, and by the end of his seven-year experiment with tobacco farming, he found himself in debt to Carey & Company to the tune of what would be roughly $60,000 today. The problem was not just the money; it was pride. He furiously negotiated for better terms and more time. "It is but an irksome thing for a free mind to be anyways hampered in debt," he wrote. As the aphorism factory Ben Franklin had already remarked, "Think what you do when you run in debt; you give to another power over your liberty."

Debt undercut Washington's prized sense of independence, directly connected to his carefully cultivated sense of honor and character. He decided to innovate his way out of the problem by declaring defeat as a tobacco farmer and switching his focus to wheat, selling superior flour, marketed under the name G. Washington, at considerable profit. His rye whiskey distillery was eventually a logical extension of this new crop. He diversified by selling shad and herring caught in the Potomac and dispatched the fish to be sold as far as the Caribbean, using the excess to fertilize the soil of Mount Vernon.

The lesson for Washington was self-sufficiency, not just for his family but for the nascent nation. He resolved that the colonies should reduce their dependence on imports and take advantage of the vast land and internal markets, investing in manufacturing and industry in addition to agriculture, so that American fortunes would not be subject to British whims.

He led by example, cutting back on imported luxuries and seeking to produce necessities at Mount Vernon. Blacksmiths were ordered to produce forks and knives, cotton was spun and woven into cloth, and a small fabric business was established. As biographer Paul Longmore explained, "In thus pursuing his own economic interests, he was subverting the goals of the British Empire: He denied English merchants a colonial market they had hitherto monopolized. He developed 'domestic' industries imperial policymakers had systematically sought to restrict."

His vision of self-sufficiency ran into conflict with Parliament, as debates over debt from the French and Indian War resulted in new colonial taxes that ultimately led to the American Revolution.

We often lionize lofty principles of the past. The fight for independence is, of course, noble. But never forget that the war for independence began as a tax protest.

Low taxation was one of the inducements that drew new residents to the British colonies. But when the Crown found itself deeply in debt after the French and Indian War, members of Parliament decided that the colonists should help pay its cost. And so the taxman came to pry a little more coin out of every man's pockets.

In 1765, the Stamp Act was imposed on the American colonists. This form of direct taxation required that any letter, pamphlet or legal document be sealed with a stamp purchased at government offices. Trial by jury was suspended for offenders, and the fines were to be paid to the Crown in the currency of silver coin.

Boston's Sam Adams, a founder of the revolutionary fraternity known as the Sons of Liberty and a former deputy tax collector, decried the Stamp Act as a "deep-laid and desperate plan of imperial despotism . . . for the extinction of all civil liberty." An effigy of the official in charge of stamp distribution in Boston, a gentleman by the name of Andrew Oliver, was hung from an old oak known as the Liberty Tree in Hanover Square and then decapitated. The flesh-and-blood Andrew Oliver was then compelled to resign his office beneath the Liberty Tree. Two weeks later, Lieutenant Governor Thomas Hutchinson saw his mansion raided and wine cellar emptied by rebellious tax protestors.

In New York City, a young Caribbean immigrant named Alexander Hamilton rose to give his first public speech at King's College, arguing that the tax protests "will prove the salvation of North America and her liberties," and warning of the results if the British refused to overturn them: "Fraud, power, and the most odious oppression will rise triumphant over right, justice, social happiness, and freedom."

In the prosperous port city of Charleston, a tax mob descended on the home of the merchant-planter (and future signer of the Declaration of Independence) Henry Laurens. Their faces blackened with soot to obscure their identities, the protestors forced their way into his home. Laurens recognized members of the mob and began calling them out by name "to their great surprise"—and, according to historian Gordon S. Wood, "won the mob over to the extent that they gave him 'three cheers,' wished his 'Lady' well and retired with 'God bless your honor, good night, Colonel.' "

The Stamp Act proved unenforceable, and Parliament was compelled to renounce the tax one year after it had been imposed. But as Parliament took the tactical step back, it simultaneously passed the Declaratory Act, which asserted its right to impose legislation on the colonies in all cases, whatsoever.

With the need for revenue still pressing, and the barrier to direct taxation now down, in 1767 Parliament approved a new set of taxes on the colonists named after the chancellor of the Exchequer, Charles Townshend. The Townshend Acts imposed taxes on everyday imported items like paper, paint, lead, glass and—most crucially—tea, which could only be purchased by colonists from the mother country.

In Virginia, George Washington led the protest effort with George Mason, forcing the colonial governor to dissolve the House of Burgesses. Washington expressed frustration regarding taxation without representation, writing a friend, "I think the Parliament of Great Britain hath no more right to put their hand in my pocket, without my consent, than I have to put my hands in yours for money."

The taxes raised only £40,000 for the Crown. In an irony of history, Parliament voted to strike down many of the offending aspects of the Townshend Acts on the same day—and hours before—the Boston Massacre lit a match to the smoldering tensions between colonizers and colonists that would spark into revolution.

Yet the tax on tea still fatefully remained, and it would have impacts beyond turning America into a nation of coffee drinkers. (Another enduring result of the revolution was to turn our drinking affections from rum to whiskey, because the latter didn't depend on molasses delivered from the British West Indies.)

A local newspaper promoted the Boston Tea Party in terms P. T. Barnum might have recognized: "Friends! Brethren! Countrymen! That worst of plagues, the detested Tea, shipped for this Port by the East India Company, is now arrived in this Harbor. The Hour of Destruction or manly Opposition to the Machinations of Tyranny stares you in the Face. Every Friend to his Country, to himself, or to Posterity is now called upon to meet in Faneuil Hall, at Nine o'Clock THIS DAY (At which Time the Bells will ring) to make a united and successful Resistance to the last, worst, and most destructive Measure of Administration."

On the night of December 16, 1773, more than fifty members of the Sons of Liberty, crudely disguised as Mohawk Indians, boarded three British ships in Griffin's Wharf. Communicating with grunts and armed with tomahawks, they cracked open 342 cases of British tea and threw their contents into the dirty water of Boston Harbor.

After their shock subsided, British officials sniffed that the price of the Americans' taxed tea was still only half the six shillings London residents shelled out. But the issue wasn't the cost of tea or even taxes anymore—they were proxies for the deeper desire for independence. As John Adams wrote, "Many persons wish, that as many dead carcasses were floating in the harbor as there are chests of tea."

The antitax insurgency moved into active rebellion and then combat between the British redcoats and a chaotic Continental Army initially based outside Boston. The economic roots of the conflict became obscured in the escalation.

General Washington's anxiety over money never really ended. He famously refused to take a salary for his role leading the army, preferring instead to have his (considerable) expenses paid by Congress. But despite the Declaration's pledge to support independence with "lives, fortunes, and sacred honor," the members of the Continental Congress found it almost impossible to support their troops during wartime.

Inflation was rampant. Amid a money crunch, the thirteen states started printing excess currency to pay off their debts. In turn, the British began issuing counterfeit continental dollars, further flooding the market and undermining trust in the currency.

By 1781, it took 167 continental dollars to purchase what one dollar had done before the start of the war. "A wagon load of money will scarcely purchase a wagon load of provision," Washington wrote with disgust. The debased paper currency issued by each of the thirteen colonies meant that already scarce basic provisions—from weapons to horses to shoes and food—were too expensive to supply with any regularity. Soldiers' pay was nothing more than an airy promise.

The individual states could not summon the collective will to support the troops. This constant strain impacted strategy, with Washington explaining to a senior aide, "We must of necessity adopt the principle of a defensive campaign, and pursue a system of the most absolute economy," while bitterly remarking that the British seemed to be "placing their whole dependence in the depreciation of our money, and the wretched management of our finances."

By the winter of 1780, the army's capable quartermaster general, Nathanael Greene, confessed that "there was never a darker hour in American prospects that this . . . our Treasury is dry and magazines empty; how we are to support the war is beyond my conception. Shillings cannot be had where pounds are wanting."

While his army was starving amid twelve-foot drifts of snow, Washington fumed that speculators profiting from the printing of paper money were living a life of luxury in Philadelphia.

For Washington, these passive war profiteers were the worst of American society. "I cannot with any degree of patience, behold the infamous practices of speculators, monopolizers, and all that tribe of gentry which are preying upon our very vitals, and for the sake of a little dirty pelf are putting the rights and liberties of this country into the most eminent danger," he wrote his cousin Lund Washington. He blamed the unnecessary duration of the war on "the depreciation of the money (which in a great measure is the consequence of it) and our own internal divisions."

Distaste turned to disgust when Washington visited Philadelphia to lobby Congress for more money to supply the troops and found that the high life was still in full swing while soldiers were starving and the currency plummeting. He resolved to school himself in the dark arts of high finance and arranged for tutorials from his friend Robert Morris, a pudgy, balding Liverpool-born Pennsylvanian who had risen to become perhaps the wealthiest man in America. A signer of the Declaration of

Independence and member of the Continental Congress, Morris leveraged his fortune to keep the rebel nation afloat, personally providing loans for soldiers' pay and ammunition. Morris was a powerful man who, uniquely among members of the Continental Congress, put his money where his mouth was.

Because Washington's travails were rooted in the debasement of currency, he absorbed basic lessons in the value of printed money and its relation to tax revenue. With the states lacking the proper mechanisms to collect taxes dedicated to the national defense, the only means of paying for goods was paper money whose value became less by the day while speculators traded scrip.

This reinforced his belief that "[l]and is the most permanent estate and the most likely to increase in value." Now he had not only experience but an economic argument to back it up: "The paper currency of this continent has, for sometime past, been upon too fluctuating a scale to receive in return for real property, unless it was to be bartered off immediately for something else of permanent value," he wrote his brother John Augustine Washington.

The cause of this conundrum was the speculator, who "makes every thing yield to his lust for gain . . . practicing every art that human craft and cunning can devise to counteract the struggles of the virtuous part of the community." And while Washington admitted privately that his opinions and positions were "not consistent with national policy," he advised John Augustine that "our money is upon too unstable a footing and fluctuating to part with land for—when the latter, we are certain, will become more valuable every day." For Washington, speculating in land was fundamentally different than the kind of financial chicanery that was driving wartime profiteers and destabilizing the nation.

The tide turned in the war when the nation's finances came under control, thanks to Robert Morris. With the colonies' credit in shambles, the Continental Congress decided to ditch its committee-based approach in favor of making Morris the superintendent of finance. He took radical actions to reduce inflation, required the states to cough up necessary cash, introduced competitive bidding for army contracts, and established the Bank of North America, the first national bank, for the sole purpose of financing the war. As Hamilton wrote to Morris at the time, "'tis by introducing order into our finances—by restoring public credit—not by gaining battles that we are finally to gain our object." These reforms helped coax foreign loans, with the French supplying six huge cash infusions while John Adams negotiated $2 million from the Dutch at a reasonable 5 percent rate.

As a result, Washington overcame his dislike of debt to accept the necessity of loans, reflecting on what he believed was the United States' unique capacity to generate future growth. A modest degree of public debt could help secure, rather than compromise, our independence. "No nation will have more in its power to repay what it borrows than this," he wrote. "Our debts are hitherto small. The vast and valuable tracts of unlocated lands . . . the advantages of every kind, which we possess for commerce, ensure to this country a rapid advancement in population and prosperity." America was a good long-term investment. And when the British finally surrendered at Yorktown in 1783, to the strains of a popular pub tune called "The World Turned Upside Down," all the desperate gambles and the overextensions seemed justified.

But even in victory, perhaps especially in victory, the fractured Continental Congress could not secure the funds to make good on their promises of back pay, or of pensions for the widows and orphans of the revolutionary soldiers, one in four of whom had died in the cause.

It was this insult at a moment of triumph that almost sparked a mutiny at Newburgh. After shaming the officers into line, Washington set out to make matters right and called for economic "justice" for his troops in his Circular Letter to the States. "The ability of the country to discharge the debts which have been incurred in its defense is not to be doubted," Washington wrote. "The path of our duty is plain before us . . . let us fulfill the public contracts, which Congress had undoubtedly a right to make for the purpose of carrying on the war."

This meant new taxes to pay down the war debt. "Who does not remember the frequent declarations, at the commencement of the war, that we should be completely satisfied, if at the expense of one half, we could defend the remainder of our possessions?" he asked. "Where is the man to be found, who wishes to remain indebted, for the defense of his own person and property, to the exertions, the bravery, and the blood of others, without making one generous effort to repay the debt of honor and of gratitude? In what part of the continent shall we find any man, or body of men, who would not blush to stand up and propose measures purposely calculated to rob the soldier of his stipend, and the public creditor of his due?" This is "more than a common debt, it is a debt of honor," Washington thundered.

★

AT MOUNT VERNON, WASHINGTON EVOLVED toward an entrepreneurial approach to nation building. The agrarian skeptic of finance and industry now believed that "a people . . . who are possessed of the spirit of Commerce, who see and who will pursue their advantage, may achieve almost anything."

From his perch overlooking the Potomac, a dream from his youth reemerged—he would build a vast canal system that would connect the Potomac with the Ohio River, creating a connection with the western frontier that would bind the nation with the mutually beneficial bonds of commerce.

Urgency for the plan increased when the Spanish closed access to the lower Mississippi for U.S. shipping, threatening to choke off western exports. Competition from the North also reared its head as New York began exploring what would become the Erie Canal system and transform the region.

Washington purchased five shares of the Potomac Canal Company and assumed the title of president of the corporation while also buying five shares of the rival James River Company. He besieged visitors to Mount Vernon with navigation tables and maps showing the possibilities of the intercoastal waterway, which could bring to market goods as distant as furs from Detroit and could collect income through tolls.

"Extend the inland navigation of the eastern waters—communicate them as near as possible (by excellent roads) with those that run westward," Washington wrote, "open these to the Ohio, and such others as extend from the Ohio towards Lake Erie; and we shall not only draw the produce of western settlers, but the fur and peltry trade of the lakes also, to our ports (being the nearest and easiest of transportation), to the amazing increase of our Exports, while we bind those people to us by a chain which can never be broken."

After a visitor named Elkanah Watson stayed at Mount Vernon for a few days in January 1785, he recounted how Washington dismissed questions about the glory days of war in favor of pivoting forward to his plans for the canal system. "Hearing little else for two days from the persuasive tongue of the great man," Watson wrote, "I confess completely infected me with the canal mania."

Washington's newfound enthusiasm managed to bring states together and formed the foundation of one of the most pivotal friendships in American history.

At the time, James Madison admired Washington from a distance. He hailed from the Blue Ridge Mountain region, some 200 miles inland from the Atlantic Ocean. He was one of the westernmost representatives of the Continental Congress and pressed for the peace treaty with England to include all land up to the Mississippi for purposes of trade and long-term stability. He feared that western settlers might be induced to secede and associate themselves with foreign powers if they could not bring their goods to market. The canal plan offered an area of mutual interest and expertise.

Madison marveled at Washington's energy on the subject of the canal project, both his political lobbying and exploration of the river on horseback and canoe, during which he occasionally tackled the rapids himself to gauge currents.

"The earnestness with which he espouses the undertaking is hardly to be described," Madison wrote Jefferson, "and shows that a mind like his, capable of grand views, and which has long been occupied by them, cannot bear a vacancy."

But in the absence of the unifying struggle, America was already show-ing signs of fraying. On opposite sides of the Potomac, Washington's native Virginia and Maryland were threatening war over control of the river. Wash-ington's enthusiasm for canals managed to turn the overheated commercial competition into cooperation—and began the birth of the U.S. Constitution.

Washington leveraged his reputation to bring political leaders from Maryland and Virginia to meet with him in Alexandria in March 1785. His personal diplomacy produced a revolutionary result: a first-of-a-kind commercial compact between the two previously feuding states, not only funding the project but also adopting uniform regulations and a common currency, functionally creating a commercial union and America's greatest public-private works project up to that point.

This success brought Washington deep satisfaction. He was overjoyed at the success of his commercial scheme, laughing at proving the merchant skeptics wrong while proposing multiple toasts, cheering "Success to the navigation of the Potomac!" as a bottle passed around the table "pretty freely."

But there were ethical headaches that came with the state's involve-ment. Washington was granted a share-based income for his efforts but grew concerned that this public profit would tarnish his reputation. A rem-edy of sorts appeared when he resolved to put the shares in a trust dedicated to "two charity schools, one on each river, for the education and support of the children of the poor and indigent."

Washington's success in spurring the Virginia and Maryland legisla-tors to coordinated action had an unintended consequence that would lead in a fitful fashion to the Constitutional Convention. The Potomac states decided to invite neighboring Delaware and Pennsylvania to subsequent meetings, enlarging the commercial union. This led to an invitation ex-tended to all states to a meeting in Annapolis to "consider how far a uni-form system in their commercial relations may be necessary." Out of this commercial meeting about something as practical as canal-based interstate commerce came the Constitutional Convention.

With a new Constitution came the unwelcome obligation to pay for a government that could secure its hard-won freedom and protect the general welfare. Old suspicions about centralized power endured, but now the founding fathers found themselves on the side of the government instead of in opposition. Even after the Constitutional Convention of 1789, Benjamin Franklin wrote a friend, "Our Constitution is in actual operation. Everything appears to promise that it will last; but in this world nothing is certain but death and taxes."

Now the new republic would have to work out a new balance between taxation and representation and some citizens would find themselves dissatisfied with the results.

In Washington's first inaugural address, statements of national unity rather than fiscal principles dominated the remarks. The pressing question of finance was still outside his comfort zone, though among the voluminous notes for the first inaugural address was a "sketch of a plan of American finance" that paid off the wartime debts of the states and made the federal government the sole taxing authority, raising revenue from a 5 percent import tariff.

As Washington cobbled together the first cabinet, Alexander Hamilton was a logical candidate to lead the new Treasury Department after Robert Morris passed on the honor to pursue personal business in addition to an inaugural Senate seat.

Hamilton believed that "power without revenue in political society is [only] a name," weaponizing Washington's maxim that "influence is not government." Having served by Washington's side during wartime and experienced the impotence of the Continental Congress, Hamilton argued that a strong central government was essential to effective governance, expressing frustration that "getting money from the states is like preaching to the dead."

Hamilton proved to be an excellent ally for the new president, decisive and energetic. He was determined to have the federal government assume responsibility for the staggering $79 million in combined state and foreign debts from the war as a means of increasing our national credit and capacity for public investment. This difficult step was necessary to show that the United States could be trusted as an independent nation on the world stage.

Hamilton believed that "a national debt, if it is not excessive, will be to us a national blessing." But the opportunities it created for internal improvements had to be balanced with a commitment to paying down those debts expeditiously. After all, excessive debt could topple empires. Prompt payments were necessary for reasons of perception as well as practicality. "In nothing are appearances of greater moment than in whatever regards credit," Hamilton wrote. "Opinion is the soul of it and this is affected by appearances as well as realities."

He presented a revolutionary plan for a modern system of finance under the modest label of a "Report on Public Credit." It was a centralized system based on the British model, which despite its recognized excellence did little to endear the plan with congressmen who howled at Hamilton's belief that financing a degree of debt could grow the nation while strengthening the central government.

Hamilton presented the plan as the "price of liberty," but it proved a particularly hard sell because it would pay the speculators who owned the soldiers' scrip. This made sense in terms of strengthening the infant nation's financial credit but it caused Washington political heartburn. Now that he had the power to secure full and direct restitution of his soldiers' back pay, he would have to refuse to fight for it as president.

The assumption of debt delighted states like New York and Massachusetts, which had seen much of the fighting. But states like Virginia, which had largely paid off its state debt, were disgruntled. This was more than an early echo of rural-versus-urban divides. It was the first decisive clash in the post-ratification fight between states' rights and a stronger central government.

There was a larger game at play. Hamilton recognized that the assumption of debt represented a larger imperative: establishing federal government's power of taxation, determining that our united responsibilities would outweigh states' rights for all time. The precedent created the power.

But the plan met powerful and persuasive opponents, and for a time it seemed as though the democratic process would doom Hamilton's ambition. As one revolutionary veteran named Joseph Martin pungently put it, "When the country had drained the last drop of service it could screw out of the poor soldiers, they were turned adrift like old worn-out horses, and nothing said about land to pasture them upon. . . . No one ever took the least care about it, except a pack of speculators, who were driving about the country like so many evil spirits, endeavoring to pluck the last feather from the soldiers."

Hamilton's Plan B for passage would have far-reaching implications. Alarmed at the prospect of defeat, he set about politicking with representatives, using New York City's position as the capital of the new nation as a bargaining chip. If this gamble had gone sidewise, residents of Trenton, New Jersey, or the Philadelphia suburb of Germantown could have found themselves basking in the nation's capital while residents of the Potomac basin were still swatting away malarial mosquitoes.

His final gambit occurred at an infamously private and pivotal boozy dinner at Jefferson's apartment at 57 Maiden Lane, during which a compromise was reached between rivals: Virginia gained the capital and the country received a strong central government in return.

The backlash was brutal but the broad coalition secured its passage. The proof was in the results: the controversial plan sparked a fiscal renaissance. Within four months of signing the National Bank into law, Washington told Congress "our public credit stands on that ground which three years ago would have been considered as a species of madness to have foretold."

While the strategic vision for economic self-sufficiency accelerated by financial instruments was in place, there was still a lack of working capital to administer the new government. Tariffs were the prime means of revenue, spurring the creation of the Coast Guard, but Hamilton understood the counterproductive danger of excessive taxes and fees: "If duties are too high, they lessen consumption—the collection is eluded and the product to the treasury is not so great as when they are confined within proper and moderate bounds." To augment the government income, Hamilton proposed a package of excise taxes. What we have come to call a "sin tax" was already an attractive revenue remedy. Pennsylvania's tax on liquor sales had already been justified as "to restrain persons in low circumstances from an immoderate use thereof." And so in 1794, a federal tax on whiskey sales was imposed.

In the capital city of Philadelphia, this might have seemed a modest proposal, equitable because of its emphasis on optional (and decadent) behavior. But in the western part of Pennsylvania, rye whiskey was a way of life, serving as currency, trade and medicine, a means of marking both births and deaths, moments of celebration and sorrow. It felt as though eastern elites from faraway cities were imposing their will on rural folks who just wanted to be left alone, a recurring theme in American culture.

And so erupted the Whiskey Rebellion, the first violent tax protest and popular uprising directed at an American president's administration. When it was over, with some 12,000 militia members assembled at Washington's command, the entire adventure cost an estimated one-third of the total amount raised by the whiskey tax.

President Washington's drive for order and stability increasingly focused him on fiscal affairs. In his 1794 address to Congress, after detailing the cost of putting down the Whiskey Rebellion, Washington declared that the time had come to pay down the national debt.

"Nothing can more promote the permanent welfare of the nation and nothing would be more grateful to our constituents. . . . Indeed whatsoever is unfinished of our system of public credit cannot be benefited by procrastination; and as far as may be practicable, we ought to place that credit on grounds which cannot be disturbed, and to prevent that progressive accumulation of debt which must ultimately endanger all governments."

This was an early and eloquent statement of Washington's warning that excessive debt was a force that could topple empires. But he had also learned that strategically deployed debt could aid the growth and stability of society.

In the past, Washington had worried about "whether foreign commerce is of real advantage to any country—that is, whether the luxury, effeminacy, and corruptions which are introduced by it are counterbalanced by the convenience and wealth of which it is productive." But now Washington had a passion for commerce, a farsighted vision of how increased international trade could channel warring passions in a way that might decrease the cost of conflicts and increase human happiness.

As he wrote to Lafayette in one of his rare flights of fancy,

> I cannot avoid reflecting with pleasure on the probable influence
> that commerce may here after have on human manners and society
> in general. On these occasions I consider how mankind may
> be connected like one great family in fraternal ties. I indulge a
> fond, perhaps an enthusiastic idea, that as the world is evidently
> less barbarous than it has been, its melioration must still be
> progressive—that nations are becoming more humanistic in their
> policy—that the subjects of ambition and causes for hostility are
> daily diminishing—and in fine, that the period is not very remote,
> when the benefits of a liberal and free commerce will, pretty
> generally, succeed to the devastations and horrors of war.

In this missive, Washington anticipated globalization by some two hundred years, envisioning an era when the ties of commerce would someday outweigh the temptations of war. Coincident with the writing of Adam Smith (whose book *The Wealth of Nations* still rests on the shelf at Mount Vernon), Washington understood that the bonds of free trade, strengthened by mutual self-interest, could reduce the passions of conquest simply because war itself would be seen as an ultimately inefficient exercise of national power. After all, it was the costs associated with the Seven Years'

War that led the British to raise taxes on the colonies, ultimately sparking the revolution.

These ideas animated Washington's actions in office—fighting for treaties with Spain and England with an eye toward increasing peace and commerce. He believed that "the spirit of trade which pervades these States is not to be restrained." Despite his military background, Washington's vision of foreign policy was focused on free and fair commerce between nations rather than advancing any particular ideology or imperial expansion.

★

GIVEN WASHINGTON'S DECADES OF GRAPPLING with debt and his own entrepreneur's belief that fiscal self-sufficiency was the key to freedom, it was no surprise that enduring economic principles would play a central role in the Farewell Address. The fact that former Treasury secretary Hamilton was acting as primary speechwriter all but ensured the emphasis and eloquence on this point.

In his Farewell, Washington warned that we must "cherish public credit . . . avoiding likewise the accumulation of debt, not only by shunning occasions of expense, but by vigorous exertion in time of peace to discharge the debts which unavoidable wars may have occasioned, not ungenerously throwing upon posterity the burden which we ourselves ought to bear."

Making a case for generational responsibility, Washington favored a policy of fiscal restraint within a limited but energetic government. The lifelong solider saw "unavoidable wars" as a significant source of expense, as they had been for civilizations throughout history. Wars of choice would have been offensive to him as a waste of precious blood and treasure.

To control costs while maximizing "strength and security," Washington counseled "avoiding occasions of expense by cultivating peace, but remembering also that timely disbursements to prepare for danger frequently prevent much greater disbursements to repel it." Practical preparation was often cheaper than desperate last-minute escalations. And when the moment of danger had passed, it was time for "vigorous exertion" in paying down wartime debts. The best time to fix a roof is when the sun is shining.

Washington understood that dealing with debts was the federal government's responsibility, but he also knew that leaders in a democracy would be disinclined to make unpopular decisions unless the public were enlightened.

"The execution of these maxims belongs to your representatives," he said—meaning the members of Congress. "But it is necessary that public opinion should co-operate. To facilitate to them the performance of their duty, it is essential that you should practically bear in mind that towards the payment of debts there must be revenue; that to have revenue there must be taxes; that no taxes can be devised which are not more or less inconvenient and unpleasant."

In other words, deal with the math. Paying down debts means raising revenue as well as cutting costs. It is a basic profit-and-loss ledger buoyed on a national level by overall economic growth. Complaining endlessly about taxes ignores their central role in securing our civilization. Blithely disregarding debt is the surest path to the poorhouse, risking freedom and independence.

After watching Robert Morris at work during the war, Washington had come to see that a degree of debt could be invaluable in getting through hard times. He and Hamilton applied those lessons to his administration with profitable results for the nation.

Ultimately, the United States' economic rise and expansion of credit was built on a foundation of real estate, the almost unlimited expanses of land that stretched west, which propped up investment capital as collateral, perfect for sale, speculation, and settlement, allowing the nation to develop and prosper quickly.

Achieving a wise balance was always Washington's aim. He was too mindful of myths like the story of Icarus to tempt fate by flying too high. Watching Robert Morris's painful reversal of fortune reminded Washington of the wisdom of his more conservative path.

Sometimes history offers up poignant twists that would stretch a story-teller's credibility. And in the last years of Washington's life, he watched dear friends and American heroes suffer the indignities that came with the overextension of uncontrolled debt. The frenzy around the construction of the federal city that bore Washington's name would play a critical role in their downfall.

With America on the rise and a future capital under construction, land speculation was in vogue and it ensnared many of the most respectable men in America, including Robert Morris. He had embarked on an ambitious—and, as it turned out, reckless—spending spree with two partners: former Pennsylvania comptroller John Nicholson and a bright-eyed, social-climbing, quasi-con man from Boston named James Greenleaf.

Their plan was to back vast land purchases with guarantees from Dutch financiers whom Greenleaf claimed to have on a leash from his first marriage to a Dutch baroness and a six-month stint as a member of the U.S. consulate in Amsterdam. Mix in Nicholson's power over Pennsylvania's purse strings and Morris's unparalleled esteem among the republican ruling class and the result was a venture grandly called the North American Land Company.

In 1795, they started out by purchasing 40 percent of the land tracts set aside in the District of Columbia, in large part funding the construction of the Pierre L'Enfant–designed capital, which was predicated on private financing. Then they cast their eyes southward, gobbling up an estimated 6 million acres throughout Kentucky, Georgia, North Carolina and South Carolina. This made the North American Land Company one of the largest landowners in U.S. history.

They propositioned Alexander Hamilton to invest (he declined) but succeeded in looping Washington's personal aide Tobias Lear into their scheme, despite the president's pointed concern that rapid westward expansion could further inflame relations with Native American tribes. All caution was dismissed until the French invasion of the Netherlands made their promised foreign backing dry up almost overnight. Greenleaf began stealing some of the partnership's money to pay his debts just as the land speculation bubble began to burst.

By late 1796, a cash crunch sparked a panic and debts were called in. The dramatic overextensions that occur amid rampant speculation brought down a number of senior statesmen, including one of Washington's original appointees to the Supreme Court, Justice James Wilson, who lost his lifetime seat when he was thrown in debtor's prison and then spent the last years of his life trying to outrun creditors. Soon they set their eyes on Morris & Company.

"I am in want of money," Morris confessed, "and when that is the case every plague follows." The Financier of the Revolution, once the richest man in America and the owner of the president's executive mansion, was caught in financial riptide. For a time, he was able to stay one step ahead of the creditors, aided by his respectable reputation and still-charming countenance. But in February 1798 the game was up. He summoned the sheriff and turned himself in, writing a tersely despairing note to his business partner Nicholson: "My money is gone, my furniture is to be sold, I am to go to prison and my family to starve. Good night."

Robert Morris was imprisoned in Philadelphia's Prune Street jail, blocks away from the mansion he once rented to the president. The financier of the revolution was a number now.

On November 12, 1798, the ex-president Washington made his way to the Prune Street prison, where he had candlelight dinner with Morris and his wife in a newly whitewashed prison cell. They were now at opposite ends of the American experience, a president and a prisoner. The cautionary tale was clear, however stoically endured. But because of their shared history, the monuments of their creation surrounding them beyond the prison walls, the shock of recognition faded a bit over the course of their meal. Washington never renounced his fallen friend and extended an invitation to his family to visit Mount Vernon. It is the only time a president has visited a friend for dinner in prison.

Virtue and Religion
THE FAITH OF THE FIRST FOUNDING FATHER

★

*Of all the dispositions and habits which lead to political prosperity, reli-
gion and morality are indispensable supports. . . . And let us with caution
indulge the supposition that morality can be maintained without religion.
Whatever may be conceded to the influence of refined education on minds
of peculiar structure, reason and experience both forbid us to expect that
national morality can prevail in exclusion of religious principle.*

You've probably seen pictures of George Washington on bended knee
at Valley Forge, deep in prayer. It is an inspiring image for the faithful,
invoked by patriotic preachers and a particular favorite of Ronald Reagan
at prayer breakfasts. It's also unfortunately a comforting myth, dreamed
up by his early biographer Parson Weems, a traveling book salesman who
never let facts get in the way of a good story.

Washington's real vision of faith, virtue and morality is far more interesting. There's no doubt that he was a Christian, raised in the Anglican Church, and served for a time as a member of his local vestry. But as
president, Washington declined to take communion, despite the protests
of prominent ministers, and he avoided specific mention of Jesus Christ
in public and private letters. Nonetheless, he regularly praised the good
fortune that "Providence" provided in a spirit of gratitude, freely acknowl-
edging the larger forces outside our control.

Washington believed virtue and morality were taught most easily by religious traditions. But he took a dim view of the intolerance that is too often excused in the name of God, writing: "Of all the animosities which have existed among mankind, those which are caused by difference of sentiments in religion appear to be the most inveterate and distressing."

Washington was a consistent defender of religious pluralism, preaching tolerance and inclusion, even to faiths beyond Christianity. In his Farewell Address and throughout his life, he championed the civic virtues that flow from faith broadly rather than any particular orthodoxy.

But evangelists have never been able to resist rewriting history to claim Washington as one of their own, trying to harness his halo to their flock. Here's the scene that spawned a thousand paintings as Parson Weems wrote it in the seventh edition of his constantly evolving, hugely popular early-nineteenth-century biography:

> In the winter of '77, while Washington, with the American army, lay encamped at Valley Forge, a certain good old FRIEND, of the respectable family and name of Potts, if I mistake not, had occasion to pass through the woods near head quarters. Treading in his way along the venerable grove, suddenly he heard the sound of a human voice, which, as he advanced, increased on his ear; and at length became like the voice of one speaking much in earnest. As he approached the spot with a cautious step, whom should he behold, in a dark natural bower of ancient oaks, but the commander in chief of the American armies on his knees at prayer! Motionless with surprise, friend Potts continued on the place till the general, having ended his devotions, arose; and, with a countenance of angelic serenity, retired to headquarters. Friend Potts then went home, and on entering his parlor called out to his wife, "Sarah! my dear Sarah! all's well! all's well! George Washington will yet prevail!"

The churchmen who knew Washington best had to admit the truth. When asked in later years whether he'd ever seen Washington "kneeling during the service," Bishop White of Philadelphia (Robert Morris's brother-in-law) responded, "I owe it to truth to declare, that I never saw him in the said attitude."

An assistant minister of Christ Church in Philadelphia got into an unhappy test of wills with Washington when he sought to raise the issue of the president's departure before communion (while his wife, Martha, stayed to take the sacrament). "I considered it my duty, in a sermon on public worship, to state the unhappy tendency of *example*, particularly of those in elevated stations, who uniformly turned their backs upon the celebration of the Lord's Supper," he explained. "I acknowledge the remark was intended for the President; and as such he received it."

A few days later, the preacher received word from a prominent U.S. senator that the president had received the message so well that he mentioned it over dinner, saying "he had received a very just reproof from the pulpit for always leaving the church before the administration of the Sacrament; that he honored the preacher for his integrity and candor; that he had never considered the influence of his example, and that he would not again give cause for the repetition of the reproof; and that, as he had never been a communicant, were he to become one then, it would be imputed to an ostentatious display of religious zeal, arising altogether from his elevated station. Accordingly he afterwards never came on the morning of sacramental Sunday, though at other times a constant attendant in the morning."

This was not the preacher's intended outcome. But Washington was not a man who would adjust his character to criticism or seem to indulge in hypocrisy for political gain.

The rituals of organized religion could bring out a rare puckish side in Washington. His diary is generally a recounting of weather and travel details, but on one occasion when he attended the Dutch Reformed Church in Manhattan, the president allowed himself a dry aside, writing that the sermon, "being in that language not a word of which I understood I was in no danger of becoming a proselyte to its religion by the eloquence of the preacher."

But unlike many Enlightenment-era contemporaries, Washington was not hostile to religion. During his two terms in office, the French Revolution called into fashionable question the influence of religion on society. In contrast, Washington was careful to invoke faith in a spirit of personal and public gratitude—choosing to devote a considerable portion of his first inaugural address to "the Almighty Being who rules over the universe" and "the Great Author."

In his 1783 Circular Letter to the States, Washington had closed with a civic prayer for our young nation. But he particularly favored invoking the term "Providence"—a nondenominational phrase favored by Deists such as Benjamin Franklin. Many of his public expressions of faith followed Masonic phraseology, such as "the master builder." And as he contemplated plans for his own postmortem, he specified that the Anglican and Masonic rites be read at his funeral service.

The founders' vision of faith was far more multidimensional than we are used to hearing on the campaign trail today. Some were Deists or quietly secular humanists, consistent with the Age of Reason they believed themselves to be living in. Benjamin Franklin quipped that "a virtuous heretic shall be saved before a wicked Christian." But all were culturally familiar with Christian doctrine and even a skeptic like Thomas Jefferson attempted to distill Jesus Christ's teaching from religious dogma in his redacted "Jefferson's Bible." John Adams took a more hard-boiled view of the benefits of religion, believing that the Bible gave the "only system that ever did or ever will preserve a republic in the world."

Washington viewed religion from a utilitarian rather than sectarian perspective. In his experience, people of faith were more likely to be constructive members of society. As he wrote in a letter to the General Assembly of Presbyterians a month after assuming the presidency, "No man, who is profligate in his morals, or a bad member of the civil community,

can possibly be a true Christian, or a credit to his own religious society."
There seemed to be a happily self-reinforcing relationship between Enlightenment-era liberalism and the early Christian virtues of "prudence,
temperance, fortitude, and justice."

During the revolution, Washington refused specific allowances for religious minorities, making Congregationalists work on the Sabbath and
discouraging pacifist Quakers from staying neutral in the fight for independence. But when some soldiers wanted to continue the British tradition
of celebrating Guy Fawkes Day, with its ceremonial burning of the pope in
effigy, Washington swiftly sent orders to forbid the offensive action, con-
demning the "ridiculous and childish custom of burning the effigy of the
Pope" and expressing his "surprise, that there should be officers and soldiers in this army so void of common sense as not to see the impropriety of
such a step at this juncture."

Washington viewed a diversity of faiths as a source of long-term stability for society. He was drawn to the *via media*—the middle path—just
as Anglicans saw themselves as standing somewhere between the Roman
Catholic Church and Calvinism.

As Madison later explained, he did "not suppose that Washington had
ever attended to the arguments for Christianity, and for the different systems of religion, or in fact that he had formed definite opinions on the subject. But he took these things as he found them existing, and was constant
in his observances of worship according to the received forms of the Episcopal church in which he was brought up."

In the colonial Virginia of Washington's youth, religion was "more of
an institution than a means of grace." As his early-twentieth-century biographer Douglas Southall Freeman recounted, by the time Washington had
reached his mid-twenties "there was for him no rock of refuge in religion.
Not once in his letters had he quoted Holy Writ or the prayer book of the
church into which he had been baptized. He believed in Providence, but
sometimes he thought the rightful name was Destiny."

There is no record of Washington owning a Bible in his library at

Mount Vernon, but we know he gained something like spiritual nourishment from a popular translation of Seneca's *Morals*—a book that contained a practical maxim Washington would draw on all his life: "There can be no Happiness without Virtue."

It was a belief he repeated often, declaring in his first inaugural address: "There exists in the economy and course of nature an indissoluble union between virtue and happiness, between duty and advantage, between the genuine maxims of an honest and magnanimous policy, and the solid rewards of public prosperity and felicity." Or, as he wrote in a presidential letter to the bishops of the Protestant Episcopal Church in New York, in August 1789: "The consideration that human happiness and moral duty are inseparably connected will always continue to prompt me to promote the progress of the former, by inculcating the practice of the latter."

Faith influenced many of the civic institutions Washington joined as he rose up the ranks of colonial society, like the Masonic Lodge of Fredericksburg, Virginia, into which he was initiated at the age of twenty. The Masons traced their lineage to the first mason of the Temple of Solomon, but their secret society began in 1717, when a group of London-based political and cultural elites gathered together to pursue philosophic and philanthropic rites, bonded by a belief in a Supreme Being and evidence of good character. Washington was attracted to this band of brothers and to the practical idealism they professed.

In 1762, settled into domestic life with Martha, Washington was elected to the vestry of Truro Parish, but even this was little more than a sign of his advancement. The vestry was preoccupied with charitable works ranging from relief for the local poor to public education, as well as the salaries and maintenance of the church. It was primarily a civic rather than religious organization.

In the run-up to the revolution, Washington sought clarity in prayer, attending two church services on Sunday, May 29, 1774, as the Virginia House of Burgesses debated a boycott of British tea as a tax protest. On

June 1, he fasted all day and went to church in Williamsburg as the rector cried, "God preserve all the just rights and liberties of America!"

When the call came from the Continental Congress for Washington to lead the ragtag band of troops then stationed in Roxbury, outside of Boston, he wrote Martha, "My Dearest . . . as it has been a kind of destiny that has thrown me upon this service, I shall hope my undertaking of it, is designed to answer some good purpose. . . . I shall rely therefore, confidently, on that Providence which has heretofore preserved and been bountiful to me, not doubting but that I shall return safe to you."

During the first siege of the war, British general Thomas Gage wrote Washington a letter invoking God as judge and jury for the "severe retaliation" and "dreadful consequences" that would come to the American army and its supporters.

Washington defiantly responded, "May that God, to whom you then appealed, judge between America and you! Under his Providence, those who influence the councils of America, and all the other inhabitants of these united colonies, at the hazard of their lives, are determined to hand down to posterity those just and invaluable privileges which they received from their ancestors." He wasn't going to cede the moral high ground and instead flipped the script to cast the moral shadow on Pharaoh's inheritors, invoking the judgment of unborn generations.

After the fall of Charleston to the British in May 1780, Washington offered up a prayer: "Providence—to whom we are infinitely more indebted than we are to our wisdom, or our own exertions—has always displayed its power and goodness, when clouds and thick darkness seemed ready to overwhelm us. The hour is now come when we stand much in need of another manifestation of its bounty however little we deserve it."

And when the war was over, Washington began his farewell to the army with a moment of appreciation and thanks to God: "We shall have equal occasion to felicitate ourselves on the lot which Providence has assigned us, whether we view it in a natural, a political, or moral point of light."

He chose to close out that first farewell address with an uncommonly
explicit prayer for his countrymen, which has subsequently been cast as
"Washington's Prayer for the United States." In at least this one case, the
hype matches the history:

> I now make it my earnest prayer that God would have you, and the
> state over which you preside, in his holy protection, that he would
> incline the hearts of the citizens to cultivate a spirit of subordination
> and obedience to government, to entertain a brotherly affection and
> love for one another, for their fellow citizens of the United States
> at large, and particularly for brethren who have served in the field,
> and finally, that he would most graciously be pleased to dispose
> us all to do justice, to love mercy, and to demean ourselves with
> that charity, humility, and pacific temper of mind which were the
> characteristics of the Divine Author of our blessed religion, and
> without an humble imitation of whose example in these things we
> can never hope to be a happy nation.

The only other time Washington was this explicit and extensive about
faith was in his first inaugural address, which he developed in close consultation with Madison. But of all the founding fathers, Madison was perhaps
the most dogmatic about the separation of church and state, declaring before the war that "religious bondage shackles and debilitates the mind and
unfits it for every noble enterprise" and later that "the Constitution of the
U.S. forbids everything like an establishment of a national religion."

And so it is notable that Washington devoted almost a third of his first
inaugural address to the subject of faith, even though the absence of a family Bible for the ceremony meant that couriers were sent scrambling to retrieve one from the local Manhattan Masonic lodge on John Street.

> It would be peculiarly improper to omit in this first official act,
> my fervent supplications to that Almighty Being who rules

over the universe, who presides in the councils of nations, and whose providential aids can supply every human defect, that his benediction may consecrate to the liberties and happiness of the people of the United States a government instituted by themselves for these essential purposes, and may enable every instrument employed in its administration to execute with success the functions allotted to his charge. In tendering this homage to the Great Author of every public and private good I assure myself that it expresses your sentiments not less than my own, nor those of my fellow-citizens at large, less than either. No people can be bound to acknowledge and adore the invisible hand which conducts the affairs of men more than the people of the United States. Every step by which they have advanced to the character of an independent nation seems to have been distinguished by some token of providential agency.

After concluding his national benediction, Washington waded through the crowds to pray at St. Paul's Chapel on lower Broadway, where his pew remains today beneath an early painting of the Great Seal of the United States, emblazoned with the national motto, *E Pluribus Unum*—Out of Many, One.

Washington believed in those native powers of pluralism and assimilation. He'd learned the lesson early in his life. As a young man working as a surveyor, he'd seen the resistance of German immigrants to move to Virginia unless they were exempted from a uniform tax that went directly into the Church of England's coffers. His beloved older brother Lawrence lobbied the legislature to amend the law, arguing against "restraints on conscience" on the ground that they were not only "cruel" but that they put Virginia at a competitive disadvantage against other states as immigrants of different faiths fled there and grew the local population, while Virginia only "increased by slow degrees except [for] Negroes and convicts." This practical as well as moral imperative left its mark on Washington's mind.

Preaching religious tolerance was Washington's most consistent and farsighted principle of faith: "Being no bigot myself, I am disposed to indulge the professors of Christianity in the church with that road to Heaven which to them shall seem the most direct, plainest, easiest, and least liable to exception."

When his colleagues at the Virginia House of Burgesses proposed a general tax to fill the church coffers before the war, Washington declared that he would not support the measure. "No man's sentiments are more opposed to *any kind* of restraint upon religious principles than mine are."

When the supervisor of his farms needed to hire new workmen, Washington sent this practical progressive message: "If they are good workmen, they may be from Asia, Africa, or Europe; they may be Mahometans, Jews, or Christians of any sect, or they may be Atheists."

This religious pluralism was not simply a matter of freedom of conscience—it was a bulwark against tyranny, consistent with the national unity that could come from diversity. As Madison wrote in Federalist 10, "A religious sect may degenerate into a political faction in a part of the Confederacy; but the variety of sects dispersed over the entire face of it must secure the national councils against any danger from that source."

As president, Washington had a bully pulpit and he devoted much time to writing to various religious denominations, assuring them of their welcome place in the new nation.

Baptists were often persecuted under British colonial rule, sometimes imprisoned on charges of child abuse for not baptizing their children soon after birth. A month after his inauguration in 1789, Washington wrote the United Baptist Churches of Virginia to assure them of their permanent welcome in the new nation. "If I could have entertained the slightest apprehension that the Constitution framed in the Convention, where I had the honor to preside, might possibly endanger the religious rights of any ecclesiastical society, certainly I would never have placed my signature to it," he wrote, "and if I could now conceive that the general government might ever be so administered as to render the liberty of conscience insecure, I beg you will be persuaded that no one would be more zealous than myself to establish effectual barriers against the horrors of spiritual tyranny and every species of religious persecution."

To the Committee of Roman Catholics, Washington overrode centuries of religious persecution in the old country: "as mankind becomes more liberal, they will be more apt to allow that all those who conduct themselves as worthy members of the community are equally entitled to the protection of civil government," Washington wrote. "I hope ever to see America among the foremost nations in examples of justice and liberality."

Perhaps Washington's most enduring ode to religious pluralism came in a letter to the Hebrew Congregation of Newport, Rhode Island, in 1790. "It is now no more that toleration is spoken of as if it was by the indulgence of one class of people that another enjoyed the exercise of their inherent natural rights," Washington wrote. "Happily, the government of the United States, which gives to bigotry no sanction, to persecution no assistance, requires only that they who live under its protection should demean themselves as good citizens, in giving it on all occasions their effectual support."

Here, in crisp, clear terms, Washington laid out the principles for religious freedom a year before the passage of the Bill of Rights, reaching beyond the condescension that can come with mere tolerance, instead insisting on equal exercise of natural rights that come from God, though they are secured by man. Not content to simply articulate that sometimes still elusive standard, in the next sentence Washington unabashedly established the United States as a beacon of religious freedom by asserting to members of a minority who so frequently found themselves persecuted around the world that America would give "bigotry no sanction" and "persecution no assistance."

The only condition that Washington put on this welcome was good citizenship. Once that was established, he added, "May the children of the stock of Abraham who dwell in this land continue to merit and enjoy the good will of the other inhabitants; while every one shall sit in safety under his own vine and fig tree, and there shall be none to make him afraid."

This reference to the "vine and fig tree" was Washington's favorite Old Testament citation. From the book of Micah, it flowed from a story of a poor farmer freed from military oppression, living free from fear on his own land in a state of contented self-sufficiency. Washington referred to the "vine and fig tree" almost fifty times in his correspondence, often mentioning it in relation to his own hopes of retirement at Mount Vernon. And it appropriately appears one last time in the Farewell Address.

Perhaps because of his native skepticism, Washington's first draft of the 1796 Farewell Address did not dwell on religion, containing only a passing mention of "heaven." But that summer, when Hamilton presented his first major draft, he waxed poetic about religion at unusual length for a man most often fixated on money matters.*

> To all those dispositions which promote political happiness, religion
> and morality are essential props—in vain, does that man claim the
> praise of patriotism who labors to subvert or undermine these great
> pillars of human happiness, these firmest foundations of the duties
> of men and citizens. The mere politician equally with the pious man
> ought to respect and cherish them—a volume could not trace all
> their connections with private and public happiness. Let it simply be
> asked where is the security for property, for reputation, for life, if
> the sense of moral and religious obligation deserts the oaths which
> are administered in the courts of justice? Nor ought we flatter
> ourselves that morality can be separated from religion. Concede
> as much as may be asked to the effect of refined education in the
> minds of peculiar structure—can we believe—can we in prudence
> suppose that national morality can be maintained in exclusion

---

* Hamilton's extended riff on religion is all the more surprising given his generally puckish approach to faith during the early years of the republic. For example, when asked why the founders had failed to include a reference to God in the U.S. Constitution, Hamilton reportedly joked, "We forgot."

of religious principles? Does it not require the aid of a generally
received and divinely authoritative religion?

Tis essentially true that virtue or morality is a main and
necessary spring of popular republican governments. The rule
indeed extends with more or less force to all free governments.
Who that is a prudent and sincere friend to them can look with
indifference on the ravages which are making in the foundation of
the fabric—religion? The uncommon means which of late have
been directed to this fatal end seem to make it in a particular of
manner the duty of the retiring chief of a nation to warn his country
against tasting of the poisonous draught.

The words were Hamilton's, but the ideas were Washington's. The
problem was the verbosity of it all. Washington valued economy of language, and he slashed the section, perhaps embarrassed by too many pro-
fessions of faith that he, in good conscience, knew he did not live up to in
either his public or private life. Washington edited Hamilton's pieties to a
manageable but meaningful 209 words:

Of all the dispositions and habits which lead to political
prosperity, religion and morality are indispensable supports.
In vain would that man claim the tribute of patriotism, who
should labor to subvert these great pillars of human happiness,
these firmest props of the duties of men and citizens. The mere
politician, equally with the pious man, ought to respect and to
cherish them. A volume could not trace all their connections
with private and public felicity. Let it simply be asked: Where is
the security for property, for reputation, for life, if the sense of
religious obligation desert the oaths which are the instruments of
investigation in courts of justice?

And let us with caution indulge the supposition that morality
can be maintained without religion. Whatever may be conceded

to the influence of refined education on minds of peculiar structure, reason and experience both forbid us to expect that national morality can prevail in exclusion of religious principle.

It is substantially true that virtue or morality is a necessary spring of popular government. The rule, indeed, extends with more or less force to every species of free government. Who that is a sincere friend to it can look with indifference upon attempts to shake the foundation of the fabric?

This was a decidedly nondenominational tribute to religion from a civic perspective, dedicated to the practical benefits that flowed from faith, the time-tested wisdom that religions hand down the generations as the surest path toward achieving good character.

But Washington also offered a gentle rebuke to those sophisticates who are inclined to dismiss religion as mere superstition, writing, "let us with caution indulge the supposition that morality can be maintained without religion." While making allowances for educated freethinkers, Washington wanted America to have the steadying benefits that come from religion writ large rather than the amoral anarchy that can come from a vast vacuum of belief.

Washington's vision of religion was practical and pluralistic. In his habitual blurring of Stoicism and Christianity, the belief that virtue and happiness are entwined, he presaged that characteristically American mix of religion and self-help that later resonated from figures as disparate as Ralph Waldo Emerson and Norman Vincent Peale.

At the same time, Washington was being elevated into a civic pantheon at the head of a new firmament of American mythology, coming to embody virtues in word and deed. A Russian visitor recounted how "every American considers it his sacred duty to have a likeness of Washington in his home, just as we have of God's saints." Washington was no saint, but he was committed to living his adult life in a way that was worthy of emulation.

In the wake of his death in 1799, Washington was praised from the pulpits. In those sermons, the Farewell Address was cited as a new form of civic scripture, suitable for repeated readings and reflection. Some parishioners were told to "bind it in your Bible next to the Sermon on the Mount, that the lessons of your two Saviors may be read together."

In the end, Washington's view of faith is consistent with our contemporary formulation that freedom *of* religion is not necessarily freedom *from* religion. An enthusiastic embrace of religious tolerance and pluralism is consistent with concepts of the common good. Washington was searching for societal stability, and he believed that virtue—which is so often elevated by communities of faith—was the surest path to the successful pursuit of happiness.

Education

"PUBLIC OPINION SHOULD BE ENLIGHTENED"

★

Promote then, as an object of primary importance, institutions for the general diffusion of knowledge. In proportion as the structure of a government gives force to public opinion, it is essential that public opinion should be enlightened.

"That Washington was not a scholar is certain," said John Adams. "That he is too illiterate, unlearned, unread for his station is equally past dispute."

That's tough talk from a second in command. Even Jefferson was more charitable when he reflected that Washington's "mind was great and powerful, without being of the very first order . . . [but] as far as he saw, no judgment was ever sounder. It was slow in operation, being little aided by invention or imagination, but sure in conclusion." This was something close to conventional wisdom among those who knew him best. Washington's personal secretary David Humphreys described his liege this way: "his talents were rather solid than brilliant."

With more than a trace of insecurity, Washington admitted his educational and intellectual deficiencies: "I have had but little leisure to read of late years," he confessed as he approached the presidency, and "I cannot indeed pretend to be so well acquainted with civil matters, as I was with military affairs." He was rarely the smartest man in the room, but character was the architect of his achievement.

Although Washington did not have the gift of wit, he possessed something more valuable—a combination of common sense and moral clarity that allowed him to steer steadily toward a fixed course, no matter the weather.

Washington was not formally educated beyond a series of boyhood schools in colonial Virginia. He could read and speak only English, unlike Adams, Jefferson and Madison, who knew Greek, Latin, French and (in the case of Madison) Hebrew. As the second son of a middling planter who died young, Washington did not have the advantage of a higher education at Harvard, William and Mary, King's College (later Columbia University) or the College of New Jersey (later Princeton), where Adams, Jefferson, Hamilton and Madison studied.

But the man who doesn't have the benefit of a formal education sometimes appreciates it the most. The surveyor turned soldier was a lifelong student, always focused on self-improvement. In colonial years it was said that Virginians were more inclined to "read men by business and conversation, than to dive into books." Accordingly, Washington was more of a man of action than reflection. But he sought a balance between a life of action and a life of the mind: "I conceive a knowledge of books is the basis upon which other knowledge is to be built."

He accumulated books from an early age with the goal of learning how to live a successful life. The most famous relic of Washington's school days was a dutiful transcription of a seventeenth-century Jesuit list of advice for young gentlemen known as "Rules of Civility & Decent Behavior in Company and Conversation."

Copied in young Washington's enviably neat rolling script, the rules ranged from table manners ("talk not with meat in your mouth") to respectable behavior ("Let your countenance be pleasant but in serious matters somewhat grave") to guidelines for picking friends ("Associate yourself with men of good quality if you esteem your own reputation; for 'tis better to be alone than in bad company"). Washington had drilled into him the premise of follow-through ("Undertake not what you cannot perform but be careful to keep your promise") and perhaps most important, the fidelity to what

Lincoln would later call "the better angels of our nature" ("Labor to keep alive in your breast that little spark of celestial fire called conscience"). The resulting rules remain in print under Washington's byline.

At the end of his life's journey, the library at Mount Vernon contained more than 900 volumes accumulated over the decades. According to an analysis by Mount Vernon, a third of his books concerned politics, law and the economy—practical topics for the first president. The next-greatest percent of his collection were books about agriculture, his favorite topic and favored profession.

Young George enjoyed literary diversions such as *Don Quixote*, *Tom Jones* and *Aesop's Fables*. As a teenager his tastes grew more ambitious, including Caesar's *Commentaries on the Gallic Wars* and Cicero's *On Duties*, which was also a favorite of John Adams. "Cicero's belief in the virtues of agrarian life, in natural law and justice; his emphasis on friendship as the political bond of states; on the civic value of education in both theory and practice; on nonpartisanship—all of these have their place in Washington's political philosophy," attests Jeffry H. Morrison in *The Political Philosophy of George Washington*.

The classical philosopher Washington most loved was Seneca. His treatise on morals included essays whose titles Washington would later live by: "There Can Be No Happiness Without Virtue" and "The Blessings of Temperance and Moderation."

Seneca's Roman Stoicism—which venerated reason, moderation, virtue, strength and self-discipline—was a particular source of comfort for Washington. From control over his fiery temper to a fatalistic embrace of "providence," Stoic virtues were also a list of Washington's own aspirations.

While Washington was a devoted reader of Shakespeare, peppering his letters with paraphrased lines from *Julius Caesar* and *Othello*, his favorite play was the tragedy *Cato*, an account of the last day of Rome's greatest Stoic hero. Washington committed whole sections to memory.

Washington's love of this play was his central literary touchstone all his life. First performed in 1713, *Cato* was the work of the celebrated British essayist Joseph Addison, whose political prose a youthful Washington eagerly devoured. *Cato* was his most successful venture into the theater, capturing a vogue for Roman history by dramatizing the rivalry between Cato the Younger and Caesar amid the fall of the Roman Republic. Though largely forgotten today, Cato was a symbol of personal virtue and republican principle, despite the play's downer of an ending, when Cato chooses to commit suicide rather than live under a tyrant.

The play was an instant hit in London, beloved by both Tories and Whigs. Published in eight American editions before 1800, it was also perhaps the best-known contemporary play among the founding fathers.

Cato provided Washington comfort in his darkest hours. Throughout the Revolutionary War, when the situation seemed hopeless, Washington repeatedly wrote his fellow generals with variations on the line, "'Tis not in mortals to command success; but we'll do more . . . we'll deserve it."*

This pep talk was sometimes combined with a rueful reminder to himself about the loneliness of ethical leadership: "the post of honor is a private station." And when Washington wrote about his hope of repose under his Bible-inspired "vine and fig tree" he often added another line about achieving mental peace in "the calm light of mild philosophy." All these lines came from *Cato*.

In the frozen dark of Valley Forge, Washington even staged a performance of *Cato* to rally the troops, with soldiers playing the parts to warm their collective courage.

Washington's references to Rome would have been as well understood by his contemporaries as movie references are today, and he was far from the only member of the revolutionary generation to find inspiration in *Cato's* words.

Many signature phrases of the American Revolution—Nathan Hale's "I only regret that I have but one life to lose for my country"; Patrick

---

* Among the generals to whom Washington sent this high-minded message was the notorious traitor Benedict Arnold.

Henry's "Give me Liberty, or give me Death"—were conscious echoes of Addison's *Cato*.

The revolutionary generation's love of the play and its Roman namesake spoke to their reverence for classical texts, especially those reimagined for contemporary ears, emphasizing the ideal of civic virtue.

But Washington wasn't the kind to retire to his tent and read texts in their original Latin for relaxation. He was a practical man, and even his interest in history was impatiently rooted in its application to the present and its guidance for the future. "We ought not to look back," he wrote, "unless it is to derive useful lessons from past errors, and for the purpose of profiting by dear-bought experience."

Perhaps because Washington's personal reading focused on self-improvement, he increasingly valued education, seeing it as the key to a country's collective self-improvement. Once the tide had turned in the war for independence and prospects for the new nation emerged, Washington focused on education as a means of strengthening the loosely united states. "The best means of forming a manly, virtuous, and happy people will be found in the right education of youth," he wrote. "Without *this* foundation, every other means, in my opinion, must fail."

His belief in the value of a liberal education shows a softer side of the sober-minded general: "The arts and sciences essential to the prosperity of the state and to the ornament and happiness of human life have a primary claim to the encouragement of every lover of his country and mankind."

In his Circular Letter of 1783, Washington framed the opportunity facing the newborn nation in terms of the progress of knowledge:

The foundation of our empire was not laid in the gloomy age of ignorance and superstition, but at an epocha when the rights of mankind were better understood and more clearly defined than at any former period, the researches of the human mind after social happiness have been carried to a great extent, the treasures of knowledge, acquired by the labors of philosophers, sages, and legislatures, through a long succession of years, are laid open for our use, and their collected wisdom may be happily applied in the establishment of our forms of government; the free cultivation of letters, the unbounded extension of commerce, the progressive refinement of manners, the growing liberality of sentiment, and above all, the pure and benign light of Revelation, have had a meliorating influence on mankind and increased the blessings of society. At this auspicious period, the United States came into existence as a nation, and if their citizens should not be completely free and happy, the fault will be entirely their own.

Washington was not generally one to wax poetic, but he understood that the opportunities of the moment were based on advancements in science and liberty beyond superstition and tyranny. And so as the young republic emerged unsteadily, the most unschooled founding father emerged as the leading proponent of national education as a means to develop an American character and our success as a self-governing people.

The best test of advice is whether it is enacted at home. And while Washington had no children of his own, he treated his stepchildren with a solicitous care that extended to their education.

His stepson Jack Custis was a constant worry, a bright but undisciplined teen whose interests, in Washington's eyes, tended toward "dogs, horses, and guns."

Attempting to remedy Jack's wayward inclination, Washington wrote to his schoolmaster with a detailed prescription for his stepson's education: "To be acquainted with the French tongue is become part of polite education; and to a man who has any idea of mixing in a large circle, absolutely necessary. Without arithmetic, the common affairs of life are not to be managed with success. . . . The principles of philosophy, moral, natural, &c. I should think a very desirable knowledge for a gentleman." For another younger stepson, he specified that a tutor must be a classical scholar, despite Washington's own disregard for classical languages.

For his step-granddaughters, especially his beloved Nelly, educational advice was emotional. He wrote to them primarily about love, cautioning them against putting too high a price on passion. In the twilight of his presidency, he warned one step-granddaughter that "in the composition of the human frame there is a great deal of inflammable matter, however dormant it may lie for a time, and . . . when the torch is put to it, that which is within you must burst into a blaze."

No apostle for romantic love, the man who married for stability and social advancement cautioned another step-granddaughter, "Love is a mighty pretty thing; but, like all other delicious things, it is cloying; and when the first transports of the passion begins to subside, which it assuredly will do, and yield—oftentimes too late—to more sober reflections, it serves to evince that love is too dainty a food to live upon *alone,* and ought not to be considered farther than as a necessary ingredient for that matrimonial happiness which results from a combination of causes; none of which are of greater importance than that the object on whom it is placed should have good sense—good dispositions—and the means of supporting you in the way you have been brought up. . . . Experience will convince you, that there is no truth more certain, than that all of our enjoyments fall short of our expectations; and to none does it apply with more force, than to the gratification of the passions."

★

WASHINGTON DISTRUSTED PASSION AND VENERATED reason as a means to achieve self-improvement. Perhaps that's why he lost few opportunities to preach the importance of education to a self-governing people. In part, this was practical. With 95 percent of Americans living on farms, Washington could see that more widespread education promised economic diversity as well as respect in the wider world of nations. But the subject of public education was also winding its way toward the mainstream of civic debate, as wartime worries gave way to peacetime responsibilities. Philadelphia's Benjamin Rush, the most prominent doctor among the founding fathers, argued in advance of the Constitutional Convention that "the business of education has acquired a new complexion by the independence of our country. The form of government we have assumed, has created a new class of duties to every American." An educated population was in the national interest.

At his first annual address to Congress, huddled in New York's Federal Hall, President Washington took advantage of the opportunity to expound on education at length, while formally introducing his greatest frustrated ambition—the creation of a national university:

> Knowledge is in every country the surest basis of public happiness. . . . To the security of a free Constitution it contributes its various ways: by convincing those who are instructed with the public administration that every valuable end of government is best answered by the enlightened confidence of the people; and by teaching the people themselves to know and to value their own rights, to discern and provide against invasions of them, to distinguish between oppression and the necessary exercise of lawful authority, between burdens proceeding from a disregard to their convenience and those resulting from the inevitable exigencies of society, to discriminate the spirit of liberty from that of licentiousness, cherishing the first, avoiding the last, and uniting a speedy, but temperate vigilance against encroachments, with an inviolable respect to the laws. Whether this desirable object will be the best promoted by affording aids to seminaries of learning already established—by the institution of a national university— or by any other expedients, will be well worthy of a place in the deliberations of the legislature.

America already had great regional colleges—Yale, Harvard and Virginia's own William and Mary were a half-century old. But Washington's idea of a national university was something new.

Congress pushed back on the president, arguing that his vision of a national university was unconstitutional. "This power should be exercised by the states in their separate capacities," said Connecticut representative Roger Sherman. Others argued that education should be a private, rather than public, pursuit. Among the less lofty anxieties expressed was not only that a national university would lead to the creation of an American elite, but that "the further children are from home . . . the more their morals would be injured." This Congressional resistance drove the focus for public education toward the creation of state universities, such as the University of North Carolina and Jefferson's beloved University of Virginia.

But Washington did not give up easily and he kept adding to his arguments over the course of his two terms, expressing concern about the foreign influence on young Americans whose families still believed they could only receive a world-class education abroad. "It has always been a source of serious reflection and sincere regret to me, that the youth of the United States should be sent to foreign countries for the purpose of education," he wrote in 1795. "Although there are doubtless many under these circumstances who escape the danger of contracting principles unfriendly to republican government, yet we ought to depreciate the hazard attending ardent and susceptible minds, from being too strongly and too early prepossessed in favor of other political systems before they are capable of appreciating their own."

Washington saw public education as a hedge against would-be demagogues and regional divisions, but he also saw a national university as a way of reducing foreign influence while creating an American character.

Washington believed that the national university should be located in what he called "the Federal City" as a matter of geographical convenience. By placing the new capital on the banks of the Potomac, Washington was not only seeking to bring the seat of national power closer to home in Virginia. Instead, its centrality could offset arguments of regional bias or favoritism. Moreover, the presence of the Potomac offered western settlers the ability to access a national capital from lands as then distant as Ohio and Pennsylvania.

Because this particular project was outside his realm of expertise, there was more than a trace of frustrated impotence in Washington's correspondence with the directors of the District of Columbia in January 1795. He grasped for concrete statements of progress and planning, justified in sensing that his priority—the creation of a national university—was not shared by other actors on the stage who would soon be supplanting him. They did not see education as matter of national urgency compared to defense, trade and development.

But it's easy to appreciate personally and politically why the establishment of a national university was of such preeminent importance to Washington at the end of his two terms. A national university was an antidote to the regional divisions he saw all around him. Future young leaders who wanted to participate in government would come to learn about civic life from the generation currently operating in the capital. This exchange would break down regional differences and create a common currency of communication and knowledge that would help stabilize the state in future years and avoid further influence of foreign powers.

It was his hope, in effect, to create a national civic culture rooted in a place of practical knowledge. He had a rooting interest, of course. As David Humphreys attested, "There is scarcely one work written in America on any art, science, or subject" that failed to make its way to Washington's study.

The goal was not just to improve the administration of government, but also to encourage the establishment of new industries, and of a distinctly American artistic community ranging from literature to painting.

As John Adams memorably put the logical progression in a letter to his wife, Abigail, "I must study politics and war that my sons may have liberty to study mathematics and philosophy. My sons ought to study mathematics and philosophy, geography, natural history, naval architecture, navigation, commerce, and agriculture, in order to give their children a right to study painting, poetry, music, architecture, statuary, tapestry, and porcelain."

This intergenerational vision was at once practical and expansive. But Washington was not satisfied to wait three generations for the development of an American literature. He had been an early booster of colonial poets who had attempted to inspire a sense of the possibility that seemed pregnant at the birth of the republic.

He corresponded with the African-American female poet Phillis Wheatley, who mailed him patriotic verses before the war and met with him in 1776. Wheatley, born in West Africa, was kidnapped on a ship named *Phillis* and arrived orphaned in Boston. The Wheatley family who purchased her encouraged their daughter to teach the slave girl Greek and Latin. Deeply gifted, she published a book of poems in London that led to a tour of England. She was a devoted advocate of independence, and in 1775 she wrote a letter to Washington containing a patriotic poem titled "His Excellency General Washington," which ended with this stanza: "Proceed, great chief, with virtue on thy side / Thy ev'ry action let the goddess guide / A crown, a mansion, and a throne that shine / With gold unfading, Washington! be thine!"

Washington was so touched that he wrote the only known letter he ever addressed to a slave, saying in part, "I thank you most sincerely for your polite notice of me in the elegant lines you enclosed; and however undeserving I may be of such encomium and panegyric, the style and manner exhibit a striking proof of your great poetical talents."

Washington was also a booster of the poet Joel Barlow, the author of an early American epic called *The Vision of Columbus*. Barlow cut almost as fascinating a figure as Wheatley, serving as a military chaplain in the Continental Army and subsequently as a foreign diplomat, where he is credited for drafting the Treaty of Tripoli in 1796, which contains the still-controversial assertion that "the government of the United States of America is not, in any sense, founded on the Christian religion." In a letter to Lafayette, Washington described Barlow as one of "those bards who hold the keys of the gate by which patriots, sages, and heroes are admitted to immortality." Washington understood the value of enduringly good PR via epic poetry, from the days of Homer to his own.

*

WASHINGTON'S EARLY CALL FOR A national university slowly gathered support. By 1795, the tide seemed to be shifting in his direction. Due to instability in the wake of the French Revolution, the scholars of the University of Geneva had been displaced from their historic Swiss home and were actively looking for a safer place to conduct their studies. In this, Jefferson saw opportunity and wrote to Washington recommending that the entire Geneva faculty be imported to the United States.

But Washington quickly identified several problems. Patiently slapping down the bright idea in a letter to Jefferson, Washington explained, "The propriety of transplanting the professors in a *body*, might be questioned for several reasons; among others, because they might not all be good characters; nor all sufficiently acquainted with our language; and again, having been at variance with the leveling party of their own country, the measure might be considered as an aristocratical movement by more than those who, without any just cause that I have been able to discover, are continually sounding the alarm bell of aristocracy."

The "alarm bell of aristocracy" line was a not-so-subtle dig at Jefferson and his fellow Democratic-Republicans, who had been attacking the alleged "Monocrats" of Washington's administration both in Congress and in the partisan press. Rather than importing the teachers wholesale, Washington decided to push again in the Farewell Address, where he felt he could make a case for a national university to posterity if not Congress.

In the summer of 1796, on the third draft, Washington instructed Hamilton to include a section on education:

I have regretted that another subject (which in my estimation is
of interesting concern to the well being of this country) was not

touched upon also: I mean Education *generally* is one of the surest means of enlightening and giving just ways of thinking to our citizens, but particularly the establishment of a university, where the youth from all parts of the United States might receive the polish of erudition in the arts, sciences, and belle lettres; and where those who were disposed to run a political course, might not only be instructed in theory and principles, but (this seminary being at the seat of the general government) where the legislature would be in session half the year, and the interests and politics of the nation of course would be discussed, they would lay the surest foundation for the practical part also.

But that which would render it of the highest importance, in my opinion, is, that the juvenile period of life, when friendships are formed, and habits established that will stick by one; the youth or young men from different parts of the United States would be assembled together, and would by degrees discover that there was not that cause for those jealousies and prejudices which one part of the union had imbibed against another part; of course, sentiments of more liberality in the general policy of the country would result from it. . . .

To show that this is no *new* idea of mine, I may appeal to my early communications to Congress; and to prove how seriously I have reflected on it since, and how well disposed I have been and still am to contribute my aid towards carrying the measure into effect . . .

Washington went so far as to suggest a placement in the address for such a section on education "after the one which relates to our religious obligations, or in a proceeding part, as one of the recommendatory measures to counteract the evils arising from geographical discriminations."

In this singular case, Hamilton resisted Washington, writing four days later from New York that "you will observe a short paragraph added respecting *education*. [But] as to the establishment of a university, it is a point which in connection with military schools, and some other things, I meant, agreeably to your desire to suggest to you as parts of your speech at the opening of the session."

Instead, Hamilton suggested that the president make it part of his final year-end address to Congress in December. "There will several things come there much better than a general address to the people which likewise would swell the address too much."

This rare conflict between speechwriter and president surfaced because Hamilton felt that such a specific policy prescription did not fit in the more lofty, principle-driven Farewell Address. There is also some sense that his contemporaries thought Washington's focus on a national university was a peculiar and impractical personal obsession, and so they treated it with a degree of patient condescension.

Ultimately, a short paragraph on education was written and literally cut and pasted into the address by Washington himself back in Philadelphia. Two inches of open space was left below the lines, apparently to allow for further ruminations, but it remained blank when the final manuscript was delivered to the printer. And so when the Farewell Address appeared, the mention of Washington's dream of a national university was reduced to one meager line, given pride of place only by its own paragraph, which read, "Promote then, as an object of primary importance, institutions for the general diffusion of knowledge. In proportion as the structure of a government gives force to public opinion, it is essential that public opinion should be enlightened."

The fact that only a single paragraph in the Farewell was devoted to Washington's obsession with education does not diminish its importance. The backstory of the back-and-forth during composition—as well as the resonance of this one brisk point throughout American history, in speeches and printed posters—makes it clear that Washington's insistence on elevating public education was based on a deep and urgent insight: that democracies' success depended on an educated and enlightened population. His proposal for a national university was driven as much by a desire to overcome regional prejudices through the personal friendships of young people as it was to create a central location to teach the art of self-governance.

Washington was not about to let his greatest late-in-life policy passion go unarticulated. And so he devoted a major portion of his final address to Congress on the subject, as Hamilton suggested.

This speech, delivered on December 7, 1796, can rightly be considered a coda to this section of the Farewell Address, reflecting specific policy prescriptions to Congress that might have seemed out of place amid the broad, enduring principles in the Farewell published two and a half months before. It was a speech of unfinished business—last requests, reminders, and recommendations—from a leader who had been transformed by retirement into something close to his postwar glory:

> I have heretofore proposed to the consideration of Congress the expediency of establishing a national university, and also a military academy. The desirableness of both these institutions, has so constantly increased with every new view I have taken of the subject, that I cannot omit the opportunity of once for all recalling your attention to them.
>
> The assembly to which I address myself, is too enlightened not to be fully sensible how much a flourishing state of the arts and sciences contributes to national prosperity and reputation. . . .
>
> Amongst the motives to such an institution, the assimilation of the principles, opinions, and manners of our country-men, by the common education of a portion of our youth from every quarter, well deserves attention. The more homogeneous our citizens can be made in these particulars, the greater will be our prospect of permanent Union; and a primary object of such a national institution should be, the education of our youth in the science of government. In a republic, what species of knowledge can be

equally important? And what duty more pressing on its legislature, than to patronize a plan for communicating it to those who are to be the future guardians of the liberties of the country?

The institution of a military academy, is also recommended by cogent reasons. However pacific the general policy of a nation may be, it ought never to be without an adequate stock of military knowledge for emergencies. The first would impair the energy of its character, and both would hazard its safety, or expose it to greater evils when war could not be avoided. Besides that, war might often not depend upon its own choice. . . . The art of war is at once comprehensive and complicated, that it demands much previous study, and that the possession of it, in its most improved and perfect state, is always of great moment to the security of a nation. This, therefore, ought to be a serious care of every government: and for this purpose, an academy where a regular course of instruction is given is an obvious expedient.

Washington's request for a national military academy—a "peace establishment"—was ultimately granted at West Point, situated on the bluffs on the western bank of the Hudson River within sight of his final revolutionary headquarters in Newburgh, New York, where he'd written his first Farewell.

As president, Washington instituted a small military school dedicated to artillery and engineering on the spot. But he could not get congressional approval for the full military academy, a frustration that he mentioned in his last letter to Alexander Hamilton, sent just days before his death in 1799. His full proposal was finally enacted when Thomas Jefferson became president, bridging the partisan divisions in Congress while initially filling the ranks of West Point with future officers loyal to the Democratic-Republican Party. This was both partisan patronage and personal insurance.

Despite Washington's persistent push for the creation of a national university, his dream was never achieved. Even the first founding father could not compel Congress to do his will at a time when the federal city that bears his name was being constructed.

Familiar congressional arguments for inaction carried the day—the timing was not quite right, the costs were too high, rural students would not travel all that way for an education. The land set aside by Washington for the national university is now occupied by the Naval Observatory, the vice presidential residence since 1974.

But Washington did have the satisfaction of seeing a university named after him, as the trustees of Liberty Hall Academy voted to do in the summer before his death. He wrote to them in July in appreciation of their honor and bequeathed a donation to their institution: "To promote literature in this rising empire, and to encourage the arts, have ever been amongst the warmest wishes of my heart. And if the donation . . . is likely to prove a means to accomplish these ends, it will contribute to the gratification of my desires." Washington Academy became Washington College in 1813 and then was named Washington and Lee five years after the Civil War, when the former leader of the Confederate Army—married to a great-granddaughter of Martha Washington—became president of the university.

Washington's commitment to the idea of a national university extended beyond the grave. In his last will and testament, he devoted considerable space to the subject and directed funds for both local and national educational efforts. Washington set aside money to the Academy in the Town of Alexandria for the support of a "Free School" designed to benefit "orphan children, or the children of such other poor and indigent persons as are unable to accomplish it with their own means." He also provided for the sons and daughters of his freed slaves to "be taught to read and write, and brought up to some useful occupation," at a time when Virginia law still made teaching slaves to read illegal.

While doing so, he repeated the case that he had made for more than two decades, calling once more for "the establishment of a UNIVERSITY in a central part of the United States, to which the youth of fortune and talents from all parts thereof might be sent for the completion of their education." Washington put his personal wealth toward the execution of this vision, attempting to will its success even after death.

The least formally schooled founding father believed that education he had been denied could help unite the nation while securing its future liberty and prosperity. The spirit of civility and self-improvement that flows from education is essential to successful self-government. To that extent, all education is civic education. Washington understood that democracy depends on an enlightened public.

A Foreign Policy of Independence
PEACE THROUGH STRENGTH

★

Observe good faith and justice towards all nations; cultivate peace and harmony with all. . . . The great rule of conduct for us in regard to foreign nations is in extending our commercial relations, to have with them as little political connection as possible. . . . The period is not far off when we may defy material injury from external annoyance; when we may take such an attitude as will cause the neutrality we may at any time resolve upon to be scrupulously respected; when belligerent nations, under the impossibility of making acquisitions upon us, will not lightly hazard the giving us provocation; when we may choose peace or war, as our interest, guided by justice, shall counsel.

The most famous phrase attributed to the Farewell Address—a warning against "entangling alliances"—doesn't appear among its fifty-four paragraphs.

Ironically, it was Thomas Jefferson who uttered those words in his first inaugural. The sage of Monticello had chutzpah. After a decade attacking President Washington's foreign policy, Jefferson finally found the wisdom of Washington's position when he assumed the presidency, proclaiming the "essential principles of our Government . . . peace, commerce, and honest friendship with all nations, entangling alliances with none."

The vindication came too late for Washington to savor. He died one year before Jefferson was elected. But Washington's wisdom had a way of converting critics when they reached the presidency.

Even future president James Monroe—whom Washington unceremoniously removed as ambassador to France for undercutting the administration's neutrality proclamation—is today best known for issuing the Monroe Doctrine, which explicitly built on Washington's principle of neutrality from European affairs by insisting on respect for our own sphere of influence, hanging a "closed for colonization" sign over the New World.

In his Farewell Address, Washington established a distinctly American foreign policy tradition—not isolation, but independence.

It was a practical vision rooted in our distance from the perpetual turmoil in Europe. As a Swedish minister told John Adams in 1784, "Sir, I take it for granted that you will have sense enough to see us in Europe cut each others' throats with a philosophical tranquility."

America was protected by an ocean from aggressors. As comedian, newspaper columnist and movie star Will Rogers joked more than a century later, "No nation ever had better friends than we have. You know who they are? The Atlantic and Pacific Oceans." As a surveyor turned soldier, Washington also appreciated the strategic advantages that came with such fundamental facts of geography.

His perspective on foreign policy was rooted in British tradition often articulated during his youth. England was also an island trading nation separated from continental Europe, prompting prime minister Robert Walpole to proclaim, "My politics are to keep free from all entanglements as long as we possibly can . . . this is a trading nation, and the prosperity of her trade is what ought to be principally in the eye of every gentleman." Of course, England did not ultimately resist the temptations of empire and playing in the great power politics of Europe. This overextension ultimately led to its fall from global dominance.

In an ironic twist of fate, George Washington helped kick off the real first world war, in the 1750s. As a young soldier—ambitious, aggressive and insecure—he was embroiled in the first combat of the French and Indian War in western Pennsylvania, which sparked the Seven Years' War in Europe, fought with a dizzying array of alliances on both sides, ranging from

European regents to Indian tribes. As Voltaire wrote, "Such was the complication of political interests that a cannon shot fired in America could give the signal that set Europe in a blaze." The danger of transatlantic alliances was clear.

★

BASED IN HIS EXPERIENCES, WASHINGTON believed America needed at least twenty years of neutrality to grow powerful enough so that independence could be reliably sustained.

He had a farmer's sense of the value of time. Growth could not be rushed. His patience was further enhanced by guerrilla warfare. As commander of the Continental Army, he learned the hard way that only rarely could he defeat the redcoats by confronting them head-on. Instead, Washington pursued a strategy to preserve his army and outlast the British. He ordered tactical retreats more often than attacks, always mindful of the need to conserve a credible force that, season after season, year after year, could harass the redcoats and wear away at London's enthusiasm for war.

When the war ended, Washington hammered home the need for military preparedness in his Circular Letter: "The militia of this country must be considered as the palladium of our security and the first effectual resort in case of hostility," he wrote, cautioning that the military must be standardized in terms of equipment and drills in all corners of the country. "No one, who had not learned it from experience, can conceive of the difficulty, expense, and confusion which result from a contrary system, or the vague arrangements which have hitherto prevailed."

As president, Washington's military experience continued to inform national strategy. While he saw commerce as key to stable foreign affairs and a satisfied domestic population, he did not do so from a naïve position that would redirect resources away from basic military preparedness. Presiding over the Constitutional Convention, he confronted delegates' deep fears that a standing army would be an invitation to tyranny, as it had throughout history. Massachusetts delegate Elbridge Gerry reached for a bawdy metaphor to describe this danger: "a standing army is like a standing member," Gerry gibed, "an excellent assurance of domestic tranquility, but a dangerous temptation to foreign adventure."

But when Gerry went from sexual innuendo to a specific proposal that an American army be limited to 3,000 soldiers, Washington indulged in a rare break from his stoic silence to mock the suggestion, sarcastically suggesting in a stage whisper, "No foreign enemy shall invade the United States, at any time, with more than three thousand troops."

In his speech to Congress in January 1790, Washington produced one of his most famous aphorisms, still quoted by candidates today: "to be prepared for war is one of the most effectual means of preserving peace." This was a powerful paraphrase of one of the most time-honored Roman maxims: *Si vis pacem, para bellum*—"If you want peace, prepare for war."

Washington's understanding of history as well as his army experience drew him to the conclusion that a strong military was essential to deter meddling nations from disrupting the American experiment. Even before the presidency, he imagined a time "when foreign nations shall be disposed to give us equal advantages in commerce from dread of retaliation." Military strength made trade a more attractive option than war.

When Washington spoke of foreign policy he often couched the relationship between the United States and other nations in personal terms: "I hold the maxim no less applicable to public than to private affairs, that honesty is always the best policy," he wrote in the Farewell Address, while making the case that existing treaties and agreements must be honored but not indefinitely extended.

It was a view he'd maintained for decades, writing Lafayette in 1786, "Nations are not influenced as individuals may be by disinterested friendships: but when it is their interest to live in amity, we have little reason to apprehend any rupture." Self-interest drove most decisions. Nations have no permanent allies, only permanent interests.

After all, Washington had already seen our closest wartime ally, France, attempt not just to interfere with our domestic policies but also try to overthrow his democratically elected government with the help of the partisan press, an over-agitated public and even his own secretary of state. Little wonder that Washington devoted so much of the Farewell Address to this warning: "Against the insidious wiles of foreign influence . . . the jealousy of a free people ought to be constantly awake, since history and experience prove that foreign influence is one of the most baneful foes of republican government."

History and experience were the guides Washington followed in his Farewell. As Madison noted in "On Ancient and Modern Confederacies," history was littered with examples of small republics losing their sovereignty through destabilization by larger powers who wormed their way into domestic politics through pretend friendships and partisan alliances.

This was not simply the stuff of history books. In 1791, inspired by the United States, Poland ratified the first written constitution in Europe, attempting to press past the polarization and paralysis of its parliamentary monarchy. The result was praised by such divergent voices as Thomas Paine and Edmund Burke. But squeezed between Russia and Prussia, Poland found its sovereignty systematically undermined by senate candidates who secretly served those neighboring states. With a weakened military, a series of partitions reduced Poland to a skeletal state.

Washington's experience with the intrigues of revolutionary France compelled him to warn in the Farewell: "A passionate attachment of one nation for another produces a variety of evils. . . . As avenues to foreign influence in innumerable ways, such attachments are particularly alarming to the truly enlightened and independent patriot. How many opportunities do they afford to tamper with domestic factions, to practice the arts of seduction, to mislead public opinion, to influence or awe the public councils? Such an attachment of a small or weak towards a great and powerful nation dooms the former to be the satellite of the latter."

This fear of "the enemy within"—which has resurfaced throughout American history—has its roots in scars sustained in the early years of the republic. But the principles Washington articulated were far older than the vicious fights over France and England. They had once been considered common sense.

Thomas Paine articulated many of the same ideas in his famous pamphlet, *Common Sense*, published in January 1776: "Any submission to, or dependence on, Great Britain tends directly to involve this continent in European wars and quarrels. . . . As Europe is our market for trade, we ought to form no partial connection with any part of it. It is the true interest of America to steer clear of European contentions."

These principles endured when John Adams was serving as America's foreign ambassador. Adams wrote to Congress to warn his fellow countrymen of the real politics behind great powers in Europe: "Not even Spain nor France wishes to see America rise very fast to power. We ought therefore to be cautious how we magnify our ideas and exaggerate our expressions of the generosity and magnanimity of any of these Powers."

This consensus was also expressed in a resolution of Congress in 1783: "The future interest of these states requires that they should be as little possible entangled in the politics and controversies of European nations."

The principles were bipartisan, articulated by men with widely varying worldviews. Washington didn't change his principles to blow with the wind of political fashion.

Washington detested the French Revolution's rush to radicalism, but he tried to keep neutral among European intrigues. He had no love for the British Crown, but he tried to make a sober distinction between the people and their rulers, guided by American self-interest. "I was opposed to the policy of [Great Britain] and became an enemy to her measures," he wrote John Ellis, "but I always distinguished between a cause and individuals: and while the latter supported their opinion upon liberal and generous grounds, personally, I never could be an enemy to them."

When the French Revolution turned violent and Lafayette was forced into exile for being insufficiently radical, Washington overruled his own personal passions and refused to intercede for his old friend's release from an Austrian prison for fear of embroiling America in foreign intrigues. This was an act of remarkable self-discipline for a man who essentially adopted Lafayette's son during his imprisonment. Washington likewise kept a portrait of the beheaded King Louis prominently on the wall of his executive mansion in silent rebuke to fans of the French Revolution.

In April 1793, Washington officially proclaimed America's neutrality in the widening European war between Britain and her allies and France, saying, "The duty and interest of the United States require, that they should with sincerity and good faith adopt and pursue a conduct friendly and impartial toward the belligerent powers."

Americans who'd been whipped up into a frenzy of support for France under the rhetoric of universal liberty and an understandable remembrance of that nation's support for American independence, albeit under a now-beheaded head of state, were offended. But their overzealousness was itself more evidence to support Washington's firm belief, articulated in the Farewell Address, that "[t]he nation which indulges towards another a habitual hatred or a habitual fondness is in some degree a slave. It is a slave to its animosity or to its affection, either of which is sufficient to lead it astray from its duty and its interest."

In 1795, Washington attempted to extend this Proclamation of Neutrality by dispatching the chief justice of the Supreme Court, John Jay, on a mission to negotiate a treaty with England. The treaty Jay returned with was far from perfect but it offered strategic benefits by giving our nation a chance to grow in strength both economically and militarily.

Among the concessions Jay received were British abandonment of six forts in the Great Lakes region, reparations to American merchants and increased access to the valuable trading ports of the West Indies (albeit with small trading vessels). Combined with Thomas Pinckney's treaty with Spain, which opened up the Mississippi for trade, these were powerful incentives for the principles of neutrality and increased foreign trade instead of involvement in foreign wars.

But the domestic debate over the Jay Treaty raged and turned violent.

Hamilton weighed in, writing public essays under the signature of Horatius, arguing for the treaty's ratification. "If you consult your true interest your motto cannot fail to be 'Peace and Trade with all Nations; beyond our preset engagements, political connection with none,'" Hamilton bellowed. "You ought to spurn from you as the box of Pandora the fatal heresy of close alliance, or in the language of *Genet*, a true *family compact* with France. This would at once make you a mere satellite of France, and entangle you in all the contests, broils, and wars of Europe. . . . 'Twere insanity to embrace such a system."

The vice president's eldest son, John Quincy Adams, already a distinguished diplomat by his late twenties, predicted, "If the Jay Treaty should not be ratified, the French will exert themselves for the purpose of hurrying us into a war. . . . Their partisans, perhaps, in declamations or in newspapers will promise wonders from their co-operation. . . . The final result of the whole matter will be, that all this tender sympathy, this amiable fraternity, this lovely coalescence of liberty, will leave us the advantage of being sacrificed to their interests, or of purchasing their protection upon the most humiliating and burdensome conditions." When it came to gifts of acerbic wit, the apple did not fall far from the Adams' family tree.

Quincy beat this drum in dispatches his father passed on to President Washington and newspaper notices published under the names Marcellus and Columbia, warning that if America were drawn into a European war, "it would be a war in which we should have everything to lose and nothing to gain."

By the fall of 1795, Washington was lobbying for the treaty's passage with arguments that would find their ultimate expression in the Farewell Address.

In October, Washington wrote Patrick Henry to explain that his guiding principle was "to keep the United States free from *political* connections with *every* other Country. To see that they *may be* independent of *all*, and under the influence of *none*. In a word, I want an *American* character, that the powers of Europe may be convinced we act for *ourselves* and not for *others;* this, in my judgment, is the only way to be respected abroad and happy at home, and not, by becoming the partisans of Great Britain or France, create dissensions, disturb the public tranquillity, and destroy, perhaps forever, the cement which binds the Union."

Two months later, days before Christmas, Washington wrote a similar screed to his friend Gouverneur Morris: "My policy has been, and will continue to be, while I have the honor to remain in the administration of the government, to be upon friendly terms with, but independent of, all the nations of the earth. To share in the broils of none. To fulfill our own engagements. To supply the wants and be carriers for them all: being thoroughly convinced that it is our policy and interest to do so. . . . For sure I am, if this country is preserved in tranquility twenty years longer, it may bid defiance, in a just cause, to any power whatever; such, in that time, will be its population, wealth, and resources."

★

IN THE END, WASHINGTON OUTMANEUVERED the Democratic-Republicans in Congress to pass the Jay Treaty, based largely on his personal prestige. "Nothing but his weight of character and reputation, combined with his firmness and political intrepidity, could have stood against the torrent," John Quincy Adams remarked. "He is now pledged, and he is unmoved. If his system of administration now prevails, ten years more will place the United States among the most powerful and opulent nations on earth."

But bitterness prevailed after the treaty passed. France was particularly unforgiving, and the French ambassador Pierre-Auguste Adet threw his most vocal advocate, Thomas Jefferson, under the carriage.

"Mr. Jefferson likes us because he detests England," Adet sneered. "Although Jefferson is the friend of liberty and of science, although he is an admirer of the efforts we have made to cast off our shackles and to clear away the cloud of ignorance which weighs down the human race, Jefferson, I say, is an American, and as such he cannot sincerely be our friend. And America is the born enemy of all the peoples of Europe."

Washington's worldview retained a core healthy skepticism about the perfectibility of man as well as concern about the inevitable overreach that comes with the temptations of empire. This was a focus of his fears about foreign wars and their high cost in blood and treasure. Instead, he approached foreign policy with a spirit of global good citizenship, maintaining friendly terms with all, driven by the mutual self-interest that can come with commerce.

The Farewell Address is a response to the second-term crises that threatened those ideals. Beneath almost every phrase, you can hear echoes of domestic political debates between the Federalists and the Democratic-Republicans and their proxy states, England and France. But even Jefferson eventually flip-flopped and found religion on the subject, writing a few months after the Farewell's publication, "Our countrymen have divided themselves by such strong affections to the French and the English, that nothing will secure us internally but a divorce from both nations. And this must be the object of every real American."

It has been a common mistake for centuries to assume that the broad foreign policy principles Washington presented—specifically the principle of neutrality—was a de facto or explicit endorsement of isolationism. Washington's immediate goal was to keep the United States out of foreign wars so that we might gain in strength and be free to pursue our own independent interests without being used as a pawn by Old World powers.

"If this country can remain in peace 20 years longer," Washington wrote in the first draft of his 1796 Farewell, "such in all probability will be its population, riches, and resources, when combined with its peculiarly happy and remote situation from other corners of the globe, as to bid defiance, in a just cause, to any earthly power whatsoever."

While Washington dropped that wording from the final Farewell Address, he kept the message intact: "The period is not far off when we may defy material injury from external annoyance; when we may take such an attitude as will cause the neutrality we may at any time resolve upon to be scrupulously respected; when belligerent nations, under the impossibility of making acquisitions upon us, will not lightly hazard the giving us provocation; when we may choose peace or war, as our interest, guided by justice, shall counsel."

"Choose peace or war, as our interest, guided by justice, shall counsel" is not an isolationists' ostrich-like mantra. It is practical advice aimed at preserving independence of action, including the use of military force when necessary.

Washington was a soldier, but he hated war as only a soldier can. In the first draft of the Farewell, he explained the context for conflict. "That we may always be prepared for war, but never unleash the sword except in self-defense, so long as justice and our essential rights and national respectability can be preserved without it."

This principle was one reason Washington enthusiastically advocated for the creation of a national war college, eventually established at West Point. Gibbon's *Decline and Fall of the Roman Empire* argued that one pivotal shift in Rome's fortunes was the rise of foreign mercenaries hired to defend the empire, as citizens grew decadent and reluctant to submit to the discipline of national defense. When citizens ceased to be soldiers and soldiers ceased to be citizens, the republic was no longer in control of its destiny.

This emphasis on a strong national defense also lends light to Washington's interpretation of the Second Amendment to the Constitution, which passed during his presidency and opens with the phrase "a well-regulated militia, being necessary to the security of a free state." Washington had served in the Virginia militia and supplemented the Continental Army with militiamen. But even the former general was reluctant to have too large a standing army, arguing in the Farewell Address that one of the many benefits of union was that the states "will avoid the necessity of those overgrown military establishments which, under any form of government, are inauspicious to liberty, and which are to be regarded as particularly hostile to republican liberty."

For Washington, the key was a "well-regulated" militia—that citizens were trained in military matters that included drills and the use of firearms, privately owned or, in case of crisis, publicly supplied. A federal military establishment was essential but it needed to be supplemented by state militias when necessary. We could not be lulled into a false sense of security simply because of our ocean barrier.

But Washington was not an advocate for expansion or overseas empires. He made it clear in a letter to James Monroe that his position of neutrality was consistent with his belief in self-determination, writing, "I have always given it as my decided opinion that no nation had a right to intermeddle in the internal concerns of another; that every one had a right to form and adopt whatever government they liked best to live under themselves."

Washington was trying to steer a middle path between what we would call isolationism and internationalism, rooted in our self-interest while respecting other nations' right to self-determination. He believed that "the cause of virtue and liberty is confined to no continent or climate," but he did not believe that the common cause should compel America to squander its unique strategic advantages.

This faith that America could do well by doing good was not naïve. In fact, it proved to be practical. As he wrote in the Farewell, "It will be worthy of a free, enlightened, and at no distant period, a great nation, to give to mankind the magnanimous and too novel example of a people always guided by an exalted justice and benevolence. Who can doubt that, in the course of time and things, the fruits of such a plan would richly repay any temporary advantages which might be lost by a steady adherence to it?"

Washington's foreign policy prescription set the precedent that other presidents would follow until the First World War. While isolationists and their inheritors strenuously argued that the first president was on their side, Washington's skepticism about foreign wars and permanent alliances was not intended to serve as a straitjacket for all his successors for all time. Washington and the other founding fathers were also far less enamored of the idea that their insights were the final word in human wisdom. As he told his nephew Bushrod—a future Supreme Court justice—during the debates to ratify the Constitution, "I do not conceive we are more in-spired, have more wisdom, or possess more virtue than those who will come after us."

While it seems safe to say that deploying American soldiers to far-flung battlefields in the Middle East or Asia would have been contrary to Wash-ington's instinctive wishes, he could not, of course, have anticipated the technological innovations that have made America far less isolated from the wider world. As the tyranny of distance has shrunk, new dangers have emerged while more enduring alliances based on cultural affinities and mu-tual interests between liberal democracies throughout the world have cre-ated national friendships, particularly with our original enemy, England.

Washington's vision of peace through strength has been vindicated over time. He believed that America should be a beacon of freedom—leading by the power of our example more than the example of our power—but we should resist the temptation to try to export democracy abroad by point of bayonet. The true message of the Farewell Address on foreign policy is not isolation but independence, striking a wise balance between realism and idealism, always remembering that the United States is a republic, not an empire.

SECTION III
THE AFTERLIFE OF THE IDEA

★

On Monday afternoon, September 19, 1796, the streets of Philadelphia were buzzing as crowds snatched up copies of the *American Daily Advertiser* and gathered to discuss the momentous news, then scattered by a sudden rainstorm that came out of the north to break the heat of late summer.

The great man was gone. Washington was rolling toward Mount Vernon with Martha by his side, but the suddenly receding figure loomed larger, the old attachments more vivid. By removing himself from power, their first founding father was leaving them a real republic. It was a final revolutionary act.

As newspaper reprints of the address cascaded up and down the colonies, the Farewell was lauded from editorial pages, state legislatures and preachers' pulpits as an almost biblical bit of wisdom, all the more dear because it was distinctly American. "The advice he gives the nation," wrote the celebrated Philadelphia diarist Jacob Hiltzheimer, "I hope will be remembered by all good citizens to the end of time."

Overseas, the Farewell was praised as well, with American diplomat William Vans Murray giving the address to colleagues at The Hague as a way of explaining the American character. "This advice is a text book in hundreds of families where the constitution of the country had never been very much studied," he explained; it is "a source of authority for great sublime and eternal political truths."

But Washington could not entirely escape the wingnuts of his time. In December, an extended letter allegedly written by a flinty Vermonter named Jasper Dwight appeared in the pages of the *Aurora,* slamming the Farewell Address as "the loathings of a sick mind," full of "evil effects."

It was a debunking of the Farewell Address from a Jeffersonian perspective, which made more sense when it became known, years later, that the author was not a rural citizen motivated by civic pride but the *Aurora*'s deputy editor, William Duane, a New York–born, Irish-raised newspaperman who'd been kicked out of the British colonial outpost of Calcutta for being a "dangerous incendiary" and remade himself into a pioneering populist pugilist in Philadelphia.

Duane took particular offense at Washington's warning to restrain partisanship, calling it "the aggravating recollections of wounded pride," arguing that "neither is it true that ill-founded jealousies and alarms are the invariable consequences of popular associations, although it is too frequently the effect of combinations among external enemies and a governmental party."

With the election of 1796 now only weeks away, Duane's screed captured the Democratic-Republicans' pushback to the broad popularity of the Farewell Address. In their eyes, Washington's claim to be above party was rank hypocrisy, expressing a frankly Federalist perspective while pretending to float above the partisan fray. Madison groused that the Farewell showed Washington was "completely in the snares of the British faction," while fellow partisans complained that its timing was designed to benefit the Federalists by giving Democratic-Republicans less than two months to organize a campaign, although it mirrored the timeline suggested by Madison four years earlier.

The publication of the Farewell kicked off the first real presidential contest in American history. As the eloquent Federalist Fisher Ames immediately saw, the address "will serve as a signal, like dropping a hat, for the party racers to start, and I expect a great deal of noise, whipping, and

1

President Washington in 1796, the year of his Farewell Address.

2

James Madison in 1792, the year he wrote the first draft of the Farewell, after Washington confided that he was frustrated with growing partisanship and felt "deficient in many of the essential qualifications" as president. Washington didn't yet know that Madison was secretly leading the opposition with Jefferson.

3

Alexander Hamilton was forty-one and already retired as Treasury secretary when he exchanged drafts of the Farewell Address with Washington between New York and Philadelphia in the summer of 1796. The prose of the Farewell Address is primarily Hamilton's; the ideas are all Washington's.

The Philadelphia executive mansion where Washington lived and worked during the last six years of his presidency. He wrote the final draft of the Farewell Address in a second floor private study overlooking Independence Hall, in a house primarily staffed by slaves.

Nelly Custis, Washington's beloved step-granddaughter, lived in the Philadelphia executive mansion as a teenager. Called a "wild little creature" by Martha, she left the only eyewitness account of Washington writing his Farewell Address by candlelight.

David Claypoole received the scoop of the century in September 1796, when Washington asked him to print the Farewell Address in the *American Daily Advertiser.* The president impulsively gave the final draft to the covetous publisher.

To the PEOPLE of the UNITED STATES:

FRIENDS and FELLOW-CITIZENS,

THE period for a new election of a Citizen, to administer the executive government of the United States, being not far distant, and the time actually arrived, when your thoughts must be employed in designating the person, who is to be cloathed with that important trust, it appears to me proper, especially as it may conduce to a more distinct expression of the public voice, that I should now apprize you of the resolution I have formed, to decline being considered among the number of those, out of whom a choice is to be made.

I beg you, at the same time, to do me the justice to be assured, that this resolution has not been taken, without a strict regard to all the considerations appertaining to the relation, which binds a dutiful citizen to his country; and that, in withdrawing the tender of service which silence in my situation might imply, I am influenced by no diminution of zeal for your future interest; no deficiency of grateful respect for your past kindness; but am supported by a full conviction that the step is compatible with both.

The acceptance of, and continuance hitherto in the office to which your suffrages have twice called me, have been a uniform sacrifice of inclination to the opinion of duty, and to a deference for what appeared to be your desire. I constantly hoped, that it would have been much earlier in my power, con-

humanly speaking, the command of its own fortunes.

Though in reviewing the incidents of my administration, I am unconscious of intentional error: I am nevertheless too sensible of my defects not to think it probable that I may have committed many errors. Whatever they may be I fervently beseech the Almighty to avert or mitigate the evils to which they may tend. I shall also carry with me the hope that my Country will never cease to view them with indulgence; and that after forty-five years of my life dedicated to its service, with an upright zeal, the faults of incompetent abilities will be consigned to oblivion, as myself must soon be to the mansions of rest.

Relying on its kindness in this as in other things, and actuated by that fervent love towards it, which is so natural to a man, who views in it the native soil of himself and his progenitors for several generations; I anticipate with pleasing expectation that retreat, in which I promise myself to realize, without alloy, the sweet enjoyment of partaking, in the midst of my fellow Citizens, the benign influence of good laws under a free government—the ever favourite object of my heart, and the happy reward, as I trust, of our mutual cares, labours and dangers.

G. WASHINGTON.

UNITED STATES, }
17th September, 1796. }

Addressed to his "friends and fellow citizens," Washington's Farewell appeared in the second and third pages of the *American Daily Advertiser* on Monday, September 19, 1796.

Washington holds the Farewell Address in this 1798 engraving, flanked by obelisks labeled "Liberty" and "Independence." The former president praised the image as "designed to perpetuate the idea of the American Revolution."

Washington's Farewell spurred memories of his resignation after winning the revolution. This 1799 engraving was modeled after a life-sized transparency exhibited at John Adams's inauguration. It shows the American Cincinnatus climbing the temple of fame as he points the way home to Mount Vernon.

The Farewell Address was celebrated as civic scripture, more widely republished than the Declaration of Independence for more than a century. This ornate print frames the text between pivotal scenes from Washington's life.

The power of Washington's example gave courage to his successors. In this cartoon by Thomas Nast in *Harper's*, the ghost of Washington comforts scandal-plagued Ulysses S. Grant with the memory of past partisan newspaper attacks, as Lincoln watches on.

This print imagines George Washington reading the Farewell Address to his family in their living room. Washington wrote his Farewell to be read in newspapers and never delivered it aloud.

CONTEST—"Washington's Farewell Address" Bridgewater, June 96

Teaching the Farewell Address was a standard part of school curriculums for decades after the Civil War, spurring public speaking and analysis contests, evidenced by this memento of the winners from an 1896 competition.

Washington's Farewell Address was so famous that its wisdom was printed on postcards through the early twentieth century.

This colorful card allowed senders to celebrate the shaded brass candlestick holder used by Washington while writing the Farewell Address. The original candlestick is now in the Smithsonian.

Emblazoned with cherries atop the Liberty Bell, Washington tells his fellow citizens to remember that "The name American, which belongs to you in our national capacity, must always exalt the just pride of patriotism, more than any appellation derived from local discriminations."

16

"Every portion of our country finds the most commanding motives for carefully guarding and preserving the Union of the Whole" — *From Washington's Farewell Address, Sept. 17, 1796.*

This souvenir from Mount Vernon quotes the Farewell to a country still healing from the Civil War: "Every portion of our country finds the most commanding motives for carefully guarding and preserving the Union of the whole."

17

1732–1799

'Tis our true policy to steer clear of permanent alliances with any portion of the foreign world. From his farewell address.

In the run up to the World War I, Washington's advice to avoid foreign wars seemed especially urgent. This postcard reminds recipients "'Tis our true policy to steer clear of permanent alliances with any portion of the foreign world."

Teddy Roosevelt's decision to run again for president in 1912 was derided as a violation of Washington's two-term precedent. This cartoon depicted T.R. decked out in Washington regalia, contemplating cutting down a cherry tree with Washington's original declaration cut in the bark: "the wise custom which limits the president to two terms regards the substance and not the form. And under no circumstances will I be a candidate for or accept another term." In 1940, T.R.'s cousin, Franklin Delano Roosevelt, broke with the tradition to win a third and a fourth term. After FDR's death, the Twenty-Second Amendment formalized the previously unwritten two-term limit.

In World War I, images of Washington were deployed by the Wilson administration to encourage a united sense of purpose, despite fierce debates about whether involvement in a foreign war violated his advice from the Farewell Address.

20

The message of the Farewell Address was twisted by members of the German American Bund at a 1939 mass rally in Madison Square Garden, which labeled Washington "the first Nazi" while urging nonintervention against Hitler. Banners hanging from the rafters read "Americans—Stop Jewish Domination of Christian America" and "Smash Jewish Communism."

The keynote speech at the Madison Square Garden Nazi rally promised to restore "America to the true Americans and to the ideals and principles given expression in the great Farewell Address of George Washington." By attempting to undermine American independence on behalf of a foreign power while pretending to be true patriots, they embodied one of Washington's core warnings in the Farewell Address.

The site of Washington's Philadelphia executive mansion in 1949, with a whisper of its outline evident on an adjoining building. The entire block was soon demolished to make way for the Liberty Mall.

The Farewell is still read in the Senate each year on Washington's Birthday. In 1949, Maine Republican Senator Margaret Chase Smith wondered whether Washington would have opposed NATO: "The objective is the same today—freedom. The only difference is the way to obtain that freedom."

4

Great Ideas of Western Man... one of a series

GEORGE WASHINGTON on knowledge in a free government

Virtue or morality is a necessary spring of popular government. The rule indeed extends with more or less force to every species of free government.... Promote, then, as an object of primary importance, institutions for the general diffusion of knowledge. In proportion as the structure of a government gives force to public opinion, it is essential that public opinion should be enlightened.

G. Washington

(FAREWELL ADDRESS, 1796)

CONTAINER CORPORATION OF AMERICA

In 1951, the Container Corporation of America published a series on The Great Ideas of Western Man in *Life* magazine. This selection excerpted Washington's Farewell on virtue, morality and education: "it is essential that public opinion should be enlightened."

Eisenhower's Farewell was the most famous presidential warning since Washington's. Addressing the nation from the Oval Office, Ike warned against the rise of the "military-industrial complex." He modeled his speech on Washington's Farewell.

Washington's Farewell Address

26

After two terms as the first President of the United States, George Washington was ready to retire from public life. In his Farewell Address, first published on September 19, 1796, Washington gave thoughtful and sound advice to the country he had served so faithfully. He emphasized the importance of an independent government dedicated to the highest ideals of morality and justice.

George Washington's final words were part of a legacy of monumental achievements. By playing a major role in centralizing the government, expanding the country to the West, and maintaining peace, Washington helped build a firm foundation for a strong and unified nation.

The historic U.S. mint stamp on this Panel features a quotation from Washington's Farewell Address. It was issued in 1960.

PHILADELPHIA, PA
SEP
19
1985
19104

On the anniversary of Washington's Farewell in 1985, the U.S. Post office reissued stamps with a quote from the Address—"Observe faith and justice toward all nations"—along with a rendering of Washington writing it with quill in hand.

27

GEORGE WASHINGTON'S
FAREWELL ADDRESS

9/19/1796
Philadelphia, PA
(first published)

Washington's Farewell achieved a kind of modern pop-culture immortality when Topps issued a baseball card commemorating the Address in 2009.

Washington's Farewell Address received the graphic novel treatment in 2014, making the Farewell come alive for a new generation of students a century after it was required reading in public schools.

The award-winning hip-hop musical *Hamilton* devoted a song to the Farewell, turning the text into lyrics. "I continue delivering it as prose, while Washington elevates it," explains playwright and lead actor Lin-Manuel Miranda, "and that's a metaphor for the relationship between Hamilton and Washington."

spurring; money, it is very probable, will be spent, some virtue and more tranquility lost; but I hope public order will be saved."

His crystal ball was better than most. The 1796 campaign birthed enduring partisan narratives. The liberal Jefferson was attacked as an effete intellectual with questionable morals and no religious faith—a revolutionary and an apostate. The more conservative Adams was called an elitist and a monarchist, "an advocate for hereditary power," hostile to the Rights of the People.

Despite Washington's warnings, the election was also divided along regional lines, with Adams representing the more urban, mercantile and abolitionist North, while Jefferson spoke for the South and its agricultural traditions, built on the backs of slaves.

The clearest difference was in the way campaigns were conducted by the candidates: Adams stayed home on his Massachusetts farm while Jefferson remained at Monticello. It was considered unseemly to campaign on your own behalf.

In the end, Adams won a narrow victory and, according to the rules of the day—which were intended to heal partisan wounds (while failing to fully anticipate partisan passions)—Jefferson served as vice president.

Washington had attempted to steer clear of electioneering. He and Adams were never close personal friends. Their temperaments were too different, with Washington favoring a soldier's personal reserve, while Adams's raging intellect was expressed through an attorney's biting asides and occasional bluster. But their shared experience in America's first administration had drawn the men of Mount Vernon and Braintree closer together. Targets of the same protests, they agreed on the dangerous excesses of the French Revolution and detested the attempts by Citizen Genêt and the Democratic-Republican Societies to undermine their government.

During his final days in office, Washington was buoyant. At a farewell dinner on March 3, 1797, Henrietta Liston, the charming wife of the British ambassador, was again selected to sit next to Washington. That night she confided to her diary her sense of the burdens about to be lifted from the president: "He has for eight years sacrificed his natural taste, first habits, and early propensities, I really believe we may truly say, solely to what he thought the good of his country. But he has become tired of his situation, fretted by the opposition often made to his measures; and his pride revolted against the ingratitude he experienced, and he was also disgusted by the scurrilous abuse lavished upon him by his political enemies. . . . He is in truth and reality, honest, prudent, and fortunate, and, wonderful to say, almost without ambition."

When the time came for Adams to take the oath of office and move into the modest executive mansion, he noted a bemused look on the face of the usually self-monitoring first founding father. To Adams, it seemed to say: "Methought I saw him think Ay! I am fairly out and you fairly in! See which of us will be happiest."

★

WASHINGTON SAVORED HIS RETURN TO Mount Vernon. He traveled without official guards and tried to keep the processional pomp and circumstance to a minimum. This effort was aided by a stubborn cold Martha was battling, providing a convenient excuse for curtailing formalities. But when Washington passed through the capital named for him, which he still called "the Federal City," the under-construction maze of muddy streets summoned up a seventeen-gun salute to its namesake.

His dream had always been a return to the "shade of my own vine and fig tree" at Mount Vernon, and Washington threw himself into the happy task of "[a]gricultural pursuits and rural amusements, which at all times have been the most pleasing occupation of my life, and most congenial with my temper, notwithstanding a small proportion of it has been spent in this way." The farms of Mount Vernon had fallen into disrepair over the eight years of his presidency and he found the attending work and want of cash a challenge "as if I had commenced an entire new establishment."

But he always found challenges invigorating and took pleasure in the development of his hometown of Alexandria, Virginia, where he had surveyed the street plan as a young man and now found new buildings and shops dotting the old untamed space. He tapped back into his old entrepreneurial instincts, expanding his whiskey distillery into one of the largest in the United States, producing some 11,000 gallons at a tidy profit of what would be nearly $142,000 today.

He wanted to put politics behind him, telling his longtime aide David Humphreys, "I shall view things in the 'calm lights of mild philosophy' and endeavor to finish my course in retirement and ease."

But old rivalries came bubbling to the surface to disturb his peace. When a letter written by Jefferson to an Italian friend, Philip Mazzei, was leaked to the press in 1797, it exposed Jefferson's contempt for the Federalists as "apostates," "men who were Samsons in the field and Solomons in the council, but who have had their heads shorn by the harlot England." Washington saw himself as one of the targets of this attack and never forgave Jefferson. Loyal Martha loathed Jefferson on her husband's behalf, calling him "one of the most detestable of mankind."

Likewise, when future president James Monroe published a book defending his aborted tenure as ambassador to France—with the assistance and encouragement of Jefferson—Washington unloaded with a barrage of uncharacteristically sarcastic notes in the book's margins, declaring Monroe's arguments "insanity in the extreme!" "an insinuation as impudent as it is unfounded" and that "none but a party man, lost of all sense of propriety, would have asked such a thing," while assuring himself, "Posterity will judge of this. Mr. Monroe's opinion is not the standard by which it will judge."

These outbursts were exceptions to the orderly rule of life at Mount Vernon. The sunset and shadow competed for his attention. He was now sixty-seven years old and feeling the physical pinch of age despite the Indian summer of excitement that came with his long-desired retirement.

Unshackled at the End

On December 14, 1799, George Washington lay dying. He asked that Martha retrieve two wills from a desk drawer. Inspecting them both closely, despite his labored breathing, Washington instructed one to be thrown into the fire, its contents lost forever in the flames. The remaining document, Washington's last will and testament, would finally release his slaves and nudge American history forward through the power of his example.

Five months before, Washington had awakened from a nightmare that seemed to foretell his death. He set to work finalizing his last will and testament. It served as a radical addendum to the Farewell Address, addressing unfinished business and completing its sweep.

The twenty-nine-page document Washington signed on July 9 was written in his rolling script, modestly identifying the author as "a citizen of the United States, and lately President of the same." He took care to emphasize with some pride that it was written without legal assistance. For such an inherently formal document, Washington chose a common imported stationery, without his personal watermark.

The document detailed his property and instructions for paying off debts. He was primarily concerned with providing for Martha, stating that her descendants should be considered as his own: "It has always been my intention, since my expectation of having issue has ceased, to consider the grandchildren of my wife in the same light as I do my own relations."

He spent paragraphs detailing his commitment to expanding education, dedicating $4,000 (the equivalent of about $75,000 today) toward the support of a free school for poor and orphan children. A more ambitious gift was the donation of his remaining stock in the Potomac Company, in a last-ditch attempt to jump-start the creation of his dream of a national university "in a central part of the United States to which the youth of fortune and talents from all parts thereof might be sent for the completion of their education in all the branches of polite literature, in arts and sciences, in acquiring knowledge in the principles of politics and good government; and (as a matter of infinite importance, in my judgment) by associating with each other, and forming friendships in juvenile years, be enabled to free themselves in a proper degree from . . . local prejudices and habitual jealousies."

This emphasis on personal relations transcending political divisions said much about the man and his understanding of civic psychology. The ultimate aim was an ambitious attempt at social engineering, though more organic than most ventures: "a plan devised on a liberal scale, which would have a tendency to spread systemic ideas through all parts of this rising empire."

The personal trumped the political as he made small specific gifts to friends and family members: to his brother Charles he gave a cherished gold-headed cane given to him by Benjamin Franklin; to Lafayette he gave a pair of steel pistols "taken from the enemy in the Revolutionary War"; to the loyal Tobias Lear he gave rent-free use of a farm; to his five nephews he gave swords, accompanied by the touching injunction "not to unsheathe them for the purpose of shedding blood, except it be for self-defense, or in the defense of their country and its rights." And to his constant companion during the Revolutionary War, his manservant William Lee, he gave immediate freedom.

The revelation in Washington's will was his final confrontation with slavery. It was a topic he had been awkwardly avoiding most of his public life. As president, he admitted to a friend that he did not "like even to think, much less talk" about slavery. He failed to mention it in his Farewell Address, choosing instead to focus on elevating national unity rather than embracing a politically and regionally divisive policy of abolition.

But a shift had taken place within Washington that led to this final declaration: "Upon the decease of my wife, it is my will and desire that all the slaves which I hold in my *own right*, shall receive their freedom."

The idealist and the realist within Washington had wrestled with the moral and practical implications of slavery since the country's birth. As he presided over the Constitutional Convention, Washington's emotions might have been more aligned with northerners Hamilton, Franklin, Jay and Adams in their desire to see slavery abolished. But his primary concern was ratification and the preservation of the fragile Union. The moral imperative of slavery was subservient to the practical imperative of preserving the Union at that time.

As president, Washington's private opinions evolved while his practical responsibilities constrained public comment and invited accusations of hypocrisy.

When Washington's slaves escaped to freedom from the Quaker-influenced capital of Philadelphia, he posted notices for their capture. But in discussions about the possibility of the future splintering of the nation along the North-South lines of slavery, the president told his fellow Virginian Attorney General Edmund Randolph that "he had made up his mind to remove and be of the Northern."

In 1796, he reportedly told a visiting British guest, "I can clearly foresee that nothing but the rooting out of slavery can perpetuate the existence of our union." It was a sentiment that gained urgency as he anticipated the end of his life, telling David Humphreys that "the unfortunate condition of the persons, whose labor in part I employed, has been the only unavoidable subject of regret. To make the Adults among them as easy and as comfortable in their circumstances as their actual state of ignorance and improvidence would admit, and to lay a foundation to prepare the rising generation for a destiny different from that in which they were born, afforded some satisfaction to my mind, and could not, I hoped, be displeasing to the justice of the Creator."

Nonetheless, by 1799, Washington's slave labor force totaled 317 people, including more than 140 children. This amounted to roughly 1 percent of all the slaves in the state of Virginia.

But unlike the apostle of international liberty, Thomas Jefferson, Washington did not purchase slaves as president and he refused to break up families. And unlike all of the nine subsequent presidents who owned slaves, he set the example of freeing his slaves, albeit after his death.

It is an understandable temptation to dismiss Washington's actions as too little, too late. He found the courage to do what he thought was right on his deathbed, when the judgment of the Lord loomed larger than the judgment of his fellow citizens or his own economic needs. But however relatively consequence-free, this action was aimed at posterity and sent a clear signal of his sentiments to his friends and fellow citizens.

Washington understood that his order might be evaded, so he spent paragraphs detailing the conditions of freedom and blocking any attempts by unscrupulous heirs to weasel out of his wishes. He "expressly forbid the sale or transportation out of the said Commonwealth of any slave I may die possessed of, under any pretense whatsoever. And I do moreover most pointedly, and most solemnly enjoin it upon my executors hereafter named, or the survivors of them, to see that *this* clause respecting slaves, and every part thereof, be religiously fulfilled at the epoch at which it is directed to take place, without evasion, neglect or delay."

Washington did not simply cut his slaves loose. The paternalist planter sought to support aged and infirm slaves through a permanent fund. He also provided for the education of the children of newly freed slaves, though this was illegal under Virginia law.

There were two crucial caveats to his newfound enthusiasm for manumission. First, Washington was not legally able to free his wife's slaves, which constituted the majority of the human property at Mount Vernon. Second, influenced by this loophole and his ever-present desire to see the farm turn a profit, he instructed that the slaves of Mount Vernon would be freed only after his wife's death. This created the apparently unintended consequence of Martha Washington living at home alongside hundreds of slaves who had an active interest in seeing her dead.

The one slave who did not seem to eager to flee the confines of Mount Vernon was the only slave to whom Washington immediately gave his freedom. Billy Lee was perhaps the most nationally prominent slave of the time, a biracial man who rode at Washington's side throughout the revolution. A house servant locally famous for being a fearless huntsman, Lee was trusted with Washington's personal effects and private papers during the war. Because of Lee's proximity to power, officers and soldiers treated him with a collegial affection not extended to other slaves. He was an eyewitness and partner in the revolution, represented in portraits as a member of the extended Washington family. He was for decades denied the freedom for which the other veterans fought.* Washington sought to rectify that with his last act on earth. But the other Mount Vernon slaves and their families would have to wait.

Six months after finishing his new will, Washington fell ill after a December day while riding in a frigid mixture of snow, hail and driving rain. Jokes with Martha and Tobias Lear about his hoarse voice turned serious when Washington's throat started to close up in the early morning of December 14.

According to a modern analysis of Washington's symptoms by Dr. White McKenzie Wallenborn, Washington died from "a classic 'textbook'

---

* After the war, repeated injuries to his knees overcame Billy Lee, and he was unable to accompany Washington as he took up the presidency. Married to a free black woman named Margaret who worked for the Washington family (but was apparently no favorite of the president), Lee was fitted for knee braces at Washington's expense but developed a dependence on alcohol, a habit he slid into to dull the pain from his damaged patellas. Despite being granted freedom and thirty dollars a month in living expenses in Washington's will, Lee chose to live at Mount Vernon's slave quarters until his death in 1828, having outlived most of the Revolutionary War veterans who would frequently visit him to trade war stories.

case of acute epiglottitis," which is characterized by "sore throat, hoarseness, dysphagia (difficulty swallowing), and respiratory distress accompanied by drooling, shortness of breath, [and] rapid pulse.... Death from this disorder is caused by obstruction of the patient's airway and is very painful and frightening."

This rare condition can still be fatal today without antibiotics. So the tincture of molasses, vinegar and butter Washington was given to open his throat was not much help, nor was a series of incisions to facilitate the supposedly beneficial effects of bleeding, which only Martha seems to have had the common sense to question. An incredible five pints of blood were drained from Washington over the course of his final day.

Ever the stoic, Washington knew he was dying and told his longtime friend and attending physician Dr. James Craik, "Doctor, I die hard; but I am not afraid to go." Around 4 p.m., he sent Martha to his room to fetch the two wills from his desk. According to Lear, "Upon looking at them he gave her one which he observed was useless, as being suppressed by the other, and desired her to burn it, which she did."

This eyewitness account suggests that the second, burned will was an older version than the one Washington had handwritten and dated in July. And while it is impossible to know exactly what the earlier will contained, it might not have included such specific instructions regarding the freeing of his slaves, as this dramatic action seems not to have been anticipated by his inner circle.

As night fell, Washington told Lear, "do not let my body to be put into the vault less than three days after I am dead," reflecting a fear of being buried alive, a horrific but not uncommon occurrence at the time.

Between ten and eleven that night at his beloved Mount Vernon, surrounded by family, old friends, doctors and slaves, George Washington died.

His last words were, "'Tis Well."

★

NEWS OF THE FIRST PRESIDENT'S death rocketed through the republic.

Americans found themselves suddenly orphaned. Amid the unprecedented outpouring of civic grief—church bells rang and shops closed; sermons, memorials and marches followed—came a renewed appreciation for the advice and example he left behind, as often occurs after the loss of any departed father figure.

"His example," wrote President Adams, "will teach wisdom and virtue to magistrates, citizens, and men, not only in the present age, but in future generations, as long as our history shall be read."

Readings of the Farewell Address were incorporated into memorial services, and reprints soared in the year after Washington's death. Historian François Furstenberg found that "of approximately 2,200 books and pamphlets to emerge from the presses in 1800, more than 400 dealt with Washington in some way." Along with the published tributes came commemorative plates, pitchers, and engravings.

Washington's last will and testament became a popular document itself, published in thirteen separate editions. It was always intended to be a public document, a final statement of principle. And it succeeded in inspiring not just abolitionists throughout the Northeast, but members of the free black community. Perhaps no tribute carries more moral weight to modern ears than that of Reverend Richard Allen, the founder of Philadelphia's African Methodist Episcopal Church, who thundered:

> Our father and friend is taken from us. . . . If he who broke the yoke of British burdens "from off the neck of the people" of this land, and was hailed his country's deliverer, by what name shall we call him who secretly and almost unknown emancipated his "bondwoman and bondmen"—became to them a father, and gave them an inheritance! Deeds like these are not common. . . . The name of Washington will live when the sculptured marble and statue of bronze shall be crumbled into dust—for it is the decree of the eternal God that "the righteous shall be had in

everlasting remembrance, but the memorial of the wicked shall rot." . . . And here let me entreat you always to bear in mind the affectionate farewell advice of the great Washington—"to love your country—to obey its laws—to seek its peace—and to keep yourselves from attachment to any foreign nation." Your observance of these short and comprehensive expressions will make you good citizens—and greatly promote the cause of the oppressed and show to the world that you hold dear the name of George Washington.

Grief nourishes myth and Washington's warnings in the Farewell were quickly elevated to the level of national scripture. Boston's Timothy Bigelow proclaimed it "an oracle of political truth . . . a palladium, which, while carefully preserved, will perpetuate our Union and independence; an amulet, which, if constantly improved, will render our body politic invulnerable, we might almost say immortal."

Other eulogists viewed the Farewell as a founding text of a civic religion: "Let it be engraven upon the tables of brass and marble, and, like the sacred Law of Moses, be placed in every church, and hall, and senate chamber, of this spacious continent, for the instruction not only of the present but of all future generations of Americans."

"Let the infant cherub suck its honey with its earliest sustenance," another declared. Awkward imagery aside, the Farewell Address was meant to be internalized. Through recitation and memorization it could not just commemorate the past but guide future decisions. Alone among the founding documents, Washington's Farewell could connect the past with the present and the future. Its talismanic power could be made real.

In the civic wilderness of life in the United States without Washington, the Farewell Address endured. It was invoked as a caution from beyond the grave, a warning with incomparable moral authority against the fractious voices calling for secession and civil war.

The 1800 presidential campaign rematch between Adams and Jefferson was even uglier than their first showdown. Opposition papers called President Adams a "hermaphrodite" and worse. Adams overreacted with the Alien and Sedition Acts, which sought to criminalize criticism of the government, taking legal action against newspaper editors like the *Aurora*'s new editor, William Duane.

In politics, every action creates an equal and opposite reaction, and the backlash against the Alien and Sedition Acts created an overreach of its own. Virginia and Kentucky passed resolutions intended to register those state legislatures' displeasure, but their language—of "interposition" and "nullification"—seeded the ground for future states' rights arguments about the constitutionality of secession, by armed rebellion if necessary. The measures were written in large part by Jefferson and Madison. In the case of Vice President Jefferson, this active encouragement could have been credibly construed as treason.

But in the aftermath of the bitter partisan presidential battle of 1800, something remarkable happened: many of the deep ideological divides that inspired attacks on President Washington suddenly evaporated. Thomas Jefferson's Democratic-Republicans were all Washingtonians now.

Washington Wins the War of Ideas

★

O n Inauguration Day, 1801, a new precedent was set—the peaceful transfer of power between two rival factions. In his inaugural address, President Jefferson took pains to change the partisan tone that had dominated his political actions in opposition, proclaiming, "Every difference of opinion is not a difference of principle. . . . We are all Republicans, we are all Federalists."

Jefferson also spoke of the danger of civil war: "If there be any among us who would wish to dissolve this Union or to change its republican form, let them stand undisturbed as monuments of the safety with which error of opinion may be tolerated where reason is left free to combat it." This warning had the added benefit of absolving Jefferson for his own partisan excesses.

It was stunning to see how quickly the man from Monticello changed once he achieved the presidency. The governing principle of foreign affairs Jefferson presented in his inaugural address might have been taken directly from the Farewell. He began with an ode to the unique benefits that come to our country from geographic distance—"kindly separated by nature and a wide ocean from the exterminating havoc of one quarter of the globe"—and then hopscotched to so concise an articulation of Washington's principle of nonintervention that he coined the phrase that would forever be associated with Washington's Farewell: "peace, commerce, and honest friendship with all nations, entangling alliances with none."

But the partisan divide persisted. Federalist reaction to Jefferson's victory was almost as panicked and petulant as Democrats' reaction to Lincoln's election sixty years later. They began talking up the possibility of secession, this time from a New England perspective. In 1807, when Jefferson imposed an embargo on exports as a means of avoiding attacks on American shipping and seizure of American sailors in the ongoing war between France and England, the northeastern coastal economy went into a tailspin, exacerbating regional resentments.

One year later, Jefferson solidified Washington's two-term precedent, explaining, "Genl. Washington set the example of voluntary retirement after 8. years. I shall follow it," while warning against the combination of comforts and vanity that makes men believe they must stay in power long after their executive expiration date: "indulgence and attachments will keep a man in the chair after he becomes a dotard."

Antipathies toward France and England reached boiling point in the War of 1812, when Jefferson's successor, President James Madison, narrowly convinced Congress to declare war on Britain. In his second inaugural address, Madison invoked some of the same arguments advanced in Washington's Farewell against France, calling out the subterranean efforts by the British to influence American policy with "attempts to disorganize our political society, to dismember our confederated Republic."

Some northeastern states and banks refused to enlist men or finance the war. One of the most popular books of the era was *The Olive Branch*, written by a Pennsylvania publisher named Mathew Carey, concerning "a conspiracy in New England, among a few of the most wealthy and influential citizens, to effect a dissolution of the union at every hazard, and to form a separate confederacy." Carey's object was "the restoration of harmony, or at least the allaying of party rage and rancor"—and to that end, the book repeatedly cited the Farewell Address as "one of the noblest efforts of human wisdom, [which] impressively urged his countrymen to frown indignantly upon any attempt to impair or dissolve the union."

The War of 1812 resulted in a stalemate, despite the United States suffer-ing the ultimate indignity of the White House consumed in flames, destroy-ing the portrait of King Louis XVI that Washington had kept as a reminder of our revolution's first allies. The national unity that emerged in the wake of the repelled invasion propelled the United States to a brief so-called Era of Good Feeling of one-party rule. The Federalists were in retreat, cut down from a national party to a regional one, while a Democratic-Republican Virginia dynasty dominated the federal government.

The ironies continued. In his second term, Madison supported the re-imposition of the hated Whiskey Tax and reestablished the National Bank, whose creation by Hamilton had so offended then-congressman Madison that it spurred the first pivotal partisan attacks on Washington's administration.

When Madison passed the presidency to James Monroe in 1816, the last president of the revolutionary generation also became a born-again Wash-ingtonian. His administration is best known for the Monroe Doctrine, which codified a policy of nonintervention in Europe in exchange for the war-weary Europeans' commitment to curtail their military adventures in the Western Hemisphere. Monroe had previously served as secretary of state but still he consulted his political patrons, Jefferson and Madison, on such a sweeping statement of national policy. They approved.

Drafted in large part by Secretary of State John Quincy Adams, who had been a supporter of American independence in foreign affairs since his passionate defense of the Jay Treaty, the Monroe Doctrine was welcomed by Simón Bolívar and other South American revolutionaries then fighting for independence from colonial powers.

Hanging a "closed for colonization" sign across the Americas also served as a deterrent to Pacific powers like Russia, which could have expanded south from its Alaskan perch. Washington's first principle of self-determination was protected and extended.

In an Independence Day address in 1821, President John Quincy Adams offered the era's most resonant defense of Washington's foreign policy vision. More than a century and a half later, his words on America's mission would still be quoted in debates over wars ranging from Vietnam to Iraq:

> She has, in the lapse of nearly half a century, without a single exception, respected the independence of other nations while asserting and maintaining her own. . . .
>
> Wherever the standard of freedom and Independence has been or shall be unfurled, there will her heart, her benedictions and her prayers be.
>
> But she goes not abroad, in search of monsters to destroy.
>
> She is the well-wisher to the freedom and independence of all.
>
> She is the champion and vindicator only of her own. . . .
>
> She well knows that by once enlisting under other banners than her own, were they even the banners of foreign independence, she would involve herself beyond the power of extrication, in all the wars of interest and intrigue, of individual avarice, envy, and ambition, which assume the colors and usurp the standard of freedom.
>
> The fundamental maxims of her policy would insensibly change from liberty to force. . . .
>
> She might become the dictatress of the world. She would be no longer the ruler of her own spirit.

A generation later Washington's Farewell Address had become national consensus, implemented by former critics and acolytes alike. Even Jefferson had relented—not only adopting its policies as president but writing to the Board of Visitors at his University of Virginia to insist that the Farewell Address be assigned in the law school as one of the "best guides" to "the distinctive principles of government of the United States."

Adams and Jefferson died on the same day—the fiftieth anniversary of the Declaration of Independence. It was a coincidence that seemed to have cosmic meaning. The old friends turned bitter rivals had reconciled in their old age. But the inheritors of their arguments did not feel pacified by their perspective.

The giants of the antebellum era—Andrew Jackson, Daniel Webster, Henry Clay and John C. Calhoun—were all students of American democracy and they honored Washington's example, even as they projected their own values onto his visage.

The Farewell Address was generally free from such subjective sentiment. Webster declared that "Washington's Farewell is full of truths, important at all times, and particularly deserving consideration at the present. With a sagacity which brought the future before him, and made it like the present, he saw and pointed out the dangers that even at this moment most imminently threaten us." The dominant debate was union versus secession and on that question the address was clear.

Andrew Jackson was a Jeffersonian in populist politics, but a boyhood admirer of Washington as a self-made soldier who fought on the frontier. He came to Congress as a Democratic-Republican from the midlands of Tennessee in December 1796.

With Washington's Farewell still fresh in the minds of his countrymen, Representative Jackson refused to be swayed by such sentiment. He was a party man and hotly opposed Washington's policy of neutrality between England and France.

"From the president's speech it would seem that the British were doing us no injury, committing no depredations, that all the depredations on our commerce was done by the French nation," he wrote his brother-in-law. And so when a House committee was tasked with writing an official congressional response to the Farewell Address, Jackson voted to refuse a formal declaration of thanks for President Washington's public service.

Jackson bitterly resented the northeastern elites, and he relished defeating John Quincy Adams for the presidency in 1828 after losing to him four years before. He threw open the doors of the White House to the public, pursuing an unapologetic policy of partisan patronage punctuated by Indian killing, famously declaring, "to the victor goes the spoils."

But once again, the office changed the man more than the man changed the office. In 1832, Jackson's vice president, South Carolina senator John C. Calhoun, engineered his home state's efforts to declare a federal tariff null and void without bothering to consult Congress or the Supreme Court. This was a direct challenge to the constitutional supremacy of the federal government over the individual states and seemed to set the stage for secession.

President Jackson's response was definitive: "Our Federal Union—It Must Be Preserved!" The president slammed states' rights extremists in a presidential proclamation, warning that nullification set the stage for secession, and secession meant civil war: "Be not deceived by names; disunion, by armed force, is TREASON. Are you really ready to incur its guilt?"

By the end of Jackson's two terms, the slave-owning, onetime states' rights supporter was committed to a strong federal union led by a powerful executive. And as he contemplated retirement, Jackson resolved to issue his own Farewell Address, formally reviving the precedent set by Washington.

Jackson sketched out his ideas and had them fleshed out in concert with a ghostwriter—in this case, Supreme Court chief justice Roger Taney. The sad-eyed, sallow-faced Marylander remains a notorious figure in American history for issuing the *Dred Scott* decision, which expanded the scope of slavery and declared that African-Americans, free or slave, could never be citizens. But Taney was a mess of contradictions—a defender of slavery who freed his own slaves and refused to defect to the Confederacy once civil war came. For the Supreme Court's chief justice, defending the Constitution meant defending the Union.

At the heart of Jackson's Farewell Address, issued on March 4, 1837, was an extended tribute to Washington's Farewell, with its prophetic warnings and enduring wisdom:

The necessity of watching with jealous anxiety for the preservation of the Union was earnestly pressed upon his fellow-citizens by the Father of his Country in his farewell address.

He has there told us that "while experience shall not have demonstrated its impracticability, there will always be reason to distrust the patriotism of those who in any quarter may endeavor to weaken its bands;" and he has cautioned us in the strongest terms against the formation of parties on geographical discriminations, as one of the means which might disturb our Union and to which designing men would be likely to resort.

The lessons contained in this invaluable legacy of Washington to his countrymen should be cherished in the heart of every citizen to the latest generation; and perhaps at no period of time could they be more usefully remembered than at the present moment. For when we look upon the scenes that are passing around us and dwell upon the pages of his parting address, his paternal counsels would seem to be not merely the offspring of wisdom and foresight, but the voice of prophecy, foretelling events and warning us of the evil to come.

Forty years have passed since that imperishable document was given to his countrymen. The federal Constitution was then regarded by him as an experiment—and he so speaks of it in his address— but an experiment upon the success of which the best hopes of his country depended, and we all know that he was prepared to lay down his life, if necessary, to secure to it a full and fair trial.

The trial has been made. It has succeeded beyond the proudest hopes of those who framed it. Every quarter of this widely extended nation has felt its blessings and shared in the general prosperity produced by its adoption.

But amid this general prosperity and splendid success the dangers of which he warned us are becoming every day more evident, and the signs of evil are sufficiently apparent to awaken the deepest anxiety in the bosom of the patriot. We behold systematic efforts publicly made to sow the seeds of discord between different parts of the United States and to place party divisions directly upon geographical distinctions; to excite the *South* against the *North* and the *North* against the *South* . . .

Has the warning voice of Washington been forgotten? Or have designs already been formed to sever the Union? Let it not be supposed that I impute to all of those who have taken an active part in these unwise and unprofitable discussions a want of patriotism or of public virtue. The honorable feeling of State pride and local attachments find a place in the bosoms of the most enlightened and pure. But while such men are conscious of their own integrity and honesty of purpose they ought never to forget that the citizens of other States are their political brethren; and that, however mistaken they may be in their views, the great body of them are equally honest and upright with themselves.

Mutual suspicions and reproaches may in time create mutual hostility, and artful and designing men will always be found who are ready to foment these fatal divisions and to inflame the natural jealousies of different sections of the country. The history of the world is full of such examples, and especially the history of republics.

What have you to gain by division and dissension? Delude not yourselves with the belief that a breach once made may be afterward repaired. If the Union is once severed, the line of separation will grow wider and wider, and the controversies which are now debated and settled in the halls of legislation will then be tried in fields of battle and determined by the sword.

Jackson argued that Washington's warnings had come to pass. The American experiment, rooted in the Constitution, had proven its worth and durability. The nation was more prosperous at home and respected abroad than anyone other than Washington would have dared hope at the end of the previous century.

But the demagogues and regional divisions that troubled Washington still afflicted the nation with "ill-founded jealousies and false alarms," spreading the flames of faction under the cover of pretend patriotism, fueled by a fundamental misreading of the Constitution.

Jackson moved Washington's Farewell forward. He took separatists' arguments and played them out, describing how a disintegration of union would not lead to peaceful competing confederations of states but to violence and foreign intrigue—even if civil war did not result. As Washington, Hamilton and Madison had taken pains to demonstrate, ancient history offered plenty of examples of this dissolution of democratic republics. It was only the broad and durable framework of national union, developed and tested over time, that made the American experiment the honorable exception.

Jackson's southern bona fides gave his admonition against secession credibility. Washington was a southerner, but he had succeeded too well in casting himself as the father of the nation. Jackson did not come with any Federalist baggage: he hailed from the southern frontier and wore his backwoods origins proudly. The old accusations that advocates of Union were proto-monarchist British apologists who did not understand the southern way of life could not stick to Andy Jackson. Their wisdom was now intertwined.

But Jackson was only able to buy more time for the Union. Civil war had been feared since the nation's founding, and now war was coming, a conflict along lines that Washington had anticipated: the struggle over slavery, deferred again and again, could not be deferred indefinitely. By not heeding Washington's warning to reason together, the bitter regional rivalry would ultimately be resolved through bloodshed.

A Farewell Fraud?

★

In the weeks after Alexander Hamilton's death in an early-morning duel with Aaron Burr, the executor of his estate found drafts of the Farewell Address in Hamilton's handwriting among his papers along with unbalanced checkbooks.

The discovery seemed a smoking gun, evidence that Washington wasn't the author of his own Farewell Address. The year was 1804 and Washington had been dead only five years. Judge Nathan Pendleton absconded with the incriminating documents and handed them over to Rufus King, a signer of the Constitution and the recent Federalist candidate for vice president, a rival to Aaron Burr and friend of the Hamilton family. King agreed to keep the papers safe at his estate in Jamaica, Queens, in the shared hope that the myth of sole authorship would be maintained.

But rumors were already working their way through New York City. An aging journalist named William Coleman maintained that Hamilton had confessed to writing it. Another old-timer, William Lewis, was accused of "constantly blabbing" about the "great secret" at coffee houses and taverns.

Hamilton's devoted widow, Elizabeth, was committed to restoring her husband's reputation, core to which was the authorship of the famous document. She often recounted the story of the day when she and Alexander were strolling down Broadway and encountered an aged Revolutionary War veteran selling reprints of the Farewell Address. "That man does not know he has asked me to purchase my own work," Hamilton told his wife with a smile.

"The unnecessary *buzz*" that Hamilton was the author of the address compelled a Washington-appointed judge Richard Peters to write John Jay on Valentine's Day, 1811. "The cat," he said, was "out of the bag."

Jay remained a Washington loyalist, always protective of his great friend's reputation. "The history (if it may be so called,) of the address is not unknown to me; but as I came to the knowledge of it under implied confidence, I doubted when I first received your letter whether I ought to disclose it," he wrote Judge Peters. "On more mature reflection, I became convinced that, if President Washington were now alive and informed of the facts in question, he would not only authorize, but also desire me to reduce it to writing; that when necessary it might be used to invalidate the imputations to which those facts give color."

Jay explained that he knew of the various drafts of the address and that some were in Hamilton's hand. He had been part of the final editing session at the New York governor's mansion before Hamilton sent the draft to Philadelphia for Washington's approval and subsequent rewriting in his own hand. But while Jay wanted to set the historical record straight, he was concerned that his testimony might be used to justify partisan whispers that Washington was ill-suited to his high station.

"Many, with affected regret and hesitation, will infer and hint that Washington had less greatness of talent, and less greatness of mind, than his friends and admirers ascribed to him," Jay wrote. "Nor will the number of those be few, who, from personal or party inducements, will artfully encourage and diligently endeavor to give currency to such imputations."

Yes, Washington had requested that close friends review the work. But the idea that the Farewell Address had sprung wholesale from Alexander Hamilton's head offended Jay's sense of not only history and accuracy, but also decency and decorum.

Of course, Washington would have consulted his close allies on the Farewell Address, precisely because of its importance. "That Address was to be presented to the whole nation, and on no common occasion; it was intended for the present and future generations; it was to be read in this country and in foreign countries; and to be criticized not only by affectionate friends and impartial judges, but also by envious and malignant enemies," Jay explained. "Who, therefore, can wonder that he should bestow more thought, and time, and pains, on that Address than on a letter? . . . He knew that authors, like parents, are not among the first to discover imperfections in their offspring, and that consideration would naturally induce him to imitate the example of those ancient and modern writers . . . who submitted their compositions to the judgment of their friends, before they put the last hand to them."

A speechwriter was no scandal. But Elizabeth Hamilton and her children were on a crusade to elevate Alexander's reputation. Her affection could overtake accuracy. In a statement about the authorship of the Farewell Address, she attested that "General Hamilton suggested to [Washington] the idea of delivering a farewell address to the people on his withdrawal from public life, with which idea General Washington was well pleased, and in his answer to General Hamilton's suggestion, gave him the heads of the subjects on which he would wish to remark."

Correspondence makes it clear that Washington raised the subject of the Farewell Address to Alexander Hamilton and used the first draft written in consultation with James Madison in 1792 as the basis for what would become the final draft. Elizabeth's loving remembrance fundamentally mischaracterizes the root of the idea and the sequence of its composition. This is no small detail.

But the widow was relentless. At first, there was the soft sell—Elizabeth requesting meetings with Jay to discuss the authorship of the Farewell Address, probing for validation, but meeting the cold caution that edits and assistance did not amount to composition. Then came a meeting with Washington's heirs at Mount Vernon, requesting old papers and correspondence for their records and an authorized biography of Hamilton. Frustrated by their failure to get back the documents that had been removed from their possession, the Hamilton family resorted to a public lawsuit against the aging Rufus King and his kin.

This result ruined the friendship between the Hamilton and King families but secured the return of the documents. It also succeeded in spilling the long-rumored controversy into the public arena.

In 1823, an enterprising correspondent wrote to ask Jefferson for his take on the debate. "With respect to his Farewell Address, to the authorship of which, it seems, there are conflicting claims; I can state to you some facts," Jefferson replied. "When, at the end of this second term, his Valedictory came out, Mr. Madison recognized in it several passages from his draft, several others we were both satisfied were from the pen of Hamilton, and others, from that of the President himself. These he probably put into the hands of Hamilton to form a whole, and hence it may all appear in Hamilton's handwriting, as if it were all of his composition."

Familiar with President Washington's manner of writing major addresses, and drawing on the experience of serving as president himself, Jefferson guessed correctly at the process of writing the Farewell Address.

Madison also weighed in from retirement at Montpelier, arguing that Washington's friends and allies "ought to claim for him the merit only of cherishing the principles and views addressed to his Country, and for the address itself the weight given to it by his sanction; leaving the literary merit, whatever it be, to the friendly pen employed on the occasion; the rather as it was never understood that Washington valued himself on his writing talent, and no secret to some that he occasionally availed himself of the friendship of others whom he supposed more practiced than himself in studied composition."

Of course, Madison had authored the first draft. He had close knowledge of its composition, but he also understood the speechwriter's code of contemporary silence: "There certainly was a species of confidence at the time in what passed, forbidding publicity, at least 'til the lapse of time should wear out the seal on it, and the truth of history should be put in a fair claim to such disclosures."

The controversy did not die. The suggestion, let alone confirmation, that Washington was not the sole author of the Farewell Address took some shine off the document even if it did not diminish its wisdom. The knowledge of the practical process of speechwriting, so unremarkable today, began to demythologize Washington just a bit, spurring the first scholarly study of its composition by Horace Binney. The Farewell Address had taken its first hit.

The Farewell for Sale

★

In 1849, Senator Henry Clay spied a small notice in a Philadelphia newspaper that the original manuscript of the Farewell Address was for sale. This was the final draft, hand-edited by Washington and impulsively given to publisher David C. Claypoole, who had jealously guarded his gift, declining to donate it to historical societies despite numerous requests. Claypoole clung to the manuscript until his death in March 1849.

Now his executors put the item up for auction, advertising the sale in a widely circulated two-paragraph notice. It appeared, for example, in the *Sunbury American* newspaper of Northumberland County, Pennsylvania, on Saturday, November 24, in the lower right corner of the front page, beneath a dispatch about "A Dog That Chews Tobacco" and beside news of a "Divorce in Connecticut." The notice read as follows:

ORIGINAL OF WASHINGTON'S FAREWELL.

The executors of Mr. Claypoole, of Philadelphia, offer for sale the original manuscript of Washington's Farewell Address. It should be purchased by the general government. The late venerable Wm. Rawle thus describes it:

Mr. Claypoole provided to me the original, and I saw with reverence and delight a small quarto book, containing about thirty pages, all in the handwriting of this great man. It bears throughout the marks of original composition. There are many erasures and interlineations, a transposition of paragraphs and other indications of it coming immediately from the hand of one unassisted individual. I counted the number of lines in the whole work which amounted to 1086 and of lines erased there were 174.

This modest announcement reignited debate over the document. The original draft had been widely thought lost. Now there was a chance to save it for public posterity.

Henry Clay argued that the Library of Congress should indeed purchase the handwritten text. "What is to become of that precious document?" he asked his colleagues in a speech on the Senate floor. "Is it to be sold, to be perhaps transferred out of the country, and made the ornament of the parlor of some of the distinguished men of Europe—men of rank or title or literary fame—or shall it remain here?"

In those days of sectional tension, making the Address public property was necessary, Clay argued:

Amidst the discordant and ungrateful sounds of disunion and discord which assail our ears in every part of this country, and in both halls of Congress—who is there that would not find refreshment and delight behind the Farewell Address of Washington to the people of this country? Who is there that would not trade the paternal and patriotic advice with pleasure which was written by his own hand—that hand which, after having grasped the sword that achieved the liberties of our country, traced with the instrument of peace the document which then gave us that advice, so necessary to preserve and transmit to posterity the treasure he had bestowed upon us? Who is there, in tracing that advice to beware of sectional divisions, to beware of demagogues, to beware of the consequences of the indulgence of a spirit of disunion—who is there, in reading those lines of truly parental advice, that will not in imagination transport himself back to the period when they were transmitted to paper by Washington, and think of the emotions, the parental and patriotic emotions, at that precious movement, which must have animated his breast?

Clay's passionate proposal confronted the kind of bureaucratic resistance that often comes to kill good ideas on Capitol Hill. Senator James A. Pearce of Maryland asked whether the Library of Congress was authorized to purchase the Farewell Address manuscript, meekly noting that it only had the authority "for the purchase of books and not of manuscripts valuable merely as relics."

Mississippi senator Jefferson Davis argued against its purchase, invoking his mentor John C. Calhoun's opposition to purchasing the papers of James Madison from the Constitutional Convention. On the surface, this opposition was made in the name of fiscal responsibility, but it is easy to see the situational ethics of men motivated by self-interest. They did not want to elevate the nation's most famous argument against secession.

Davis told his fellow senators, "This is but a corrected copy of his farewell address, known not to have been entirely the result of his own mind, and if what we desire is merely manuscripts of Washington, we have enough of them to satisfy more than moderate desire. . . . Are we, the representatives of the people, and making appropriations from the treasury, to be governed by feeling, and to draw money out of the public treasury to gratify our sentiment? Certainly not. We should regard no such feelings, but should act as practical men." Seen from any historical perspective, this argument was penny-wise but pound-foolish.

The words of Tennessee senator Andrew Johnson were an even greater rebellion against common sense. To him, the push to purchase the Farewell Address was "merely a scheme to extort money from the public treasury." He asked, "why may not someone come to Congress hereafter for the purchase of a uniform, or the sword of General Washington, or for the cracked brandy-bottle said to have belonged to him?" As the nation would soon discover, Johnson knew a thing or two about cracked brandy bottles.

But his argument found supporters even outside the South, sparking national debate. The editors of the *Dollar* newspaper editorialized against the Farewell Address's purchase by picking up a strange mix of Jefferson Davis's and Andrew Johnson's claims: "We certainly venerate Washington's farewell address," the editors wrote. "But why should we venerate a paper and ink of the manuscript from which the printer gave that address to the world? It is probably in the handwriting of Washington's private secretary; for Washington, retiring from the presidency, was doubtless too much occupied by the duties of Commander-in-Chief to perform the sergeant's duty of preparing a copy for the press. . . . At what point do we object to the taxation of the people for a museum of revolutionary pots and pans? When will it stop?"

Pennsylvania's *Lewisburg Chronicle and West Branch Farmer* took on the *Dollar's* reasoning with acerbic wit:

> There is a wide difference between the original Farewell Address and cobwebs in Washington's library, the snuff from his candles, bits of the old mill in which the paper was made, and the clay in which the types were cast and which it was printed—almost as great a difference as there is between mind and matter. In the one case, the association of ideas is more elevated and intellectual. You were brought into as direct and intimate communion as possible with the mind, and the heart and soul of the mighty dead. . . .
>
> It is not blind superstition nor any approach to it, that places a high value upon this document, or that always leads visitors to the National Capital, off on a pilgrimage to Mount Vernon, and the Tomb of Washington. But it is because standing on the spot where he lived and lies buried, the associations of the place enable them to call up the living breathing presence of departed greatness more

vividly before their mental visions, and realize more deeply the original cost and present value of our free institutions. . . .

Suppose we take the opposite principle as stated by the "Dollar Paper," and run it out in a similar style, to the same ultra-conclusions, and what will be the result? Why, you must discard all the mementos and associations connected with the personal existence and identity of Washington, and treasure up and reverence only his thoughts, principles, intentions and deeds, and the direct consequence would be to make him, not a mortal man that once lived and moved and acted on this earth like other men, but an ideal image merely of the brain: And, a few centuries hence, he would become to our descendants an intangible abstraction like Thor and Woden, the mythic demigods of ancient Scandinavia, and they would doubtless deny his existence altogether except as a mythological representation of republican principles.

Now all this is manifestly absurd for there is no danger that will ever be the case—and yet it is not a hint more ridiculous than the assertion that because Congress wished to buy and preserve the manuscript of the farewell address, therefore the American people will straightaway become heathen and idolaters.

Sadly, the *Lewisburg Chronicle*'s reasoning did not carry the day in Congress. The world's most deliberative body dithered and missed the auction date. Instead, the famous document was purchased by a reclusive New York philanthropist and bibliophile named James Lenox via proxy for the price of $2,300 in late February 1850. The son of a wealthy Scottish immigrant merchant, the bearded and bespectacled Lenox was a lifelong bachelor whose primary passion was purchasing rare books and manuscripts, which he displayed in a limestone library overlooking Central Park. Lenox's library was later merged into the New York Public Library, where the manuscript remains preserved and available to the public today.

Washington in Blue and Gray

★

A s the Civil War loomed, Washington's Farewell Address remained at the forefront of debate, invoked by politicians on both sides of the North-South divide.

During the 1860 presidential campaign, the nominee of the newly formed Republican Party, Abraham Lincoln, cited the Farewell Address repeatedly in his stump speech. From his famous oration at New York's Cooper Union to lesser-known stops in New Hampshire and New Haven, Connecticut, Lincoln said:

> Some of you delight to flaunt in our faces the warning against
> sectional parties given by Washington in his Farewell Address.
> Less than eight years before Washington gave that warning,
> he had, as President of the United States, approved and signed
> an act of Congress, enforcing the prohibition of slavery in the
> Northwestern Territory, which act embodied the policy of the
> Government upon that subject up to and at the very moment
> he penned that warning; and about one year after he penned it,
> he wrote Lafayette that he considered that prohibition a wise
> measure, expressing in the same connection his hope that we
> should at some time have a confederacy of free States.
>
> Bearing this in mind, and seeing that sectionalism has since
> arisen upon this same subject, is that warning a weapon in your

hands against us, or in our hands against you? Could Washington himself speak, would he cast the blame of that sectionalism upon us, who sustain his policy, or upon you who repudiate it? We respect that warning of Washington, and we commend it to you, together with his example pointing to the right application of it.

The prairie lawyer was pulling a political judo move, flipping his political opponents' arguments against them, undercutting the secessionists who claimed the mantle of Washington as a rebellious southern plantation owner and decried the newfound Republicans as a regional protest party, unable to unite the nation.

Lincoln's response turned the question of progressive versus conservative on its head: "You say you are conservative—eminently conservative—while we are revolutionary, destructive, or something of the sort. What is conservatism? Is it not adherence to the old and tried, against the new and untried? We stick to, contend for, the identical old policy on the point in controversy which was adopted by 'our fathers who framed the Government under which we live'; while you with one accord reject, and scout, and spit upon that old policy, and insist upon substituting something new." Abolitionist Republicans were fulfilling the purpose Washington had expressed, at least implicitly, in his last will and testament.

In the heat of the presidential campaign, Lincoln presented himself as Washington's heir, defending his legacy against the secession-threatening southern Democrats who formed the core of both men's opposition. Lincoln nailed the hypocrisy of men who tried to twist history to their advantage while ignoring original intentions, "calling, not the sinners, but the righteous to repentance—such as invocations to Washington, imploring men to unsay what Washington said, and undo what Washington did."

The repeated references to Washington and the Farewell Address would be forgotten next to his thundering closing sentence: "Let us have faith that right makes might, and in that faith, let us, to the end, dare to do our duty as we understand it."

One month after Lincoln was inaugurated, the southern states launched the Civil War by firing on Fort Sumter in South Carolina. Washington's worst fear had come to pass.

But the Farewell Address remained a means of rallying what was left of the Union. With the war raging, citizens of Philadelphia petitioned Congress to read "that immortal Farewell Address which even in the pages of British history is pronounced 'unequaled by any composition of uninspired wisdom'" to commemorate Washington's first birthday celebration since the rebellion's outbreak.

In response, Lincoln issued a presidential directive that Washington's Birthday be commemorated in 1862 with readings of the Farewell Address nationwide. General orders went out to the army that "the President of the United States, Commander in Chief of the Army and Navy, orders that the following extracts from the Farewell Address of George Washington be read to the troops at every military post and at the head of the several regiments and corps of the Army."

The extensive excerpts selected by Lincoln focused, logically enough, on the need to maintain a strong national union. Washington's words took on renewed urgency against the backdrop of civil war:

> The unity of government which constitutes you one people is also
> now dear to you. It is justly so, for it is a main pillar in the edifice
> of your real independence, the support of your tranquility at home,
> your peace abroad; of your safety; of your prosperity; of that very
> liberty which you so highly prize. But as it is easy to foresee that,
> from different causes and from different quarters, much pains will
> be taken, many artifices employed to weaken in your minds the
> conviction of this truth; as this is the point in your political fortress
> against which the batteries of internal and external enemies
> will be most constantly and actively (though often covertly and
> insidiously) directed, it is of infinite moment that you should
> properly estimate the immense value of your national union to

your collective and individual happiness; that you should cherish
a cordial, habitual, and immovable attachment to it; accustoming
yourselves to think and speak of it as of the palladium of your
political safety and prosperity; watching for its preservation with
jealous anxiety; discountenancing whatever may suggest even a
suspicion that it can in any event be abandoned; and indignantly
frowning upon the first dawning of every attempt to alienate any
portion of our country from the rest, or to enfeeble the sacred ties
which now link together the various parts.

The unity of government was now threatened in fact rather than theory.
Now its fate would be determined on battlefields, as soldiers confronted the
ultimate attempt to "alienate any portion of our country from the rest."

While Union soldiers gathered to listen to the Farewell read by their
commanders in the field, a grand procession was occurring underneath the
U.S. Capitol dome, which was still under construction. Lincoln ordered
members of the House and Senate as well as cabinet officials and justices
of the Supreme Court to witness a reading of the Farewell Address that
Saturday, February 22, at noon.

Lincoln could not attend the event as he was still mourning the death
of his beloved eleven-year-old son, Willie. But it was the president's suggestion to have captured Confederate flags hung in the Capitol while
the Farewell Address was read, confronting the symbols of treason with
Washington's enduring appeal to reason.

When the rebel battle flags were brought into the House of Representatives, there was a formal objection by Representative John Crittenden, a former United States attorney general and now a member of the
secession-rejecting Unionist Party from Kentucky. Crittenden declared
that the flags of "pirates and rebels" should not be allowed to sully the
Capitol, and the motion carried.

The crowd resented being denied the spectacle and a fistfight broke out in
the gallery. A captain of the Capitol Police named Nathan Darling arrested

two people and was later indicted by a grand jury for assault with "force of arms" and endeavoring to "beat and ill-treat" the protestors. Lincoln later pardoned the captain for "supposing he was doing his official duty."

The *New York Times* weighed in, agreeing that Confederate emblems were best kept out of the Capitol, declaring that "the bastard flags" should "rot as the memory of the wicked whose cause they symbolize will rot."

Lincoln's decision to elevate the Farewell Address on Washington's Birthday proved a powerful rallying point for a nation at war with itself and kicked off the bipartisan tradition of its annual reading under the Capitol dome that continues to this day.

The Farewell retained its diplomatic utility overseas as well. In 1863, at the height of the Civil War, France requested that America join them in an international condemnation of Russia tamping down a Polish uprising. Secretary of State William Seward refused the request by invoking Washington's Farewell and defending "our policy of non-intervention—straight, absolute, and peculiar as it may seem to other nations . . . the American people must be content to recommend the cause of human progress by the wisdom with which they should exercise the powers of self-government, forbearing at all times, and in every way, from foreign alliances, intervention, and interference."

The *New York Herald* proclaimed, "Never in the history of our country have we had so much cause to revere the memory of Washington as now." In Union Square, where Washington had met New Yorkers on Evacuation Day, the flag that flew over Fort Sumter was laid in the hands of his statue. New editions of the Farewell Address were published to newfound popularity. On the west coast, the *San Francisco Bulletin* called the Farewell "a magnificent chapter of prophecy," a "triumph of loyalty over treason . . . of the Constitution over insurrection."

But Confederate rebels were unwilling to cede the mantle of Washington to the Union. To them, he was a southern symbol of resistance to tyranny. One Confederate delegate even proposed they call their breakaway country the Republic of Washington.

Confederate president Jefferson Davis chose Washington's Birthday to take his oath of office in Richmond, beneath a statue of Washington seated on horseback, which became the model for the Seal of the Confederacy. In his inaugural address, Davis declared, "On this the birthday of the man most identified with the establishment of American independence, and beneath the monument erected to commemorate his heroic virtues and those of his compatriots, we have assembled to usher into existence the permanent government of the Confederate States. . . . We are in arms to renew such sacrifices as our fathers made to the holy cause of constitutional liberty."

Washington's portrait was placed on Confederate fifty- and hundred-dollar bills. Envelopes issued by the Confederate States of America portrayed Washington's face under the slogan "One of the Rebels," framed by the phrase "The Southern Gentleman and Slaveholder."

Even Washington's last will and testament became a casualty of the Civil War.

When Virginia seceded, the Fairfax County Courthouse, which held the document, was controlled by Confederate forces, but Union troops raided the location at the outset of the war. Amid the skirmishes, the Court Clerk, Alfred Moss, removed Washington's will for safekeeping.

Moss was a slave-owning Confederate sympathizer, hailing from an old Virginia family, and one of his uncles had served as a pallbearer at Washington's funeral. Moss secretly carried the will twenty-nine miles to his wife's family home, where she sewed the will into a large pocket hidden inside the hem of a dress.

Seeking greater safety as Union troops marched closer, Moss sealed the dress along with valuable court documents in a trunk, and locked it in an underground wine cellar. Moss was captured by Union troops, but the will remained hidden, and after his release in a prisoner swap, he unearthed the trophy and deposited it in a courthouse in the Confederate capital of Richmond. At war's end, the will was returned, damaged but intact, to its original resting place, where it remains today.

As the war raged in his home state, Washington's legacy became a battlefield of its own, each side claiming his symbolic benediction. But seen with any sense of perspective, Washington could not be claimed by traitors. The core message of his public life, codified in the Farewell Address, was the necessity of national union in the face of factions and regional rivalries. But then there was no modesty or perspective in the Confederacy's choice of role models: its chosen motto was *Deo Vindice*—God Vindicates.

He eventually did, with the Confederates' defeat in the spring of 1865 and the subsequent Thirteenth Amendment to the Constitution, which abolished slavery.

*

AFTER LEE'S SURRENDER TO GRANT at Appomattox Courthouse, reuniting the nation became America's most urgent task. As Washington's Farewell had been quoted to argue for unity before the war, it was used to heal the country's wounds in its aftermath.

With Lincoln's Good Friday assassination at Ford's Theatre, the presidency fell to Vice President Andrew Johnson, a southerner who opposed secession, which had qualified him for the Union presidential ticket with Lincoln in 1864. Expectations were set when Johnson showed up for Lincoln's second inauguration drunk.

Before the war, Johnson had dismissed congressional attempts to purchase the Farewell Address. As president, he honored it for "containing all the principles by which he sought to be guided," at a meeting of the National Monument Society, whose work on the Washington Monument had stalled during the war.

As Johnson warred with Radical Republicans over the course of Reconstruction, there were few figures who retained respect across the Mason-Dixon Line. Northerners had a hero in the martyred president, and reciting the Gettysburg Address began to replace the Farewell Address as standard-issue patriotic fare at public events. To many in the South, Lincoln was the leader of an invading army.

Now Washington's symbolic appeal to both sides became a powerful force for reunification. Condensed versions of the Farewell Address, simplified for children, had been standard in grammar textbooks before the war and now those verses proliferated in schoolhouses throughout the South.

One textbook, edited by the pioneering women's educator Emma Willard, called the address "A Father's Counsel," summarizing its 6,000 words in 57: "Good faith and equal justice should be observed towards all. Honesty, no less in public, than in private affairs, is the best policy. Religion and morality are the pillars of human happiness. These great truths, with others, were taught us, as parting precepts, by our paternal friend, whose fame, for wisdom, gathers brightness as time passes on."

These sentiments were lovely, but battles over Washington's memory still continued with remarkable bitterness. On his birthday in 1867, the Augusta, Georgia, *Daily Constitutionalist* published an editorial titled "George Washington—Rebel," in which the authors called for the national holiday to be abolished, because of "the despotism which our northern brethren force upon the South, making Great Britain a saint of freedom by comparison." In the midst of all the fireworks and parades, the Georgia editors protested that "the teachings of Washington have been spurned; his glorious example denied, and the Republic he founded destroyed."

But the *Indianapolis Star* declared Washington's birthday a "secular Sabbath," and "a safe harbor in still troubled times." In Chicago, at the Wigwam convention center, where Lincoln had been nominated, the Farewell Address was read before a massive audience.

In New York's Trinity Baptist Church, a sermon declared that "[George Washington's] character has been better appreciated in the last few years of our national history, years of trial and darkness through which our nation has passed." Celebrations of his birthday in Manhattan inspired a ball at a local armory, which contained "the graceful forms of elegantly attired 'demoiselles and their stately cavaliers as, locked in each other's arms, they glided in dreamy ecstasy through the mazes of the dance, their twinkling feet keeping time," as an inspired reporter in the

New York Herald described "the happy hours they chased into oblivion on Washington's birthday."

In the run-up to the 1868 election, the *Herald* suggested that former Union general Ulysses S. Grant run on a ticket with former Confederate general Robert E. Lee, who was then leading Washington University in Virginia. And when Grant's two-term presidency was coming to a scandal-plagued, recession-scarred end, amid the populist anger that often accompanies economic downturns, *Harper's Weekly* printed a full page illustration by the legendary cartoonist Thomas Nast of Grant being comforted by the ghost of Washington, carrying a reminder of the bitter attacks directed at him by the *Aurora* and other newspapers.

Washington was now the symbol of perspective in our politics, a source of strength for his successors.

In 1889, centennial celebrations of Washington's inauguration crowded the streets of New York and captivated the nation. The founding father's face was slapped on commemorative prints and pitchers, stained glass and statuary. As the hundredth anniversary of the Farewell Address drew nearer, *Harper's Weekly* printed a testament to its relevance: "The utterances today are the very commonplace of political wisdom. In his own days, the beginnings of a government threw a glamour over these utterances which lent them color. In these days of jingoism and of financial madness it is well to hark back to the simple and sincere propositions of the address. The warnings against foreign entanglements, against faction and abuse of the instruments of government against national dishonor and sectional strife are as pertinent today as they were in 1796."

With the Civil War slowly receding from living memory, Washington's warning about the dangers of regional rivalries lost some of its urgency. But with America's rise as a world power, his warnings on foreign policy moved to the center of political debate.

World Wars and the
Temptation of Empire

★

In 1885, the first Democratic president since the Civil War took the oath of office.

New York's Grover Cleveland reaffirmed Washington's Farewell in his inaugural address, pledging himself to "the scrupulous avoidance of any departure from that foreign policy commended by the history, the traditions, and the prosperity of our Republic. It is the policy of independence, favored by our position and defended by our known love of justice and by our power. It is the policy of peace suitable to our interests. It is the policy of neutrality, rejecting any share in foreign broils and ambitions upon other continents and repelling their intrusion here. It is the policy of Monroe and of Washington and Jefferson—'Peace, commerce, and honest friendship with all nations; entangling alliance with none.' "

But now that the West had been won and the continent conquered, the United States was a great power, no matter how much it wished to avoid great power politics.

When a South American border dispute flared up between Venezuela and British Guiana, the British wanted a chance to mediate. Cleveland's secretary of state, Richard Olney, smacked down that suggestion: "Today the United States is practically sovereign on this continent. . . . Its infinite resources, combined with its isolated position, render it master of the situation and practically invulnerable as against any or all other powers." This pronouncement extended the Monroe Doctrine's sphere of influence, going well beyond neutrality and noninterventionism. America was the great power in the New World.

In 1898, Olney pushed beyond even this reframing of Washington's great rule of foreign policy, arguing that the time had come to "shake off the spell of the Washington Legend and cease to act the role of the sort of international recluse."

"The Washington rule, in the sense in which it has been commonly understood and actually applied, could hardly have been adhered to more faithfully if it had formed part of the text of the Constitution," the now former secretary of state bellowed to Harvard students:

> Though the nation is still young, it has long since ceased to be feeble or lack the power to command its own fortunes. It is just as true that the achievements in modern science have annihilated the time and space that once separated the Old World from the New. In these days of telephones and railroads and ocean cables and ocean steamships it is difficult to realize that Washington could write to the French ambassador at London in 1790, "We at this great distance from the northern parts of Europe hear of wars and rumors of wars as if they were events or reports of another planet." . . . Nothing can be more obvious, therefore, than that the conditions for which Washington made his rule no longer exist. The logical, if not the necessary result is that the rule itself should also now be considered as nonexistent.

This was well-reasoned heresy and it perfectly anticipated the challenges of the twentieth century. The sturdy Ohio Republican William McKinley was in the White House, delivering a more interventionist foreign policy than had ever been seen in the United States, extending victory in the war against the Spanish in Cuba to annexation of the Philippines.

The Anti-Imperialist League, formed to protest the action, often invoked Washington's Farewell to bolster its argument. But even McKinley could not avoid paying lip service to the Farewell Address: "Following the precepts of Washington, we cannot err. The wise lessons in government which he left us it will be profitable to heed. He seems to have grasped all the possible conditions and pointed the way safely to meet them. He has established danger signals all along the pathway of the nation's march. . . . His wisdom and foresight have been confirmed and vindicated after more than a century of experience."

The moral authority of the Address was hammered home in public schools. In 1901, the Chicago Board of Education's paperback series "Four Penny Classics" published the Farewell Address paired with Lincoln's first inaugural, declaring, "Its logic and beauty and grace can hardly fail to impress anyone who reads it. The prophecies contained in it have been fulfilled. . . . This address should be read and re-read by every pupil in the public schools. It furnishes instruction in the duties and importance of true patriotism and high-minded citizenship."

The Farewell also became the subject of turn-of-the-century oratory and analysis contests in many schools, with the hopes that its inculcation might save the nation from numerous ills, both past and present. Wilson L. Gill, president of the Patriotic League, was among the advocates who praised its teaching in public schools, saying, "If the last generation of our people had been taught the wisdom of Washington's admonition in his Farewell Address, the War of '61 would have been impossible. Had the present generation understood and heeded his instructions, the municipal affairs throughout the United States would not have fallen into the hands of thieves. If the children of the present and future are thoroughly taught and trained in the spirit and wisdom of that address, we need have no fear of anarchy or the destruction of our common welfare."

Soon after the new century dawned, America's first hero of a foreign war paced the floors of the White House, committed to extending his assassinated predecessor William McKinley's strenuous foreign policy. Theodore Roosevelt delighted in the wide arena of foreign affairs, winning a Congressional Medal of Honor for leading the Rough Riders in a much-publicized charge up Cuba's San Juan Hill, as well as winning a Nobel Peace Prize for negotiating an end to the Russo-Japanese War as president. TR loved the African proverb, "Speak softly and carry a big stick," but the big stick was the sixteen battleships of the "Great White Fleet" he sent to flex America's muscle at ports across the Pacific Ocean. Roosevelt idolized Washington, but he tended to disregard precedents that limited his power.

Many of Roosevelt's Republican allies in Congress, though, still saw the Farewell Address as the keystone of American policy—particularly his lifelong friend, Massachusetts senator Henry Cabot Lodge. This patrician part-time historian, author of a four-volume biography of Washington, was a conservative in that he was reluctant to ditch the wisdom of tradition. After TR regretted following Washington's two-term precedent and decided to run for reelection in 1912 against his chosen successor, he was derided for trying to overturn Washington's wisdom.

After TR lost the 1912 election, Lodge squared off against progressive president Woodrow Wilson, also a Washington biographer, in one of the epic battles in American political history: the argument over the League of Nations. And so the foundational debate over the direction of American foreign policy in the twentieth century was carried out by two warring Washington scholars, debating to what extent the Farewell Address remained stable ground for national policy in the new century.

Wilson was raised in the South and remembered seeing Robert E. Lee ride by his house on horseback and watching Jefferson Davis paraded in chains down the street by Union troops. The son and grandson of Presbyterian ministers, the bookish boy chose academic lectures over the pulpit and first rose to fame as a professor of the Constitution and Congress at Princeton University. His academic work was chiefly distinguished by its disdain for the inefficiencies of the system of checks and balances so carefully laid out by the founding fathers.

Wilson's 1896 Washington biography was fawning and florid; today, it's interesting primarily as an assessment of the first president from the man who would become the twenty-eighth president. But his tribute to the Farewell Address captured the document's sentimental hold on the generation that had grown up in the ashes of the Civil War:

> The circumstances which had given his services a temporary value, he told them, were passed; they had now a unified and national government which might serve them for great ends. He exhorted them to preserve it intact, and not to degrade it in the using; to put down party spirit, make religion, education, and good faith the guides and safeguards of their government, and keep it national and their own by excluding foreign influences and entanglements. 'Twas a noble document. No thoughtful man could read it without emotion, knowing how it spoke in all its solemn sentences to the great character of the man whose career was ended.

Wilson understood the precepts of the Farewell Address and was destined to violate them. "It would be an irony of fate if my administration had to deal chiefly with foreign problems," Wilson confided to a friend shortly after his election in 1912. Irony abided.

While Wilson's immediate predecessors sometimes gloried in expressing America's growing power on the world stage, they did not embark on a full-fledged embrace of foreign alliances. This was not Wilson's style or intention either. When German atrocities in the 1914 invasion of Belgium began to galvanize a portion of the American public, Wilson promised to remain committed to a policy of neutrality "in word and deed."

His secretary of state, William Jennings Bryan, was a populist pacifist and dedicated to neutrality. Powerful Democrats in Congress, like Virginia's James Hay, tried to enforce isolation by blocking efforts to modernize and expand the U.S. military. Hay took a page from the Farewell Address, arguing, "isolated as we are, safe in our vastness, protected by a great navy, and possessed of an army sufficient for any emergency that may arise, we may disregard the lamentations and predictions of the militarists." Senator Lodge retorted "the ocean barrier which defended us in 1776 and 1812 no longer exists. Steam and electricity have destroyed it."

As war raged across Europe and horror stories were dominating the American press, Washington's Farewell was invoked as a trump card of antiwar activists. The American Peace Society was formed to argue against American involvement in the Great War, and while speaking to their organization Wilson warned against growing militarism, asking whether Americans had "forgotten the sound advice of George Washington that we should not meddle in the affairs of other countries; that, above all things, we should avoid entangling foreign alliances?"

While the term *isolationism* would not appear in the *Oxford English Dictionary* until 1922, the sentiments were alive, and the terminology was tiptoeing toward its ultimate expression.

The blind senator Thomas Gore, Democrat of Oklahoma and grandfather of novelist Gore Vidal, thundered against war on the Senate floor: "I still believe in the policy of no entangling alliances," he said. "I believe our policy of isolation is our best security." His colleague, Arizona senator Henry Ashurst, railed against the temptation of foreign alliances, arguing that America should never enter into "any sort of alliances with any country for any reason. It is a dangerous thing, and the admonition of Washington should be religiously followed. The European war, with all its horrors, should serve as a warning of the penalty of alliances."

In this, Senator Ashurst, wonderfully nicknamed "the Silver-Tongued Sunbeam of the Painted Desert," had a point. A tangle of alliances between European powers had lit the powder keg of a war that it seemed few actually wanted. Millions died. But isolation was becoming a theory rather than a reality.

In 1915, the sinking of the passenger ship *Lusitania* by a German submarine, with 128 American passengers aboard, made Wilson's arguments for neutrality harder to keep, especially because the ship contained rifle-cartridges and shell cases for the British in its hull. Wilson quickly condemned the German attack, provoking the huffy resignation of Secretary of State Bryan, who feared that a one-sided condemnation could drag the nation into war.

Wilson campaigned for reelection in 1916 under the banner "He Kept Us Out of War." But the president was already contemplating a vision of America as a mediator of European conflicts from our safe perch across the Atlantic.

In the spring of 1916, Wilson spoke at the convention of the League to Enforce Peace, chaired by William Howard Taft, the president he had defeated four years before. Wilson thrilled the audience with his declaration, "We are participants, whether we would or not, in the life of the world. The interests of all nations are our own also. We are partners with the rest."

Henry Cabot Lodge was eager to play his role as a conservative congressional foil to the progressive president. At a Washington's Birthday dinner in Wilson's home state of New Jersey, he associated himself with the time-honored wisdom of Washington's policy of neutrality in measured contrast to the president.

"While I am far from thinking that all wisdom died with our forefathers, I am perfectly certain that all wisdom was not born yesterday," Lodge told the crowd. "The fact that Washington had never seen an automobile or flying machine or received a wireless message does not alter in the least his judgment as to forms of government or as to the conduct of nations in their relations to each other."

"Washington was not only a great but a very wise man of large experience who had reflected much on all these subjects," Lodge continued.

He laid down certain fundamental doctrines, from some of which we have never swerved. . . . I think that from his calm wisdom we all, yes, even the youngest and wisest among us, can learn much today. The country has never suffered from following Washington's leadership and counsel, whether in his own lifetime or since. In dealing with questions where the underlying conditions, like human nature in international relations, are in their essence constant, I do

not think we shall gravely err if we consider his advice today, and I
think that in many directions it is just as applicable now as when he
was President of the United States.

Lodge directed his fire not only at international adventurists, but also
at those who, through a combination of innocence and ignorance, urged
America to disarm to affirm its peaceful intentions. "The chief argument
of the extreme pacifists is that a well-prepared national defense is an incen-
tive to war. This Washington regarded as false. He puts his demand for
preparedness on the ground that it will preserve peace. . . . The people who
mistake the frail conventions of civilization for the realities of human existence, who wholly fail to realize that domestic peace and law and order rest
on the organized force of the community are dangerous guides to trust or
follow. They are like children playing on the glittering surface of a frozen
river, unconscious of the waters beneath."

*

IN JANUARY 1917, SOON AFTER his narrow reelection over New York governor Charles Evans Hughes, President Wilson ventured to the Senate and
proposed the creation of a "World League of Peace." But he was careful to
frame the unprecedented proposal as a global extension of the principles of
Washington's Farewell and the Monroe Doctrine.

> I am proposing that all nations henceforth avoid entangling
> alliances which would draw them into competitions of power,
> catch them in a net of intrigue and selfish rivalry, and disturb their
> own affairs with influences intruded from without. There is no
> entangling alliance in a concert of power. When all unite to act in
> the same sense and with the same purpose, all act in the common
> interest and are free to live their own lives under a common
> protection. . . . These are American principles, American policies.

This was a clever rhetorical move, but opponents of war were not swayed.

Senator William Borah, a populist Republican from Idaho, declared that there must be "no alliances, no leagues, no entanglements. We have abandoned the policy of nearly a century and a half and entered directly and at once upon that policy which was condemned by the Father of our Country in the very beginning of the Government. . . . Had it not been for Washington's policy, had he yielded in the fateful hour when urged to form a European alliance, we would have participated in every war which has torn and tormented Europe from that hour to this."

One hundred and twenty years after it was published, Washington's Farewell Address was still, perhaps for the last time, defining the broad terms of the debate.*

Lodge was willing to listen to the president's reasoning on the need to confront Germany on the side of England and France, but he slammed the naïveté of Wilson's suggestion that peace could be achieved through a permanent international alliance. He argued that while he had "no superstition in regard to Washington's policy," he believed that "we should not depart from it without the most powerful reasons and without knowing exactly where that departure would lead."

Then the Zimmermann Telegram exploded American assumptions of isolation. When British intelligence intercepted a coded telegram from the German foreign minister Arthur Zimmermann, offering a secret diplomatic deal to Mexico to "make war together, make peace together"—and with the promise of not just "generous financial support" but also the return of Mexico's former territory in Texas, New Mexico, and Arizona.

Wilson released the text of the Zimmermann Telegram on February 28,

---

* A satirical cartoon by Lute Pease published on Washington's birthday in 1917 showed pacifist protestors rejecting the first president's warning that "if we desire to secure peace, we must be prepared for war." The marchers reply: "My friends, that militarist jingo is way out of date."

1917, inflaming nationalist feelings, which were heightened in the weeks to follow by Germany's sinking of five American merchant marine vessels. Thirty-three days later, President Wilson asked Congress for a formal declaration of war.

As Congress prepared to vote on our first European continental war, antiwar Nebraska representative C. Frank Reavis walked heavy-hearted along the National Mall and noted that he was "not surprised to note that the towering [Washington] monument, erected to him who advised against entangling alliances, had hidden its head in the mist and fog."

In the end, only 54 representatives opposed the war resolution: 35 Republicans, 18 Democrats, and 1 Socialist, with members of the Party of Jefferson largely falling into line behind their progressive president, Wilson.

America had now inserted itself in a sprawling foreign war. President Wilson's wartime propaganda department was nonetheless careful to invoke the first founding father in its rally-round-the-flag posters, depicting Wilson flanked by Washington and casting soldiers as the inheritors of the Revolutionary generation.

In public schools, the Farewell was reemployed as a core part of a standardized curriculum on patriotism. "Patriotic exercises should be held in every school house in this country at least once a month," advised the Pennsylvania superintendent of public instruction. "Washington's Farewell Address, Lincoln's Gettysburg Speech, Second Inaugural Address and Wilson's messages to Congress should be read by the older pupils and they should be urged to read and discuss them in their homes. Teachers should be loyal and they should make a public declaration of their loyalty. Being public officials, if they cannot support the government heartily, they should resign."

In Brooklyn, eighth graders memorized Washington's key points with the help of an acrostic:

F—oreign entanglements

A—gainst bitter politics

R—emain Americans

E—ach one pay taxes

W—ar avoided

E—ncourage little borrowing

L—earning to be spread

L—ive and let live

The propaganda-driven patriotic surge was vindicated by the relatively swift victory that followed entry into the Great War, making the doomsayers look superstitious rather than sage.

Wilson was triumphant, bounding into the Paris Peace talks resplendent in his beaver top hat, eager to embrace what he hoped would be the progressive moment on the world stage. He was on his way to winning a Nobel Peace Prize. But as often happens, pride comes before the fall.

Wilson rejected advice to create a bipartisan U.S. delegation to the Paris peace conference, needlessly polarizing the triumph at home while compounding the effects of a midterm election loss to the Republicans.

He also found that the continental powers who suffered through the Great War were far less interested in implementing grand plans and alliances for peace. They were all operating out of self-interest, driven by necessity. Seventy-three percent of French troops had either been killed, wounded or captured during the conflict. Idealism took a backseat to realism at the negotiating table, where massive (and ultimately unwise) German reparations were the goal, as punishment competed with the practical need to rebuild cities pounded into dust.

Wilson staked all his political capital on the creation of the League of Nations, a farsighted if somewhat soft-minded attempt to create an armed international coalition to make the world safe for democracy. This would institutionalize entangling alliances.

The Republican-controlled Senate would have to approve the treaty but Wilson was not in a mood to compromise. Despite the midterm results, he felt that American sentiment was on his side. But his failure to compromise on one particular provision would deny him the international legacy he craved.

Article 10 of the League's covenant committed member states to a collective security obligation. America could be drawn into another European war, regardless of whether our interests were at stake. The article seemed to supersede congressional authority on matters as broad as war and peace and as specific as immigration and trade policy. Unsurprisingly, some people had a problem with this.

Still, members of the Senate seemed willing to listen to reason; nevertheless, Wilson was unwilling to reason with them: "I will consent to nothing," he told reporters. "The Senate must take its medicine." Behind closed doors, administration aides could not seem to answer basic questions as to how the treaty would work in practice.

Led by Lodge, Republicans responded with fourteen amendments to clarify America's obligations and sustained sovereignty in the League of Nations.

Wilson responded by having a stroke on a transcontinental train tour while trying to sell his version of the treaty. The resulting stalemate meant that America would not join the League of Nations, which its president had done more than anyone else to champion.

The pace of change from Washington's precepts had been too abrupt to sustain and Wilson's disdain for compromise had doomed the measure. To add insult to Wilson's injury, a vocal opponent of the treaty, the charming but vapid Ohio senator Warren G. Harding, was elected president to succeed him. Democrats would be shut out of power for the next decade.

Washington's talismanic influence over American policy and political culture was fading, but the Farewell Address remained a powerful touchstone for politicians. Even when they departed from the first president's foreign policy prescriptions, they offered up Washington's example as evidence that they were on the side of the Founding Fathers.

But in the wake of World War I, it suddenly became chic to cut George Washington down to size and a handful of critical popular biographies were published, describing Washington's passions, weaknesses and insecurities. Evidently not infallible in matters of policy, he no longer seemed invincible as a person.

A strict reading of the Farewell Address still had its defenders, particularly in the isolationist wing of the Republican Party. More fairly described as noninterventionists, these Republicans balanced fidelity to the Founding Fathers with a nativist conviction that engagement in the problems of the wider world would inevitably mean overextension. The evolution of one such Republican tells their story.

Arthur Vandenberg began his career as the crusading editor of Michigan's *Grand Rapids Herald*. A proud progressive Republican, he was a devotee of Theodore Roosevelt. But his real political crush was Alexander Hamilton. Vandenberg set about trying to revive Hamilton's faded reputation with a biography titled *Alexander Hamilton: The Greatest American* and a series of editorials ultimately combined into a 1923 book, *If Hamilton Were Here Today*. It was an extended mash note to Hamilton's writings in both the Federalist Papers and the Farewell Address, pointing out how applicable they remained to America's present-day crises.

Vandenberg saw Hamilton as a prophet, blessed with transcendent insight, and he quoted the Federalist Papers to prove the point. "Publius" had written: "Should a war be the result of a precarious situation of European affairs, and all the unruly passions attending it be let loose on the ocean, our escape from insults and depredations not only on that element but every part of the other bordering on it would be truly miraculous." Vandenberg concluded: "That could have been said the day Austrian nobility was assaulted at Sarajevo in 1914, as truthfully as in 1787."

Vandenberg refused to interpret Washington's Farewell as solely a doctrine of isolationism. Instead he interpreted it as a mechanism for achieving a wise balance between extremes. Hamilton, he wrote, "was not the astigmatized isolationist who fools himself into thinking that America is wholly immune to the effects of eruption, economic or political, in other continents. Neither was he the anesthetized internationalist who drinks himself into the notion that America must make common lot with all the uneasy, quarrelsome—and frequently imperialistic—powers on earth. . . . He would say again that, as Europe should keep out of America, so America should keep out of Europe unless Americanism itself is to be served by voluntary exception to this age-old rule. His 'League of Nations' primarily would be Pan-American, not inter-Continental." Vandenberg was trying to update Washingtonian wisdom for a new age, a reasonable interpretation without the straitjacket of literalism.

In 1928, Vandenberg was rudely plucked from journalism—a calling his contemporary H. L. Mencken called "the Life of Kings"—and dropped into the U.S. Senate, selected to serve out the term of a dead incumbent. At age forty-four, he became one of five former journalists serving in the Senate, and he quickly picked up the torch for the Hamiltonian tradition, becoming an enthusiastic participant in the annual reading of Washington's Farewell Address. Vandenberg's Senate career spanned four decades, and he rose through the ranks of Republican leadership on the Foreign Relations Committee.

Among conservative critics of the New Deal, quoting the founding fathers provided comfort that they were fighting the good fight against liberal collectivism.

★

FORMER PRESIDENT HERBERT HOOVER INVOKED the Farewell Address to call attention to his successor Franklin Delano Roosevelt's occasional disdain for the separation of powers, perhaps most evident in his attempt to pack the Supreme Court. "Liberty is crumbling over two-thirds of the world," Hoover lectured. "And, mark you this—in every instance the persuaders have professed to be acting for the people and in the name of progress. . . . Once political power makes use of the court, its strength and its moral prestige are irretrievably weakened." Obliquely referencing the

Farewell Address, Hoover reminded contemporaries that Washington had warned, "One method of assault may be to effect in the form of the Constitution alterations which may impair the energy of the system and thus undermine that which cannot be directly overthrown."

But his successor, the polio-afflicted, patrician political master, Franklin Delano Roosevelt, also tried to wrap himself in the cloak of Washington, declaring that "despite what happens in continents overseas, the United States of America shall and must remain, as long ago the Father of our Country prayed that it might remain—un-entangled and free."

In 1935, public interest in the Farewell Address enjoyed a revival with the publication of the first comprehensive history of the address in all its drafts, edited at the New York Public Library by historian Victor Hugo Paltsits. The careful documentation of each version of the address allowed historians and citizens to trace its development and immediate impact, laying to waste a century's worth of stubborn rumors that Washington had been an author in name only. The publication of this definitive collection of documents reinforced just how central the Farewell Address remained in the American psyche. But it could be appropriated for definite political ends.

As Hitler rose to power in Germany and storm clouds returned to Europe, the Farewell Address was frequently invoked as a staple of isolationist literature, quoted on color postcards mailed out by the Southwest National Bank of Wichita, Kansas, to pamphlets produced by members of the Old South Meeting House in Boston, which traced its civic participation to the Revolutionary War. The passage most frequently excerpted was Washington's warning, "Real patriots, who may resist the intrigues of the favorite, are liable to become suspected and odious; while its tools and dupes usurp the applause and confidence of the people to surrender their interests."

Here was the Farewell Address as cold comfort for self-styled patriots who felt cast out by the tides of the times. The sting came from their sense that sinister forces were castigating them as culturally suspect for insisting on first principles against political fears and fashionable emotions. This attitude contained the embryo of contemporary conservatism as well as conspiracy theories.

Today, insistence on neutrality in the face of Hitler looks like a cartoon version of moral relativism. But in the fog of war, these opinions had influential advocates.

The hugely popular radio priest, Father Charles Coughlin, declared that Americans should "bow our heads in shame for desecrating the final words bequeathed to us by the Father of our Country—'*no European entanglements.*'"

The antiwar movement attracted luminaries ranging from movie star Lillian Gish to Teddy Roosevelt's daughter, Alice Roosevelt Longworth, to the nationally syndicated columnist Irving S. Cobb. The U.S. ambassador to Britain, Joseph P. Kennedy Sr., warned Roosevelt against war with Germany, pronouncing Britain a lost cause. "Mr. Republican," Senator Robert Taft of Ohio, the son of the former president, declared that intervention was futile and targeted both Republicans and Democrats. "The war party—and I do not mean to identify that with either political party . . . has urged one argument after another upon the people in a frank effort to change their convictions and develop an excitement and hysteria for war."

Anne Morrow Lindbergh, the wife of isolationist celebrity-aviator Charles Lindbergh, now perhaps best known for her inspirational book, *Gift from the Sea*, wrote: "Who is pushing behind Communism? What is behind the Fascism in Italy? What is behind Nazism? Is it nothing but a 'return to barbarism' . . . to be crushed at all costs by a 'Crusade'? Or is some new and perhaps even ultimately good conception of humanity coming to birth—or *trying* to come to birth, through these evil and horrible forms, these abortive attempts?" Her glass-half-full view of totalitarianism has not aged well.

But the low point for Washington's Farewell Address can be set to a specific date: February 20, 1939.

The German American Bund, an organization ostensibly dedicated to ethnic pride and entrepreneurs, held a rally at New York's Madison Square Garden to celebrate Washington's Birthday two days early. Posters proclaimed the event as a "Pro-American Rally" and a "Mass Demonstration for True Americanism."

In the Garden that night there were dozens of American flags and a massive thirty-foot banner of George Washington behind the podium. Any resemblance to a purely patriotic rally stopped there. Beside Washington were Nazi flags emblazoned with the swastika and banners that hung from the rafters that read: "Americans—Stop Jewish Domination of Christian America" and "Smash Jewish Communism."

Passed among the crowd was a pamphlet proclaiming "George Washington: The First Nazi," presenting him as an Aryan superhero, a self-made soldier and gentleman farmer.

Twenty thousand Nazi-sympathizing Americans filled the floor, offering straight-arm salutes after the national anthem was sung in a decidedly German accent. A Nazi color guard goose-stepped between the seats to kick off the ceremonies while the keynote speaker, James Wheeler-Hill, the Bund's national secretary, called for a return to the advice of Washington's Farewell—though from his opening greeting, "My Fellow Christian Americans," he twisted the text to his own purposes.

George Washington, whose birthday we are celebrating today— when bidding farewell to the people said: BE UNITED! BE AMERICANS! Let there be no sectionalism, you are all dependent on one another, and should be in one Union. Beware attacks upon the Constitution. Keep the departments of government separate, promote education, cherish the public credit, avoid debt. Observe justice and good faith toward all nations; and be independently politically of all. IN ONE WORD, BE A NATION, BE AMERICANS, AND BE TRUE TO YOURSELVES.

Never were such admonitions more timely than TODAY!

Reviewing the State of the Nation today, in the light of this historic observation: WHAT DO WE FIND? A nation of TRUE Americans? UNITED? . . . in a noble common cause? PATRIOTIC? . . . free from class hatred and sectionalism and political discrimination? The CONSTITUTION . . . has it been free from attack? ARE we avoiding public debt? Exercising good faith toward ALL nations? Are we politically independent?

I am asking YOU, my Fellow Countrymen?

Speaking for myself, much to my regret, I must confess that we are utterly and completely disregarding the Admonition of George Washington, TODAY. There is more than ample evidence in support of this contention! Let us reason from FACTS that cannot be challenged: Who will deny this part of radicalism with its inspired class hatred, racial sectionalism, political abuses, its moral erosion and subsequent disintegration of our national unity in thought, decision and action??? Who will deny the attacks that have been made upon the Constitution? Who is NOT familiar with the billion-dollar yardstick that is required to measure the stupendous total of our national public debt. The billions spent in excess of our national income: have they done away with the pitiful relief situation after six years? Have they put back to work the 12 million unemployed that are walking the streets of the richest nation in the world? Have there not been passionate attacks on other nations? . . . And is there not a very definite trend toward entangling alliances? . . .

No wonder thinking people are beginning to ask embarrassing questions and to cry for a new leadership.

WHAT would George Washington think . . . and do, were he alive today?

Would he not plead with thinking, the loyal and law-abiding people, the true Christian Americans? In noble words of his own:

"Let us raise the standard to which the wise and honest can repair"?

Would he not re-advocate strict adherence to the noble principles voiced in his farseeing political testament?

My Fellow Countrymen! WE German Americans are unequivocally committed to the defense of the Flag, Constitution and Sovereignty of our United States. WE STAND BEFORE YOU—loyal and law-abiding, to be here dedicated together with you, to the great task of national and social reconstruction, and resolved as you are resolved to restore America to the true Americans and to the ideals and principles given expression in the great farewell address of George Washington.

FREE AMERICA!

The German American Bund's odious appropriation of the Farewell Address failed on multiple fronts. Far from showing respect for the sovereignty of the United States, members of the Bund were receiving regular cash infusions from Hitler's government. While calling for a true Americanism they were acting as foreign agents in the United States, attempting to undermine our independence while pretending to be true patriots—precisely what Washington warned about in the Farewell Address.

Their plan backfired. Their leader was imprisoned on financial fraud charges and the Nazi government cut off funding for its American fifth column. "The best British Ambassador we ever had in the U.S. was Adolf Hitler," remarked Robert Bruce Lockhart, who led England's wartime propaganda department. "The crass stupidity of Nazi propaganda, which reached the height of insolent absurdity in a pamphlet entitled *George Washington, the First Nazi,* did more than any British statement could have done."

But while the Nazi government ditched the embarrassing German American Bund, they continued to try to influence the direction of American foreign policy. The German chargé d'affaires at the embassy in Washington, Hans Thomsen, worked feverishly to encourage isolationist voices in both parties, offering bribes, suggesting language for antiwar newspaper advertisements and attempting to sway the party platforms, even using a German-American spy embedded in the office of U.S. representative Hamilton Fish.

★

IN 1940, AS DRUMBEATS OF war turned to Panzers across Poland and France, President Franklin Delano Roosevelt was glumly contemplating retirement at the end of his second term.

There was no legal limit to how long a president might serve, though the two-term tradition set by Washington in the Farewell Address was considered part of the "unwritten constitution." But FDR was still popular after a landslide reelection in 1936 and he did not want to give up the power that gave him a sense of purpose. The unfinished business of the Great Depression, combined with war in Europe, made him begin to drop hints that he might run again.

If he defied the two-term precedent while planning to engage the nation in another foreign war, FDR would be a double apostate to Washington's Farewell Address advice.

"We shun commitments which might entangle us in foreign wars," FDR assured American audiences while calming similar concerns in his own administration. "Don't worry about maintaining the non-intervention policy," he told his Secretary of War Harry Woodring, while nudging him out the door. "We are certainly going to do just that."

Despite his grinning denials, some folks weren't inclined to take FDR at his word. In part, it was personal: even FDR's devoted speechwriter Raymond Moley acknowledged his boss's "lack of sincerity and directness."

Between the world wars there was widespread regret about abandoning Washington's wisdom and listening to Wilson. During the 1930s, Congress passed four "Neutrality Acts" that attempted to update Washington's original proclamation, forbidding arms trade or bank loans to warring nations. A Senate committee led by North Dakota's Gerald Nye investigated accusations that banking interests and the munitions industry had agitated for U.S. involvement in the First World War, elevating profits over American lives. Other senators embraced arguments for inaction by railing against the history of British and French imperialism while bestselling books like *Merchants of Death* drove home similar popular sentiments.

University students picked up the mantle, determined to avoid becoming the next generation of cannon fodder. At Yale Law School, a future president and a future Supreme Court justice—Gerald Ford and Potter Stewart—were active members of a nationally known student group that demanded a negotiated peace with Hitler. The *Wall Street Journal* echoed these calls with a June 1940 editorial titled "A Plea for Reason," arguing that "European totalitarianism has made obsolete our American way of life, temporarily at least; permanently, unless we modernize our thinking and our national planning." The same day, Nazi general Erwin Rommel cornered more than 45,000 French and British troops in Normandy.

FDR began to quietly prepare for a third term by cutting down would-be rivals in the Democratic Party while publicly denying that he was interested in renomination up until the night before he was formally nominated at the party convention. At the same time, he elevated hawkish Republicans, and onetime critics, like Hoover cabinet member Henry Stimson and Frank Knox, a newspaper publisher and the 1936 GOP vice presidential nominee, to serve as secretary of war and secretary of the navy. He was preparing for war and reelection by building a bipartisan interventionist cabinet.

But Republicans refused to follow the script. Arthur Vandenberg had thrown his hat in the ring, fighting for the nomination alongside his fellow isolationist Taft and thirty-eight-year-old Manhattan District Attorney Thomas Dewey. But the GOP rank and file broke with tradition and gravitated to the ultimate dark horse: a backslapping, Indiana-raised, onetime Democrat Wall Street lawyer named Wendell Willkie, who campaigned unapologetically as a pro-business liberal Republican committed to confronting Hitler's aggression overseas.

The dashing first-time candidate railed against party bosses on both sides of the aisle and took aim at FDR's abandonment of the two-term tradition, attacking "the assumption by this President, in seeking a third term, of a greater public confidence than was accorded to our presidential giants, Washington, Jefferson, Jackson, Lincoln, Cleveland, Theodore Roosevelt, and Woodrow Wilson."

Willkie's campaign "to preserve American democracy" pulled personal punches against FDR compared to the Republican National Committee, which issued one widely disseminated pamphlet that declared "a third term opens the door to dictatorship" and "violates the American safeguard against usurpation of power as established by Washington," while warning darkly that "you may never go to the polls again in a free election."

Faced with two nominees who seemed to welcome involvement in another world war, isolationists found themselves politically homeless. In September 1940, the America First Committee was founded. Its leaders spanned the left and right, from perennial socialist presidential candidate Norman Thomas to auto tycoon Henry Ford. With free membership, the organization soon claimed some 800,000 members and oversized pictures of Washington were frequent props behind the podium at their meetings.

But the organization suffered from its association with anti-Semites and extremist fringe groups like the Nazi-admiring "silver shirts." When their hero Charles Lindbergh let loose in a radio address, declaring Jewish Americans "responsible for changing our national policy from one of neutrality and independence to one of entanglement in European affairs," the dog whistle attempted to echo Washington.

Even after FDR won an unprecedented third term, organized opposition to U.S. involvement in the war against Hitler persisted, with Senator Taft declaring that 1941 would be the year to oppose intervention in the war.

Then came Pearl Harbor.

The Japanese surprise attack rendered most isolationist sentiment instantly irrelevant. America was at war. Leading Republican voices for nonintervention like Senator Vandenberg quickly became converts to internationalism out of practical and political necessity. After the war, Vandenberg voted for America to join the United Nations. And when President Harry Truman unveiled the Marshall Plan, Vandenberg famously declared, "Partisan politics ought to end at the water's edge." With this statement, Vandenberg may have been riffing off a distant memory from his book about Hamilton, published almost four decades before: "His allegiance stopped at the American shore-line; but his vision roamed the world."

Harry Truman knew that Washington would be invoked against his efforts to build a postwar world informed by the mistakes made after World War I. As he wrote in his memoirs, "Throughout my years in the Senate I listened each year as one of the senators would read Washington's Farewell Address. It served little purpose to point out to the isolationists that Washington had advised a method suitable under the conditions of *his* day to achieve the great end of preserving the nation."

Washington's Farewell was written under conditions that no longer existed, Truman argued.

> It was a long way to Europe and we were defended by two oceans that were hard to navigate, the Atlantic and the Pacific, and that created the idea of an isolationist Western Hemisphere. And at that time, the three million people scattered from Maine to the southern boundary of Georgia were not in a position to become a loud voice in foreign affairs, anyway.
>
> The strongest countries at this point in history were France and England, of course, and they were at each other's throat much of the time. . . . Washington, therefore, was trying to reach a balance between those two countries so as to protect the new government of the United States, and he thought that the less they meddled in the foreign affairs of Europe—that's all they looked at then, the foreign affairs of Europe—the better off we'd be.
>
> But that was then, and this is now.

Truman sarcastically described the Farewell as a "biblical text" for isolationists. But the president who believed that "the only thing new in the world is the history you don't know" was clear-eyed about his own departures from the dictum when he announced the Marshall Plan: "I was convinced that the policy I was about to proclaim was indeed as much required by the conditions of my day as was Washington's by the situation in his era and Monroe's doctrine by the circumstances which he then faced."

World events undercut the moral clarity of Washington's Farewell on foreign affairs, but the speech remained a core part of public school curriculums through the 1950s. FDR's rebuke of Washington's two-term precedent was corrected in 1951, when the Twenty-Second Amendment passed, forbidding any future president from serving more than Washington's traditional two terms.

Ike's Inspiration

★

One of the boys who grew up idolizing George Washington was a football-playing army enthusiast from Abilene, Kansas, named Dwight David Eisenhower.

"Washington was my hero," Ike recalled in his post-presidential memoir *At Ease*. "The qualities that excited my admiration were Washington's stamina and patience in adversity, first, and then his indomitable courage, daring, and capacity for self-sacrifice. The beauty of his character always inspired me. While the cherry tree story may be pure legend, his Farewell Address, his counsels to his countrymen on the occasions such as his speech at Newburgh to the rebellious officers of his Army, exemplified the human qualities I frankly idolized."

After securing a spot at West Point, the future commander in chief served a stint as chief of staff and chief speechwriter to General Douglas MacArthur in the Philippines before the Second World War—becoming perhaps the most distinguished ghostwriter since Madison and Hamilton. For all Ike's reputation for meandering malapropisms in presidential press conferences, he was a clear writer and decisive editor. "You know that General MacArthur got quite a reputation as a silver-tongued speaker when he was in the Philippines," Ike later boasted. "Who do you think wrote his speeches? I did."

Ike's identification with Washington only increased once he achieved the presidency. When an admiring former vice president, Henry Wallace, wrote Ike a note comparing him to Washington as a soldier-turned-statesman, Eisenhower expounded on the metaphor in a letter, dismissing "those who so glibly deprecate [Washington's] intellectual qualities. I think that too many jump at such conclusions merely because they tend to confuse facility of expression with wisdom; a love of the limelight with depth of perception."

This was a not-so-hidden form of projection: "I've often felt the deep wish that The Good Lord had endowed me with [Washington's] clarity of vision in big things, his strength of purpose and his genuine greatness of mind and spirit."

Eisenhower also identified with Washington as an independent-minded president, and even considered running for reelection as an independent because he was so exasperated by conservatives' constant attacks on the first Republican administration in twenty years. "I have no patience with the extreme rightists who call everyone who disagrees with them a Communist, nor with the leftists who shout that the rest of us are all heartless money-grubbers," he wrote. "The middle of the road is all of the usable surface," Ike believed. "The extremes, left and right, are in the gutters."

Ike's identification with Washington was complicated by the fact that he presided over the creation of the North Atlantic Treaty Organization, NATO, perhaps the ultimate expression of entangling alliances by design.

He was not alone in debating whether the new alliance violated first principles. At the inception of NATO, the ghost of Washington hung over the proceedings. "I don't care whether entangling alliances have been considered worse than original sin since George Washington's time," declared State Department director of European affairs John Hickerson in 1948. "We've got to negotiate a military alliance with Western Europe in peacetime and we've got to do it quickly."

Senator Margaret Chase Smith—the first woman elected to the Senate in her own right, as a Republican from Maine—wrote after reading the Farewell Address to her colleagues on Washington's Birthday in 1949: "As I read this, I wondered what our first President would think if he were about today.

Would he condemn a proposed North Atlantic Pact as an entangling alliance? The objective is the same today—freedom. The only difference is the way to obtain that freedom."

When the end of Eisenhower's two terms were in sight, he took one last inspiration from his boyhood hero. In May 1959, he pulled aside his chief speechwriter, Malcolm Moos, and said, "I want to say something when I leave here." He envisioned a ten-minute Farewell Address to the American people. Moos recalled, "I think the statement was prompted by a book . . . that Alexander Hamilton drafted Washington's Farewell Address."

This spark of insight was relit by White House speechwriter Frederic Fox in a memo to Moos, dated April 5, 1960:

> As the time for the president's retirement draws near, I recommend your re-reading the "Farewell Address" of George Washington. It is a beautifully wise and modest piece by a faithful public servant who loved his country.
>
> I was struck by its relevance to our day: the call for Constitutional obedience; the warnings about sectionalism; the dangers of "overgrown military establishments" but the necessity of maintaining a "respectable defensive posture"; the realistic attitude towards "that love of power and proneness to abuse it which predominate in the human heart"; the unhappy tendency of mankind "to seek security and repose in the absolute power of an individual"; the necessity for an enlightened public opinion; the ungenerous habit of one generation to spend beyond its means and to throw "upon posterity the burden which we ourselves ought to bear"; the broad diplomatic advice. And much more.

Eisenhower's Farewell Address offered a defiant coda to his presidency on his own terms, highlighting his own political ambitions to serve above the partisan fray while uniting the nation, speaking to the American people directly, rather than through the filter of an address to Congress. But what he most borrowed from Washington was the frame of the Farewell as a warning to future generations.

Ike's Farewell went through twenty-nine drafts. The president worked especially hard rewriting the opening paragraphs, asking his brother Milton, the president of Johns Hopkins University, to take an active role in editing.

Eisenhower wanted to warn his fellow Americans about the growing strength of what he first called "the military-industrial-congressional complex," defining a new trend in American government. Ike ultimately decided to drop "congressional" from the troika, out of concern that it would polarize his message and limit its influence. But the outgoing president identified the emerging issues of our era long before the advent of the Internet or the time when the number of Washington lobbyists would outnumber members of Congress.

"We must guard against the acquisition of unwarranted influence, whether sought or unsought, by the military-industrial complex," Ike said from the Oval Office on the night of January 17, his light gray suit flickering on the black-and-white TV sets of the time. "The potential for the disastrous rise of misplaced power exists and will persist. We must never let the weight of this combination endanger our liberties or democratic processes."

Eisenhower's Farewell Address echoed Washington's onetime warning against "those overgrown military establishments which, under any form of government, are inauspicious to liberty, and which are to be regarded as particularly hostile to republican liberty." The fact that two of our most famous generals-turned-presidents took time to warn about the military establishment's instinct to increase its power is a sobering commentary on the culture they knew so well. They were in unique positions to offer an honest critique: no serious politician could credibly accuse Washington or Eisenhower of being weak on national defense.

Ultimately, the overarching prescription from President Eisenhower was similar to what Washington had counseled as the ultimate check and balance: vigorous citizenship.

In a democracy, political father figures are never the last source of responsibility. "Only an alert and knowledgeable citizenry," Ike advised, "can compel the proper meshing of the huge industrial and military machinery of defense with our peaceful methods and goals, so that security and liberty may prosper together."

Ike's advancement of the Farewell Address gave it renewed relevance in an atomic age. The true message of the Farewell Address endured. This was a document directed not at a narrow interpretation of foreign affairs but a wide survey of the strengths and weaknesses that come with democracy.

Eisenhower also sounded the clarion call for generational responsibility: "As we peer into society's future, we—you and I, and our government—must avoid the impulse to live only for today, plundering for our own ease and convenience, the precious resources of tomorrow. We cannot mortgage the material assets of our grandchildren without asking the loss also of their political and spiritual heritage. We want democracy to survive for all generations to come."

More than a century and a half later, Washington's Farewell Address was still inspiring successors to follow its precedent—a presidential warning to future generations about the forces poised to derail our democratic republic.

The Farewell Echoes On

★

When John F. Kennedy took the oath of office three days after Ike's farewell address, the young president called for global engagement. His inaugural reenergized a nation with a bipartisan commitment to winning the Cold War, but it was also a full-throated rejection of Washington's limits on global ambition, one that some liberals would come to regret by the end of the decade.

Throughout the 1960 campaign, the dashing forty-three-year-old Kennedy often invoked the founding fathers as a way of dismissing concerns about his youth. After all, Kennedy pointed out, Thomas Jefferson was only thirty-three when he wrote the Declaration and the average age of the men at the Constitutional Convention was forty-two. JFK was not as fond of name-checking George Washington. As president, he quoted the Farewell Address only once—at an obscure African Freedom Day reception on April 15, 1961, in the drawing room of the State Department.

Speaking to the assembled ambassadors of postcolonial countries, Kennedy said, "All of you who are citizens of countries who have newly emerged to freedom, can find some inspiration in the Farewell Address of George Washington." Calling the Farewell a text "alive with the spirit of liberty," Kennedy ran through its central tenets. Washington, the president noted, "told our forefathers to reject permanent, inveterate antipathies against particular nations and passionate attachments for others, and said any nation failing in this is to some degree a slave. He warned against foreign influences which seek to tamper with domestic factions, who practice the arts of seduction, to mislead public opinion. His rule for commercial relations was to have with them as little political connection as possible."

Kennedy's invocation of the Farewell as applicable to any new nation was a novel extension of its advice. But like any great text, different facets of applicable wisdom emerge when it is viewed from different perspectives. When Lyndon Johnson assumed the presidency after Kennedy's assassination, he embraced Washington's Farewell as a unifying text in a time of domestic division.

At the height of the 1964 presidential campaign, with GOP nominee Barry Goldwater opposing the Civil Rights Act and declaring that "extremism in defense of liberty is no vice," Johnson cited the Farewell at a Democratic Party dinner in Pennsylvania.

"The one division our forefathers most feared, the division that they warned us against, was the division of extreme factionalism," Johnson drawled. "Jefferson warned against it, Hamilton and Madison warned against it. In his Farewell Address, the first President, George Washington, warned against allowing parties to become 'Northern and Southern, Atlantic and Western.' He told us to beware of that kind of partisanship which, in his words, 'agitates the community with ill-founded jealousies and false alarms . . . kindles the animosity of one party against the other . . . foments occasionally riot and insurrection.' "

Johnson liked to describe himself as a free man, an American, a public servant and a Democrat—in that order. He had served as Senate majority leader, alternately battling and working with President Eisenhower and congressional Republicans to pass legislation. He was earthy and expansive, could be rude and ruthless, and he loved the game of politics.

At a 1967 dinner honoring his sometime Republican ally Illinois senator Everett Dirksen, with whom he worked to pass landmark civil rights and voting rights legislation, Johnson again reached to the Farewell Address's warning to fight factions. "I think all Americans should appreciate the problems of the leader of the opposition—as well as the temptations. I know because I have been there," Johnson said.

> The problem is to stand firmly with the administration on a foundation of common idealism, while dissenting from those measures that do not fulfill these ideals. In other words, the first allegiance of any American is to our heritage—to its protection—to its preservation and to its enlargement. As George Washington put it in his Farewell Address: "The name American, which belongs to you in your national capacity, must always exult the just pride of patriotism . . . with slight shades of difference, you have the same religion, manners, habits, and political principles. . . . The independence and liberty you have possessed are the work of joint counsels and joint efforts; of common dangers, sufferings, and successes.

As Johnson escalated the war in Vietnam while attempting to build "the Great Society" at home, Washington's warnings against foreign wars and excessive spending were not easily accessible for his advocacy. But the proud graduate of Southwest Texas State Teachers' College found special kinship with the Farewell's commitment to public education.

Speaking at the dedication of the Smithsonian Institution's Museum of History and Technology, Johnson reminded the audience that "[i]t was also Washington who said, in his Farewell Address: 'promote, then, as an object of primary importance, institutions for the general diffusion of knowledge. In proportion as the structure of a government gives force to public opinion it should be enlightened.' " It was the first time in decades that a president cited the Farewell's comments on public education. Another insight had been rediscovered.

Johnson's vast liberal domestic ambitions were undercut by Vietnam. Members of a generation that had been born and raised in American suburbs found themselves being drafted to fight and possibly die in a jungle war driven by distant geopolitical considerations.

The protestors, driven by a combination of youthful idealism and understandable self-interest, took to the streets to oppose the war. The cries of protest only increased as Johnson's successor, Richard Nixon, revealed that his campaign's "secret plan to end the war" involved initial escalation.

While some protestors romanticized communist revolutionaries from Che Guevara to Ho Chi Minh, the more thoughtful among them reached back to the tradition of Washington's Farewell to make the case that their antiwar position was not anti-American or isolationist, as Nixon & Company often contended, but in fact offered a more direct connection to the wisdom of the founding fathers.

The Farewell could cut through the culture-war politics of the time, the mutual suspicions and reactive resentments, to return the debate to first principles. For an antiwar movement often tarred as unpatriotic, appealing to Washington was a subversive and substantive move.

"What is most important about Washington's testamentary address to his country is not its supposed isolationism, but its antiwar sentiment warning against militarism," argued Garry Wills in his 1969 book, *Nixon Agonistes*.

The principal burden of Washington's valedictory address is not that America should remain isolated, but that it should avoid war. His moral opposition to warfare has been blunted by those who read, and then dismiss, the Address as an attempt to forestall dealings of any sort with other nations. The Address expressly rejects that impossible ideal. . . . What Washington objected to was the establishment of rigid blocs, forever at enmity, the situation of "cold war": "Nothing is more essential than that permanent antipathies against particular nations [*read, today: Russia?*] and passionate attachments to others [*read, perhaps: South Vietnam?*]

should be excluded." The plight of America, at the mercy of either Saigon or Hanoi, or of both at the same time, is a perfect example of this situation. . . . Naturally, Washington knew that an illusion of selfless devotion could sway nations—he had experienced the pressures of those who would join France's crusade in Europe for liberté, fraternité, égalité. But he deplored such interests, which run counter to the sober estimate of national interest, set up conflicting standards, and make for erratic policy, for diplomatic instability. He predicted the outcome of such idealistic belligerence. His words could be directly applied to our involvement in Vietnam.

For a rising generation, the Vietnam quagmire was a vindication of the founders' wisdom. In the endless debate of history, the arguments proved hard to refute. The excesses of the antiwar movement—domestic bombings by the Weather Underground, reports of spitting on returning soldiers—undercut its moral authority. But nonetheless, the protestors began to win the argument, as Congress began to question both the wisdom and winnability of the war. Nixon ended the draft and drew down American forces, as the burden shifted to the South Vietnamese, who were eventually overrun. This scarring episode—which cost some 58,000 American lives—served as a cautionary tale about the dangers of ignoring Washington's advice.

Nixon's insistence that his conservative cadre represented all that was upright and decent in contemporary American culture took a considerable hit when he resigned after a break-in at the Democratic National Committee headquarters at Washington's Watergate hotel and office complex and a subsequent cover-up was connected to his White House.

In the wake of Watergate and Vietnam, trust in government was broken for many in the baby boom generation. As culture wars between the crew-cuts and long-hairs escalated, Republicans tried to reconstitute their party's appeal with faith-based political outreach and religious themes. And with that, a new angle to the Farewell Address was rediscovered.

President Gerald Ford had the unenviable task of cleaning up after

Nixon, and as evangelicals began to flex their political and cultural muscle, the unelected president quoted the Address in a speech to the National Religious Broadcasters' congressional breakfast.

"The electronic era of communications, which is only beginning—as the age of the book was only beginning when Gutenberg printed his Bible—holds unlimited opportunities for those today who tell and re-tell the good news of God's love for man," Ford declared. Quoting the Farewell, he added that "of all the dispositions and habits which lead to political prosperity religion and morality are indispensable supports. . . . Reason and experience both forbid us to expect that national morality can prevail in the exclusion of religious principle."

Ford pointed out to his evangelical audience, "President Washington urged all 'mere politicians' to respect and cherish the principles of religion and morality. It has been my experience in the Congress over the 25 years that most of us 'mere politicians' really do." Speaking six months after Nixon's resignation, the statement must have stained credulity even amid that devout audience.

The real political star of the religious right was Ronald Reagan, who was elected in 1980, four years after he challenged Ford for the Republican nomination.

Reagan was especially fond of quoting Thomas Paine's admonition that "we have it in our power to begin the world anew"—though he would have detested Paine's militant atheism. His appropriation of the Farewell Address was another example of cherry-picking sentiments and grafting them onto his political philosophy.

Reagan quoted the Farewell Address's warning on religion frequently, often when arguing for a constitutional amendment to allow prayer in schools. But Reagan's most eloquent invocation of the Farewell came during his speech at Moscow State University in 1988.

It was a moment loaded with high drama: the conservative cold warrior speaking to students in the heart of the Soviet Union about his hopes for lasting peace amid the reforms of perestroika and a thawing Cold War, even as America and Russia kept nuclear weapons trained on each other's cities.

"Freedom, it has been said, makes people selfish and materialistic, but Americans are one of the most religious peoples on Earth," Reagan said.

Because they know that liberty, just as life itself, is not earned but a gift from God, they seek to share that gift with the world. "Reason and experience," said George Washington in his Farewell Address, "both forbid us to expect that national morality can prevail in exclusion of religious principle. And it is substantially true, that virtue or morality is a necessary spring of popular government." Democracy is less a system of government than it is a system to keep government limited, un-intrusive; a system of constraints on power to keep politics and government secondary to the important things in life, the true sources of value found only in family and faith.

The actor-turned-statesman then went on to quote Dostoyevsky and *Doctor Zhivago,* as well as to recount a scene from the movie *Butch Cassidy and the Sundance Kid.* For Republicans spreading the gospel of freedom to an officially atheist state, Washington's counsel about the role of faith and morality in a democracy took on new relevance.

As the Berlin Wall fell and millions were liberated from communist oppression, America's example of liberal capitalist democracy seemed globally ascendant.

President Bill Clinton, a baby boom opponent of the Vietnam War turned political thoroughbred southern governor, presided over a decade of prosperity with centrist policies, driven by a tech explosion and punctuated by self-inflicted scandals. Clinton kept a copy of the Farewell Address in his private study off the Oval Office, and he invoked its wisdom at the end of his second term.

"In George Washington's first draft of his Farewell Address he wrote, 'We may all be considered as the children of one common country,' "

Clinton said at a conference on African development in 2000. "The more I think about globalization and the interdependence it promises and demands, the more I share that sentiment. Now we must think of ourselves as children of one common world. If we wish to deepen peace and prosperity and democracy for ourselves, we must wish it also for the people of Africa."

Clinton went beyond JFK to make the promises of the Farewell Address universal. And in the final weeks of his administration, his speechwriter Jeff Shesol turned to Washington's Farewell as a model for Clinton's last presidential speech.

When it came time to draft the final speech, "The first thing I sat down and read was Washington's Farewell," Shesol explained. "Then I read Eisenhower's farewell. Then I went back into the Clinton canon to see what I could draw from his own early speeches, his inaugural and his campaign speeches, to sort of close the circle for him, but I wanted to have the context of what the twin peaks of presidential farewells had done."

As his White House colleagues packed boxes, Shesol reflected on the tradition of outgoing presidents offering a word of warning to their fellow citizens. "We were concerned obviously about the direction of the country under the incoming president," he said, particularly on two fronts that had concerned George Washington as well: fiscal discipline and foreign affairs. "We had invested so much political and intellectual and rhetorical capital in making the case for fiscal responsibility and of course had built a surplus that with all the talk of massive tax cuts during the campaign it was quite clear that was going to be one of the first priorities of the Bush Administration." In addition, Shesol recounted, "we felt that there was an isolationist push in the Republican Party. It was not coming from George W. Bush, but there were other parts of the party that were pushing back against what they saw as an overly interventionist foreign policy on our part"— referring back to congressional Republican resistance to Bosnian intervention and fights over paying United Nations dues—"and they were looking to sort of withdraw, or withdraw support, from multilateral institutions.

And so to address that concern, I kind of picked up the line about entangling alliances from Washington/Jefferson to address that question and deliver their sort of warning as well."

The draft sent to President Clinton's desk specifically referenced Washington's warnings: "There's a long-standing tradition that a president's farewell address should contain a word of warning to future generations. It's a tradition worth keeping. I'm more confident than ever that America's best days lie ahead but I'm also convinced that our decisions today will shape our tomorrows. I want to say simply that America's security and prosperity depend, above all else, on our willingness to lead the world."

The draft sat untouched on the president's desk for days. Clinton canceled multiple speech prep meetings, for the first time Shesol could recall. "He was basically pulling all-nighters. He was exhausted. He was trying to get every last thing done and I thought that he did not want to confront his political mortality by focusing on his final speech."

On the afternoon of the Farewell Address, with network television time booked, Clinton dug into the speech from the private residence, making a flurry of edits that he finalized in a speech prep meeting in the Cabinet Room two hours before he was to give the address. "A word of warning to future generations" was turned into a softer set of "thoughts about the future." A line about "entangling alliances"—accurately attributed to Jefferson's first inaugural—remained, tempered by the caution that, "[i]n our times, America cannot and must not disentangle itself from the world. If we want the world to embody our shared values, then we must assume a shared responsibility."

"A lot of what I felt was the kind of poetry of it and the symmetry of it fell out, but such is the lot of a speechwriter," says Shesol. But the process illustrated that the influence of Washington's Farewell Address endures from the eighteenth century to the twenty-first. "These speeches are so often a dialogue among presidents across the generations. Inaugural addresses are very much like that. Farewells can be too."

★

DIALOGUES ACROSS THE GENERATIONS ARE, of course, for citizens as well as presidents. The Farewell continues to be read each year on Washington's Birthday in the Senate, and senators still write personal notes in the back of the leather-bound volume that holds the text, sometimes highlighting messages of fiscal discipline but often focusing on the fight against factions in an era of increasing hyper-partisanship.

The Farewell Address found a new popular audience in 2015, when the hip-hop musical *Hamilton* arrived on Broadway to rapturous reviews and praises by the Obamas. According to playwright Lin-Manuel Miranda, who also starred in the title role, the biggest applause of the night usually comes for the song "One Last Time," which recounts the writing of Washington's Farewell Address and includes the text in its lyrics.

Miranda chose to put the Farewell to music because for him, the moment married "the personal and the political" for Hamilton and Washington as "the culmination of their careers together." In the song, Washington asks Hamilton to "Pick up a pen, start Writing / I wanna talk about what I've learned / The hard wisdom that I've earned." "We're going to teach them how to say goodbye," Washington tells Hamilton, explaining that "If I say goodbye, the nation learns to move on / It outlives me when I'm gone."

"It's the most audacious American act," explains Miranda. "Establishing our democracy by ensuring that there's a peaceful transition of the leadership. That's a huge deal—and that's the thing that the French Revolution doesn't get right."

The song bullets Washington's key points: "I want to talk about partisan fighting," "I want to talk about neutrality." But as Miranda explains, turning the Farewell into a song inspired a creative marriage between form and function: "The moment where we break into Washington's actual speech is a really nice arc, because I am writing prose that Washington is turning into song," Miranda explains. "I kind of continue delivering it as prose, while Washington elevates it. And that's a metaphor for the relationship between Hamilton and Washington: Hamilton was the idea guy and Washington elevated it by virtue of embodying it."

Among the sections of the speech Miranda put to music are unexpected excerpts from the final two paragraphs of the Address:

> Though, in reviewing the incidents of my administration, I am unconscious of intentional error, I am nevertheless too sensible of my defects not to think it probable that I may have committed many errors. . . . I shall also carry with me the hope that my country will never cease to view them with indulgence; and that, after forty five years of my life dedicated to its service with an upright zeal, the faults of incompetent abilities will be consigned to oblivion, as I myself must soon be to the mansions of rest. . . . I anticipate with pleasing expectation that retreat in which I promise myself to realize, without alloy, the sweet enjoyment of partaking, in the midst of my fellow-citizens, the benign influence of good laws under a free government, the ever-favorite object of my heart, and the happy reward, as I trust, of our mutual cares, labors, and dangers.

This doesn't read like typical Broadway lyrics. But Miranda explained why he found this closing portion of the Farewell so inspiring: "These guys did not get marble commandments from a mountaintop," he said. "Every single line in our founding documents is a result of humanity and thus it's flawed. And what Washington basically says, in the part we musicalized, is, 'I've probably fucked up a lot. I'm not aware of fucking up but I am human and so there are errors and they are mine. And I hope that you will forgive the errors and remember the stuff I tried to do.' And that's exactly in keeping with the theme of our show, which is: one, it's a miracle it happened; and two, every step of it was created by people who were flawed and human and made compromises and talked shit and made mistakes. That's the sand in the oyster. . . . We feel patriotic while knowing it's coming from a guy who does not have a guilt-free record.

This is a man who owned other people, who is singing beautifully and eloquently about freedom. And there's no shying away from that contradiction. We embrace the contradiction. . . . There is some kind of beautiful irony at work in the cosmos."

★

AT TIMES, WASHINGTON'S FAREWELL HAS been at the forefront of debates over foreign policy, at other times serving as a touchstone for domestic debates about religion, public education or the dangers of hyper-partisanship. For Lin-Manuel Miranda, it's a reminder of the flawed humanity of the founders, which removes them from their pedestal to make them relevant to a new generation that might only see slave owners.

Certainly that's the message sent to visitors at the site of Washington's executive mansion. During the Democrats' 2016 convention in Philadelphia, in which they nominated the first woman to succeed the first African-American president, tourists wearing Hillary Clinton and Bernie Sanders T-shirts wandered around the open-air brick outlines of the building's foundation, reading plastic-covered placards and watching videos dedicated exclusively to the story of slavery.

This overdue examination at the corner of the Liberty Mall offers some degree of poetic justice for those forgotten souls who toiled for the first president and his family. It is a sign of America's fitful progress that the original sin of slavery takes center stage on the ground where so much history took place.

But in the exhibits on this still-active archaeological excavation site, there is no mention of the Farewell Address. A document designed to be "importantly and lastingly useful" is considered literally unremarkable.

Washington might have taken it in stride. Toward the end of the Farewell, Washington tempered his hopes for the endurance of his advice:

I dare not hope they will make the strong and lasting impression I could wish; that they will control the usual current of the passions, or prevent our nation from running the course which has hitherto marked the destiny of nations. But, if I may even flatter myself that they may be productive of some partial benefit, some occasional good; that they may now and then recur to moderate the fury of party spirit, to warn against the mischiefs of foreign intrigue, to guard against the impostures of pretended patriotism; this hope will be a full recompense for the solicitude for your welfare, by which they have been dictated.

Washington could of course never "control the usual current of the passions," but his Farewell has proven more than "some partial benefit, some occasional good." From whatever perspective Washington's Farewell is seen, it retains the ability to offer insight.

During the twentieth century, much of the debate over the Farewell centered on foreign affairs, trying to divine which first principles could apply to a growing power in a shrinking world. In the nineteenth century, during the decades surrounding the Civil War, Washington's warning against domestic forces of disunion and faction rose to prominence. His prescience could not stop the bloodshed, but it did help the nation heal in the aftermath.

The twenty-first century's symbolic start with the fiery destruction of the World Trade Center hammered home that isolation from the wider world was no longer an option. But even still, we strive to seek the wise balance between self-interested independence and global engagement, liberty and security.

Many of Washington's warnings have taken on new urgency. The dysfunctional polarization of government can open the door to demagogues in a democracy. As Washington cautioned, "The disorders and miseries which result gradually incline the minds of men to seek security and repose in the absolute power of an individual . . . on the ruins of public liberty." Likewise, we see new cyberspace manifestations of foreign attempts to influence our elections and government. These are new variations on an old game—which, as Washington warned, aim to "mislead public opinion, to influence or awe the public councils"—but the stakes remain the same.

On January 10, 2017, President Barack Obama carried forward the tradition begun by George Washington in his Farewell Address, warning his fellow citizens about threats to our democracy. In front of an adoring crowd of thousands that packed Chicago's McCormick Place convention center, Obama quoted the first farewell to a new generation:

In his own farewell address, George Washington wrote that self-government is the underpinning of our safety, prosperity, and liberty, but "from different causes and from different quarters much pains will be taken . . . to weaken in your minds the conviction of this truth"; that we should preserve it with "jealous anxiety"; that we should reject "the first dawning of every attempt to alienate any portion of our country from the rest or to enfeeble the sacred ties" that make us one.

We weaken those ties when we allow our political dialogue to become so corrosive that people of good character are turned off from public service; so coarse with rancor that Americans with whom we disagree are not just misguided, but somehow malevolent. We weaken those ties when we define some of us as more American than others; when we write off the whole system as inevitably corrupt, and blame the leaders we elect without examining our own role in electing them.

It falls to each of us to be those anxious, jealous guardians of our democracy; to embrace the joyous task we've been given to continually try to improve this great nation of ours. Because for all our outward differences, we all share the same proud title: Citizen.

Over many drafts of the speech President Obama wrote with his chief speechwriter, Cody Keenan, Washington's words remained.

"It was in his consciousness, especially given the Washington Farewell's focus about warning against hyperpartisanship and the importance of national unity," Keenan later explained.

> Of course, it galled him to have to sit there with Trump in the Oval Office and to have to be polite to a guy that had spent years trolling in Birtherism and tearing down democratic norms and institutions. But he reveres the office, and if there is one democratic norm that Barack Obama had complete control over preserving, it was the peaceful transfer of power . . . The reason we used that Washington line was because a lot of times we all fall prey to this: we just accept people trying to divide us and tear us apart and convince us that one aspect of American society is inevitably corrupt or not to be trusted. And it is entirely up to us to believe that or not.

Across the span of two and a half centuries, our country's slave-owning first president and his African-American successor found common ground and continuity of purpose. Confronting the dangers of division to democracy, both Washington and Obama understood this transcendent truth: our independence as a nation is inseparable from our interdependence as a people.

The challenges we face are serious but small compared to those faced by Washington and the revolutionary generation when America was fragile and unformed. Following the counsels of the Farewell Address, adjusted to the realities of our time, might still "prevent our nation from running the course which has hitherto marked the destiny of nations."

Conclusion

★

For more than a century, Washington's Farewell Address guided American leaders and drove civic debates, called upon at pivotal moments to provide a standard to which the wise and honest could repair. Its endurance was a minor miracle, spanning the time when horse and carriage gave way to steamship and railway, the car and the airplane. Then it suddenly seemed to be on the wrong side of history.

But while the Farewell Address has faded from the frontal lobe of American politics, its durable wisdom is starkly relevant and due for resurgence. It is the foundational American policy document, containing broad prescriptions that have proven their worth outside the context in which they were created. Now its advice resonates with renewed urgency. Look at America's challenges in the early decades of the twenty-first century: Hyper-partisanship? Check. Excessive debt? Check. Endless entanglements and foreign wars? Check and check.

The Farewell Address is that rarest of things: a memo from our first founding father to future generations about the forces he feared could destroy our democratic republic. But Washington was too much a man of action to simply reflect on problems. He steered us toward solutions, offering renewable sources of strength he felt could save us from descending on history's path of failed republics. Washington understood that applying enduring principles to changing times, balancing realism with idealism, is how imperfect people can form a more perfect union.

The fact that so much energy was spent during the twentieth century debating whether Washington was endorsing isolationism missed the Farewell's larger point: Washington's goal was always to give the United States enough time to strengthen so that we could stand upright on the world stage as an independent nation. He never intended his advice to be a straitjacket that constrained his successors from recognizing changing realities. Principles provide guidance, not rigid requirements.

Each generation can find meaning in the Farewell Address according to the struggles they face. Amid these ebbs and flows of specific applicability, Washington's warnings against hyper-partisanship have particular urgency in our era.

Our two political parties have become polarized along ideological and geographic lines, as Washington feared, breaking down faith in the effectiveness of our government and turning fellow citizens against those who "ought to be bound together by fraternal affection."

Washington was an independent president, but he did not think that political parties were inherently destructive. Instead, he believed that because there was "constant danger of excess" from factions, "the effort ought to be by force of public opinion, to mitigate and assuage it. A fire not to be quenched, it demands a uniform vigilance to prevent its bursting into a flame, lest, instead of warming, it should consume." Vigilant citizens are required to keep parties focused on serving the people rather than the unprincipled pursuit of power that divides in order to conquer.

There are some who look at the bitter partisan fights between the Founding Fathers and see only that politics has always been dirty. They cite the worst moments of the early republic as a way of rationalizing whatever hyper-partisan activity they want to excuse from their side of the aisle. But they ignore the larger lesson: while dissent is necessary to democracy, we dishonor ourselves when we degenerate into vicious, self-interested factions. Jefferson's surreptitious funding of the venomous *National Gazette*, Madison's topsy-turvy relationship with the national interest, Hamilton's enthusiasm for office politics and Washington's own frustrations that spilled out in thin-skinned drafts of the Farewell Address—all these were deviations from their best selves. They are cautionary tales.

Jefferson, Madison and their Democratic-Republican inheritors switched many of their positions once they achieved the presidency. Their reflexive opposition often reflected anxieties and resentments. When they achieved power, with the responsibility to uphold the Constitution and unite the nation, they advocated many policies they once attacked. Washington won the debate from beyond the grave.

Seen with a sense of perspective, the fights that forged the Farewell Address show that the deeper divisions in American politics have been remarkably consistent throughout the centuries, though they parade under different partisan banners at different times. The dividing lines were evident at the debate over ratifying the Constitution and the early days of the republic, pitting largely urban advocates of national unity and a stronger central government against rural populists who passionately defended states' rights as a proxy for protecting their way of life against forces of economic and cultural change. Both sides believed they were fighting for freedom. With his Farewell Address, Washington sought to heal those divides by helping his fellow citizens see that their interdependence was essential to their independence, urging a wise balance between the extremes.

In our polarized times, it's common to hear moderation dismissed as a weak, split-the-difference position rather than a decisive middle path, the basis for principled compromise. That's why it's essential to remember that for Washington, moderation was a virtue: a position of strength confirmed by centuries of classical wisdom. In his Farewell, Washington warned against being unwisely off-center in politics, finance and foreign policy, risking the real liberty that comes from self-sufficiency.

It's time to resurrect this tradition. Armed with a sense of perspective, we can take some comfort that our domestic divisions too shall pass. As the influential columnist Walter Lippmann once cracked: "to be partisan today as between Jefferson and Hamilton is like arguing whether men or women are more necessary to the procreation of the race."

Republicans and Democrats have cited the Farewell in recent debates over the dangers of party polarization, debt reduction and foreign wars. They have found common ground in Washington's vision of faith, virtue and education.

Washington's warning about how demagogues have historically exploited divided, dysfunctional democracies—"The disorders and miseries which result gradually incline the minds of men to seek security and repose in the absolute power of an individual"—has proven darkly prescient as well. "Sooner or later the chief of some prevailing faction, more able or more fortunate than his competitors, turns this disposition to the purposes of his own elevation, on the ruins of public liberty," he wrote. At a time when liberal democracies are being challenged by authoritarian alternatives led by self-styled strongmen around the world, Washington's Farewell offers an urgent reminder of democratic republics' Achilles' heel throughout history. Against this broad backdrop, the value of Washington's enduring wisdom is again revealed.

The good news is that a new generation is just starting to discover Washington's Farewell for themselves. On Election Night, 2012, *The Daily Show with Jon Stewart* invoked the Farewell Address's warning against factions via a pint-size hologram George Washington, who slammed the rise of hyper-partisanship as "nothing but a recipe for petty politicking at best and national discord at worst." Even Hamilton's reputation has seen an overdue resurgence courtesy of a celebrated biography that inspired the Tony Award–winning hip-hop musical, which salutes the Farewell in song.

What had faded into obscurity is now creeping back into the national conversation in new formulations, offering a chance to make the old stories new again. The Farewell is returning from the possession of a rarefied debating society of academics and politicians and back into the hands of the people, to whom it was always addressed.

Now a new generation of Washingtonians is needed, following the philosophy of political independence expressed in the Farewell Address: a strong and inclusive government, guided by the governing principle of moderation, balancing individual liberty with a sense of generational responsibility, rejecting overextension and separatism from whatever the source. This is a time to reflect on first principles and project them forward, affirming the idea that there is always more that unites us than divides us as Americans.

The Farewell Address still can inspire reflection and some needed course correction, providing a useful lens for assessing our own decisions as we face the future. The United States is not immune from the larger lessons of history. Washington understood that there are life cycles for nations rooted in human nature, and like the Founding Fathers, we should study the mistakes that toppled empires and republics before us.

History is a story we learn, add our own chapter, and then pass to the next generation. Rediscovering Washington's Farewell can once again re-center our nation, inspiring a new generation to find common ground and common purpose. It is now our story to carry forward, as friends and fellow citizens.

APPENDIX
Washington's Farewell Address

Friends and Fellow Citizens:

The period for a new election of a citizen to administer the executive government of the United States being not far distant, and the time actually arrived when your thoughts must be employed in designating the person who is to be clothed with that important trust, it appears to me proper, especially as it may conduce to a more distinct expression of the public voice, that I should now apprise you of the resolution I have formed, to decline being considered among the number of those out of whom a choice is to be made.

I beg you, at the same time, to do me the justice to be assured that this resolution has not been taken without a strict regard to all the considerations appertaining to the relation which binds a dutiful citizen to his country; and that in withdrawing the tender of service, which silence in my situation might imply, I am influenced by no diminution of zeal for your future interest, no deficiency of grateful respect for your past kindness, but am supported by a full conviction that the step is compatible with both.

The acceptance of, and continuance hitherto in, the office to which your suffrages have twice called me have been a uniform sacrifice of inclination to the opinion of duty and to a deference for what appeared to be your desire. I constantly hoped that it would have been much earlier in my power, consistently with motives which I was not at liberty to disregard, to return to that retirement from which I had been reluctantly drawn. The strength of my inclination to do this, previous to the last election, had even led to the preparation of an address to declare it to you; but mature reflection on the then perplexed and critical posture of our affairs with foreign nations, and the unanimous advice of persons entitled to my confidence, impelled me to abandon the idea.

I rejoice that the state of your concerns, external as well as internal, no longer renders the pursuit of inclination incompatible with the sentiment of duty or propriety, and am persuaded, whatever partiality may be retained for my services, that, in the present circumstances of our country, you will not disapprove my determination to retire.

The impressions with which I first undertook the arduous trust were explained on the proper occasion. In the discharge of this trust, I will only say that I have, with good intentions, contributed towards the organization and administration of the government the best exertions of which a very fallible judgment was capable. Not unconscious in the outset of the inferiority of my qualifications, experience in my own eyes, perhaps still more in the eyes of others, has strengthened the motives to diffidence of myself; and every day the increasing weight of years admonishes me more and more that the shade of retirement is as necessary to me as it will be welcome. Satisfied that if any circumstances have given peculiar value to my services, they were temporary, I have the consolation to believe that, while choice and prudence invite me to quit the political scene, patriotism does not forbid it.

In looking forward to the moment which is intended to terminate the career of my public life, my feelings do not permit me to suspend the deep acknowledgment of that debt of gratitude which I owe to my beloved country for the many honors it has conferred upon me; still more for the steadfast confidence with which it has supported me; and for the opportunities I have thence enjoyed of manifesting my inviolable attachment, by services faithful and persevering, though in usefulness unequal to my zeal. If benefits have resulted to our country from these services, let it always be remembered to your praise, and as an instructive example in our annals, that under circumstances in which the passions, agitated in every direction, were liable to mislead, amidst appearances sometimes dubious, vicissitudes of fortune often discouraging, in situations in which not unfrequently want of success has countenanced the spirit of criticism, the constancy of your support was the essential prop of the efforts, and a guarantee of the plans by which they were effected. Profoundly penetrated with this idea, I shall carry it with me to my grave, as a strong incitement to unceasing vows that heaven may continue to you the choicest tokens of its beneficence; that your union and brotherly affection may be perpetual; that the free Constitution, which is the work of your hands, may be sacredly maintained; that its administration in every department may be stamped with wisdom and virtue; that, in fine, the happiness of the people of these States, under the auspices of liberty, may be made complete by so careful a preservation and so prudent a use of this blessing as will acquire to them the glory of recommending it to the applause, the affection, and adoption of every nation which is yet a stranger to it.

Here, perhaps, I ought to stop. But a solicitude for your welfare, which cannot end but with my life, and the apprehension of danger, natural to that solicitude, urge me, on an occasion like the present, to offer to your solemn contemplation, and to recommend to your frequent review, some sentiments which are the result of much reflection, of no inconsiderable observation, and which appear to me all-important to the permanency of your felicity as a people. These will be offered to you with the more freedom, as you can only see in them the disinterested warnings of a parting friend, who can possibly have no personal motive to bias his counsel. Nor can I forget, as an encouragement to it, your indulgent reception of my sentiments on a former and not dissimilar occasion.

Interwoven as is the love of liberty with every ligament of your hearts, no recommendation of mine is necessary to fortify or confirm the attachment.

The unity of government which constitutes you one people is also now dear to you. It is justly so, for it is a main pillar in the edifice of your real independence, the support of your tranquility at home, your peace abroad; of your safety; of your prosperity; of that very liberty which you so highly prize. But as it is easy to foresee that, from different causes and from different quarters, much pains will be taken, many artifices employed to weaken in your minds the conviction of this truth; as this is the point in your political fortress against which the batteries of internal and external enemies will be most constantly and actively (though often covertly and insidiously) directed, it is of infinite moment that you should properly estimate the immense value of your national union to your collective and individual happiness; that you should cherish a cordial, habitual, and immovable attachment to it; accustoming yourselves to think and speak of it as of the palladium of your political safety and prosperity; watching for its preservation with jealous anxiety; discountenancing whatever may suggest even a suspicion that it can in any event be abandoned; and indignantly frowning upon the first dawning of every attempt to alienate any portion of our country from the rest, or to enfeeble the sacred ties which now link together the various parts.

For this you have every inducement of sympathy and interest. Citizens, by birth or choice, of a common country, that country has a right to concentrate your affections. The name of American, which belongs to you in your national capacity, must always exalt the just pride of patriotism more than any appellation derived from local discriminations. With slight shades of difference, you have the same religion, manners, habits, and political principles. You have in a common cause fought and triumphed together; the independence and liberty you possess are the work of joint counsels, and joint efforts of common dangers, sufferings, and successes.

But these considerations, however powerfully they address themselves to your sensibility, are greatly outweighed by those which apply more immediately to your interest. Here every portion of our country finds the most commanding motives for carefully guarding and preserving the union of the whole.

The North, in an unrestrained intercourse with the South, protected by the equal laws of a common government, finds in the productions of the latter great additional resources of maritime and commercial enterprise and precious materials of manufacturing industry. The South, in the same intercourse, benefiting by the agency of the North, sees its agriculture grow and its commerce expand. Turning partly into its own channels the seamen of the North, it finds its particular navigation invigorated; and, while it contributes, in different ways, to nourish and increase the general mass of the national navigation, it looks forward to the protection of a maritime strength, to which itself is unequally adapted. The East, in a like intercourse with the West, already finds, and in the progressive improvement of interior communications by land and water, will more and more find a valuable vent for the commodities which it brings from abroad, or manufactures at home. The West derives from the East supplies requisite to its growth and comfort, and, what is perhaps of still greater consequence, it must of necessity owe the secure enjoyment of indispensable outlets for its own productions to the weight, influence, and the future maritime strength of the Atlantic side of the Union, directed by an indissoluble community of interest as one nation. Any other tenure by which the West can hold this essential advantage, whether derived from its own separate strength, or from an apostate and unnatural connection with any foreign power, must be intrinsically precarious.

While, then, every part of our country thus feels an immediate and particular interest in union, all the parts combined cannot fail to find in the united mass of means and efforts greater strength, greater resource, proportionably greater security from external danger, a less frequent interruption of their peace by foreign nations; and, what is of inestimable value, they must derive from union an exemption from those broils and wars between themselves, which so frequently afflict neighboring countries not tied together by the same governments, which their own rival ships alone would be sufficient to produce, but which opposite foreign alliances, attachments, and intrigues would stimulate and embitter. Hence, likewise, they will avoid the necessity of those overgrown military establishments which, under any form of government, are inauspicious to liberty, and which are to be regarded as particularly hostile to republican liberty. In this sense it is that your union ought to be considered as a main prop of your liberty, and that the love of the one ought to endear to you the preservation of the other.

These considerations speak a persuasive language to every reflecting and virtuous mind, and exhibit the continuance of the Union as a primary object of patriotic desire. Is there a doubt whether a common government can embrace so large a sphere? Let experience solve it. To listen to mere speculation in such a case were criminal. We are authorized to hope that a proper organization of the whole with the auxiliary agency of governments for the respective subdivisions, will afford a happy issue to the experiment. It is well worth a fair and full experiment. With such powerful and obvious motives to union, affecting all parts of our country, while experience shall not have demonstrated its impracticability, there will always be reason to distrust the patriotism of those who in any quarter may endeavor to weaken its bands.

In contemplating the causes which may disturb our Union, it occurs as matter of serious concern that any ground should have been furnished for characterizing parties by geographical discriminations, Northern and Southern, Atlantic and Western; whence designing men may endeavor to excite a belief that there is a real difference of local interests and views. One of the expedients of party to acquire influence within particular districts is to misrepresent the opinions and aims of other districts. You cannot shield yourselves too much against the jealousies and heartburnings which spring from these misrepresentations; they tend to render alien to each other those who ought to be bound together by fraternal affection. The inhabitants of our Western country have lately had a useful lesson on this head; they have seen, in the negotiation by the Executive, and in the unanimous ratification by the Senate, of the treaty with Spain, and in the universal satisfaction at that event, throughout the United States, a decisive proof how unfounded were the suspicions propagated among them of a policy in the General Government and in the Atlantic States unfriendly to their interests in regard to the Mississippi; they have been witnesses to the formation of two treaties, that with Great Britain, and that with Spain, which secure to them everything they could desire, in respect to our foreign relations, towards confirming their prosperity. Will it not be their wisdom to rely for the preservation of these advantages on the Union by which they were procured ? Will they not henceforth be deaf to those advisers, if such there are, who would sever them from their brethren and connect them with aliens?

To the efficacy and permanency of your Union, a government for the whole is indispensable. No alliance, however strict, between the parts can be an adequate substitute; they must inevitably experience the infractions and interruptions which all alliances in all times have experienced. Sensible of this momentous truth, you have improved upon your first essay, by the adoption of a constitution of government better calculated than your former for an intimate union, and for the efficacious management of your common concerns. This government, the offspring of our own choice, uninfluenced and unawed, adopted upon full investigation and mature deliberation, completely free in its principles, in the distribution of its powers, uniting security with energy, and containing within itself a provision for its own amendment, has a just claim to your confidence and your support. Respect for its authority, compliance with its laws, acquiescence in its measures, are duties enjoined by the fundamental maxims of true liberty. The basis of our political systems is the right of the people to make and to alter their constitutions of government. But the Constitution which at any time exists, till changed by an explicit and authentic act of the whole people, is sacredly obligatory upon all. The very idea of the power and the right of the people to establish government presupposes the duty of every individual to obey the established government.

All obstructions to the execution of the laws, all combinations and associations, under whatever plausible character, with the real design to direct, control, counteract, or awe the regular deliberation and action of the constituted authorities, are destructive of this fundamental principle, and of fatal tendency. They serve to organize faction, to give it an artificial and extraordinary force; to put, in the place of the delegated will of the nation the will of a party, often a small but artful and enterprising minority of the community; and, according to the alternate triumphs of different parties, to make the public administration the mirror of the ill-concerted and incongruous projects of faction, rather than the organ of consistent and wholesome plans digested by common counsels and modified by mutual interests.

However combinations or associations of the above description may now and then answer popular ends, they are likely, in the course of time and things, to become potent engines, by which cunning, ambitious, and unprincipled men will be enabled to subvert the power of the people and to usurp for themselves the reins of government, destroying afterwards the very engines which have lifted them to unjust dominion.

Towards the preservation of your government, and the permanency of your present happy state, it is requisite, not only that you steadily discountenance irregular oppositions to its acknowledged authority, but also that you resist with care the spirit of innovation upon its principles, however specious the pretexts. One method of assault may be to effect, in the forms of the Constitution, alterations which will impair the energy of the system, and thus to undermine what cannot be directly overthrown. In all the changes to which you may be invited, remember that time and habit are at least as necessary to fix the true character of governments as of other human institutions; that experience is the surest standard by which to test the real tendency of the existing constitution of a country; that facility in changes, upon the credit of mere hypothesis and opinion, exposes to perpetual change, from the endless variety of hypothesis and opinion; and remember, especially, that for the efficient management of your common interests, in a country so extensive as ours, a government of as much vigor as is consistent with the perfect security of liberty is indispensable. Liberty itself will find in such a government, with powers properly distributed and adjusted, its surest guardian. It is, indeed, little else than a name, where the government is too feeble to withstand the enterprises of faction, to confine each member of the society within the limits prescribed by the laws, and to maintain all in the secure and tranquil enjoyment of the rights of person and property.

I have already intimated to you the danger of parties in the State, with particular reference to the founding of them on geographical discriminations. Let me now take a more comprehensive view, and warn you in the most solemn manner against the baneful effects of the spirit of party generally.

This spirit, unfortunately, is inseparable from our nature, having its root in the strongest passions of the human mind. It exists under different shapes in all governments, more or less stifled, controlled, or repressed; but, in those of the popular form, it is seen in its greatest rankness, and is truly their worst enemy.

The alternate domination of one faction over another, sharpened by the spirit of revenge, natural to party dissension, which in different ages and countries has perpetrated the most horrid enormities, is itself a frightful despotism. But this leads at length to a more formal and permanent despotism. The disorders and miseries which result gradually incline the minds of men to seek security and repose in the absolute power of an individual; and sooner or later the chief of some prevailing faction, more able or more fortunate than his competitors, turns this disposition to the purposes of his own elevation, on the ruins of public liberty.

Without looking forward to an extremity of this kind (which nevertheless ought not to be entirely out of sight), the common and continual mischiefs of the spirit of party are sufficient to make it the interest and duty of a wise people to discourage and restrain it.

It serves always to distract the public councils and enfeeble the public administration. It agitates the community with ill-founded jealousies and false alarms, kindles the animosity of one part against another, foments occasionally riot and insurrection. It opens the door to foreign influence and corruption, which finds a facilitated access to the government itself through the channels of party passions. Thus the policy and the will of one country are subjected to the policy and will of another.

There is an opinion that parties in free countries are useful checks upon the administration of the government and serve to keep alive the spirit of liberty. This within certain limits is probably true; and in governments of a monarchical cast, patriotism may look with indulgence, if not with favor, upon the spirit of party. But in those of the popular character, in governments purely elective, it is a spirit not to be encouraged. From their natural tendency, it is certain there will always be enough of that spirit for every salutary purpose. And there being constant danger of excess, the effort ought to be by force of public opinion, to mitigate and assuage it. A fire not to be quenched, it demands a uniform vigilance to prevent its bursting into a flame, lest, instead of warming, it should consume.

It is important, likewise, that the habits of thinking in a free country should inspire caution in those entrusted with its administration, to confine themselves within their respective constitutional spheres, avoiding in the exercise of the powers of one department to encroach upon another. The spirit of encroachment tends to consolidate the powers of all the departments in one, and thus to create, whatever the form of government, a real despotism. A just estimate of that love of power, and proneness to abuse it, which predominates in the human heart, is sufficient to satisfy us of the truth of this position. The necessity of reciprocal checks in the exercise of political power, by dividing and distributing it into different depositaries, and constituting each the guardian of the public weal against invasions by the others, has been evinced by experiments ancient and modern; some of them in our country and under our own eyes. To preserve them must be as necessary as to institute them. If, in the opinion of the people, the distribution or modification of the constitutional powers be in any particular wrong, let it be corrected by an amendment in the way which the Constitution designates. But let there be no change by usurpation; for though this, in one instance, may be the instrument of good, it is the customary weapon by which free governments are destroyed. The precedent must always greatly overbalance in permanent evil any partial or transient benefit, which the use can at any time yield.

Of all the dispositions and habits which lead to political prosperity, religion and morality are indispensable supports. In vain would that man claim the tribute of patriotism, who should labor to subvert these great pillars of human happiness, these firmest props of the duties of men and citizens. The mere politician, equally with the pious man, ought to respect and to cherish them. A volume could not trace all their connections with private and public felicity. Let it simply be asked: Where is the security for property, for reputation, for life, if the sense of religious obligation desert the oaths which are the instruments of investigation in courts of justice? And let us with caution indulge the supposition that morality can be maintained without religion. Whatever may be conceded to the influence of refined education on minds of peculiar structure, reason and experience both forbid us to expect that national morality can prevail in exclusion of religious principle.

It is substantially true that virtue or morality is a necessary spring of popular government. The rule, indeed, extends with more or less force to every species of free government. Who that is a sincere friend to it can look with indifference upon attempts to shake the foundation of the fabric?

Promote then, as an object of primary importance, institutions for the general diffusion of knowledge. In proportion as the structure of a government gives force to public opinion, it is essential that public opinion should be enlightened.

As a very important source of strength and security, cherish public credit. One method of preserving it is to use it as sparingly as possible, avoiding occasions of expense by cultivating peace, but remembering also that timely disbursements to prepare for danger frequently prevent much greater disbursements to repel it, avoiding likewise the accumulation of debt, not only by shunning occasions of expense, but by vigorous exertion in time of peace to discharge the debts which unavoidable wars may have occasioned, not ungenerously throwing upon posterity the burden which we ourselves ought to bear. The execution of these maxims belongs to your representatives, but it is necessary that public opinion should co-operate. To facilitate to them the performance of their duty, it is essential that you should practically bear in mind that towards the payment of debts there must be revenue; that to have revenue there must be taxes; that no taxes can be devised which are not more or less inconvenient and unpleasant; that the intrinsic embarrassment, inseparable from the selection of the proper objects (which is always a choice of difficulties), ought to be a decisive motive for a candid construction of the conduct of the government in making it, and for a spirit of acquiescence in the measures for obtaining revenue, which the public exigencies may at any time dictate.

Observe good faith and justice towards all nations; cultivate peace and harmony with all. Religion and morality enjoin this conduct; and can it be, that good policy does not equally enjoin it—It will be worthy of a free, enlightened, and at no distant period, a great nation, to give to mankind the magnanimous and too novel example of a people always guided by an exalted justice and benevolence. Who can doubt that, in the course of time and things, the fruits of such a plan would richly repay any temporary advantages which might be lost by a steady adherence to it? Can it be that Providence has not connected the permanent felicity of a nation with its virtue? The experiment, at least, is recommended by every sentiment which ennobles human nature. Alas! is it rendered impossible by its vices?

In the execution of such a plan, nothing is more essential than that permanent, inveterate antipathies against particular nations, and passionate attachments for others, should be excluded; and that, in place of them, just and amicable feelings towards all should be cultivated. The nation which indulges towards another a habitual hatred or a habitual fondness is in some degree a slave. It is a slave to its animosity or to its affection, either of which is sufficient to lead it astray from its duty and its interest. Antipathy in one nation against another disposes each more readily to offer insult and injury, to lay hold of slight causes of umbrage, and to be haughty and intractable, when accidental or trifling occasions of dispute occur. Hence, frequent collisions, obstinate, envenomed, and bloody contests. The nation, prompted by ill-will and resentment, sometimes impels to war the government, contrary to the best calculations of policy. The government sometimes participates in the national propensity, and adopts through passion what reason would reject; at other times it makes the animosity of the nation subservient to projects of hostility instigated by pride, ambition, and other sinister and pernicious motives. The peace often, sometimes perhaps the liberty, of nations, has been the victim.

So likewise, a passionate attachment of one nation for another produces a variety of evils. Sympathy for the favorite nation, facilitating the illusion of an imaginary common interest in cases where no real common interest exists, and infusing into one the enmities of the other, betrays the former into a participation in the quarrels and wars of the latter without adequate inducement or justification. It leads also to concessions to the favorite nation of privileges denied to others which is apt doubly to injure the nation making the concessions; by unnecessarily parting with what ought to have been retained, and by exciting jealousy, ill-will, and a disposition to retaliate, in the parties from whom equal privileges are withheld. And it gives to ambitious, corrupted, or deluded citizens (who devote themselves to the favorite nation), facility to betray or sacrifice the interests of their own country, without odium, sometimes even with popularity; gilding, with the appearances of a virtuous sense of obligation, a commendable deference for public opinion, or a laudable zeal for public good, the base or foolish compliances of ambition, corruption, or infatuation.

As avenues to foreign influence in innumerable ways, such attachments are particularly alarming to the truly enlightened and independent patriot. How many opportunities do they afford to tamper with domestic factions, to practice the arts of seduction, to mislead public opinion, to influence or awe the public councils. Such an attachment of a small or weak towards a great and powerful nation dooms the former to be the satellite of the latter.

Against the insidious wiles of foreign influence (I conjure you to believe me, fellow-citizens) the jealousy of a free people ought to be constantly awake, since history and experience prove that foreign influence is one of the most baneful foes of republican government. But that jealousy to be useful must be impartial; else it becomes the instrument of the very influence to be avoided, instead of a defense against it. Excessive partiality for one foreign nation and excessive dislike of another cause those whom they actuate to see danger only on one side, and serve to veil and even second the arts of influence on the other. Real patriots who may resist the intrigues of the favorite are liable to become suspected and odious, while its tools and dupes usurp the applause and confidence of the people, to surrender their interests.

The great rule of conduct for us in regard to foreign nations is in extending our commercial relations, to have with them as little political connection as possible. So far as we have already formed engagements, let them be fulfilled with perfect good faith. Here let us stop. Europe has a set of primary interests which to us have none; or a very remote relation. Hence she must be engaged in frequent controversies, the causes of which are essentially foreign to our concerns. Hence, therefore, it must be unwise in us to implicate ourselves by artificial ties in the ordinary vicissitudes of her politics, or the ordinary combinations and collisions of her friendships or enmities.

Our detached and distant situation invites and enables us to pursue a different course. If we remain one people under an efficient government, the period is not far off when we may defy material injury from external annoyance; when we may take such an attitude as will cause the neutrality we may at any time resolve upon to be scrupulously respected; when belligerent nations, under the impossibility of making acquisitions upon us, will not lightly hazard the giving us provocation; when we may choose peace or war, as our interest, guided by justice, shall counsel.

Why forego the advantages of so peculiar a situation? Why quit our own to stand upon foreign ground? Why, by interweaving our destiny with that of any part of Europe, entangle our peace and prosperity in the toils of European ambition, rivalship, interest, humor or caprice?

It is our true policy to steer clear of permanent alliances with any portion of the foreign world; so far, I mean, as we are now at liberty to do it; for let me not be understood as capable of patronizing infidelity to existing engagements. I hold the maxim no less applicable to public than to private affairs, that honesty is always the best policy. I repeat it, therefore, let those engagements be observed in their genuine sense. But, in my opinion, it is unnecessary and would be unwise to extend them.

Taking care always to keep ourselves by suitable establishments on a respectable defensive posture, we may safely trust to temporary alliances for extraordinary emergencies.

Harmony, liberal intercourse with all nations, are recommended by policy, humanity, and interest. But even our commercial policy should hold an equal and impartial hand; neither seeking nor granting exclusive favors or preferences; consulting the natural course of things; diffusing and diversifying by gentle means the streams of commerce, but forcing nothing; establishing (with powers so disposed, in order to give trade a stable course, to define the rights of our merchants, and to enable the government to support them) conventional rules of intercourse, the best that present circumstances and mutual opinion will permit, but temporary, and liable to be from time to time abandoned or varied, as experience and circumstances shall dictate; constantly keeping in view that it is folly in one nation to look for disinterested favors from another; that it must pay with a portion of its independence for whatever it may accept under that character; that, by such acceptance, it may place itself in the condition of having given equivalents for nominal favors, and yet of being reproached with ingratitude for not giving more. There can be no greater error than to expect or calculate upon real favors from nation to nation. It is an illusion, which experience must cure, which a just pride ought to discard.

In offering to you, my countrymen, these counsels of an old and affectionate friend, I dare not hope they will make the strong and lasting impression I could wish; that they will control the usual current of the passions, or prevent our nation from running the course which has hitherto marked the destiny of nations. But, if I may even flatter myself that they may be productive of some partial benefit, some occasional good; that they may now and then recur to moderate the fury of party spirit, to warn against the mischiefs of foreign intrigue, to guard against the impostures of pretended patriotism; this hope will be a full recompense for the solicitude for your welfare, by which they have been dictated.

How far in the discharge of my official duties I have been guided by the principles which have been delineated, the public records and other evidences of my conduct must witness to you and to the world. To myself, the assurance of my own conscience is, that I have at least believed myself to be guided by them.

In relation to the still subsisting war in Europe, my proclamation of the twenty-second of April, 1793, is the index of my plan. Sanctioned by your approving voice, and by that of your representatives in both houses of Congress, the spirit of that measure has continually governed me, uninfluenced by any attempts to deter or divert me from it.

After deliberate examination, with the aid of the best lights I could obtain, I was well satisfied that our country, under all the circumstances of the case, had a right to take, and was bound in duty and interest to take, a neutral position. Having taken it, I determined, as far as should depend upon me, to maintain it, with moderation, perseverance, and firmness.

The considerations which respect the right to hold this conduct, it is not necessary on this occasion to detail. I will only observe that, according to my understanding of the matter, that right, so far from being denied by any of the belligerent powers, has been virtually admitted by all.

The duty of holding a neutral conduct may be inferred, without anything more, from the obligation which justice and humanity impose on every nation, in cases in which it is free to act, to maintain inviolate the relations of peace and amity towards other nations.

The inducements of interest for observing that conduct will best be referred to your own reflections and experience. With me a predominant motive has been to endeavor to gain time to our country to settle and mature its yet recent institutions, and to progress without interruption to that degree of strength and consistency which is necessary to give it, humanly speaking, the command of its own fortunes.

Though, in reviewing the incidents of my administration, I am unconscious of intentional error, I am nevertheless too sensible of my defects not to think it probable that I may have committed many errors. Whatever they may be, I fervently beseech the Almighty to avert or mitigate the evils to which they may tend. I shall also carry with me the hope that my country will never cease to view them with indulgence; and that, after forty five years of my life dedicated to its service with an upright zeal, the faults of incompetent abilities will be consigned to oblivion, as myself must soon be to the mansions of rest.

Relying on its kindness in this as in other things, and actuated by that fervent love towards it, which is so natural to a man who views in it the native soil of himself and his progenitors for several generations, I anticipate with pleasing expectation that retreat in which I promise myself to realize, without alloy, the sweet enjoyment of partaking, in the midst of my fellow-citizens, the benign influence of good laws under a free government, the ever-favorite object of my heart, and the happy reward, as I trust, of our mutual cares, labors, and dangers.

Geo. Washington.

AUTHOR'S NOTE

This book is intended to be a work of popular and practical history. Almost four years of research and writing have gone into it, occupying weekends and vacations, balanced by a more than full-time job as editor in chief of *The Daily Beast* as the busy bliss of being a new dad to Jack and, in the book's closing months, Toula Lou. All of which is to say that I owe huge debt to my beautiful bride, Margaret, and all my friends and fellow Beasts.

I am, of course, also hugely indebted to the Washington chroniclers who have come before me, whether they published their work in academic journals, compilers of the founding fathers' correspondence, or the historians who have been able to devote years to their subject and receive much-justified acclaim. Getting the chance to go deep with the founding fathers means joining a fun and purposeful club. The endnotes supply a full sense of the sources cited, but I want to acknowledge several works that provided excellent companionship and guidance on this journey.

Looking back, a high school library stumble upon Garry Wills's *Cincinnatus* while procrastinating provided the seeds to this book. Its elegant insights and inspired prose still hold up more than a quarter century later. Another Wills book, *Lincoln at Gettysburg*, offered evidence that a book about a single speech can both entertain and educate. The other prime early influence is the incandescent Richard Hofstadter, whose *The Idea of a Party System* provided an early touchstone and whose *The Paranoid Style in American Politics* inspired my earlier book, *Wingnuts*. James Thomas Flexner and

Douglas Freeman are justifiably famed for their multivolume biographies, as are Richard Norton Smith and Ron Chernow for their single volumes. Jeffry H. Morrison's *The Political Philosophy of George Washington* and Paul K. Longmore's *Invention of George Washington* delve deeply into Washington's early influences. Carl J. Richard's *The Founders and the Classics* is a definitive work that deserves more regular reading from twenty-first-century citizens. Paul Leicester Ford's *The True George Washington* must be taken with a grain of salt, but it remains a refreshingly human early portrait of the man behind the mask. François Furstenberg's more recent *In the Name of the Father* deserves to be regarded as a modern classic, an engaging work of scholarship with particular relevance to the Farewell Address. Matthew Spalding and Patrick Harrity's *A Sacred Union of Citizens* offers an engaging perspective on the address and its more contemporary context. Ron Chernow's *Alexander Hamilton* deserves its obligatory tag of "magisterial" and the Broadway play it inspired has been something of a soundtrack to final drafts of this book.

But the greatest debt to anyone diving into Washington's Farewell Address belongs to the distant figure of Hugo Paltsits, whose 1935 book for the New York Public Library brought together all the drafts of the Farewell Address and associated correspondence, deftly separating fact from fiction. They continue to have most definitive drafts, and Thomas Lannon and Ann Thorton were very kind in letting me access the documents directly, which was a thrill. Certainly, for anyone researching Washington, the NYPL stands second only to Mount Vernon itself, whose gracious library director, Mark Santangelo, has been a constant encouragement at the beautiful new library and archives. Laura Ping has been a valued, steadfast research assistant on this book from its earliest days and Rob Goodman provided a thorough and thoughtful second set of eyes on the manuscript. My friend Matt Pottinger, godfather to my children, was also an invaluable second read, as is my wife, always, who gamely listened to me read the entire book aloud before it went to galleys.

None of this would be possible without the encouragement of my agent, Ed Victor. He was a giant of grace, tact, experience and intuition. He was in fine form at the Fraunces Tavern party that launched this book in January of 2017. By June, he was gone, survived by his beloved wife, Carol, and his children. He is deeply missed but will not be forgotten. Simon & Schuster president Jonathan Karp deserves special thanks for believing in the book and encouraging that it be published just before President Obama's Farewell. Stuart Roberts was a patient and invaluable aide during the reediting process. And it almost goes without saying that it is a great honor to work with my editor, Alice Mayhew. She is that rarest of things: a legend who lives up to her reputation while also being a delight to deal with on things big and small.

I'd like to offer a special word of thanks to the people who made me feel that history was not too huge a topic to tackle, particularly my mother, who always read biographies to me as a child; my grandparents, who gave me a sense of the obligation to the opportunities they provided as immigrants and Americans. More broadly, the work of David McCullough, Robert Caro, Edmund Morris and Douglas Brinkley have provided inspiration on the biographical front, while the late great Jim Harrison and Martin Amis dependably deliver a shot in the arm whenever I read them.

This book was written in many places in stolen hours, from the east coast to the west. It began in an apartment in New York City on Pine Street that overlooked the site of Federal Hall, where Washington took the oath of office, just down the street where Hamilton edited the Farewell. I always enjoy my time at the Hoover Institution, but it was a particular pleasure to utilize their unparalleled archives for this book's third section. A crucial final draft was edited at Bagehot Backs, courtesy of our friends Lynn and Evelyn. Lin Manuel Miranda was the hottest ticket on Broadway when he agreed to speak with me, and I appreciate that he made time for an interview. The professional and the personal are always entwined and I'd be remiss not to thank the people I've had the honor of working for longest in my career to date: Rudy Giuliani, Tina Brown and Barry Diller.

I'll leave the last word to the now-three-year-old Jack's favorite baby book biography of Washington, given to us by our friend Elise Jordan, which summed up the Farewell with touching simplicity: "George was a good president for eight years. Then George said, 'I'm tired. I want to go home.' "

NOTES

ABBREVIATIONS

AFP *Adams Family Papers: An Electronic Archive*. Massachusetts Historical Society. http://www.masshist.org/digitaladams/.

AP Avalon Project. Yale Law School. http://avalon.law.yale.edu/19th_century/jefinaul.asp.

APP American Presidency Project. http://www.presidency.ucsb.edu.

FO Founders Online. National Archives. http://founders.archives.gov.

FWS Fred W. Smith Library for the Study of George Washington. Mount Vernon, Virginia.

GWMV George Washington's Mount Vernon. http://www.mountvernon.org/.

LOC Library of Congress. http://www.memory.loc.gov.

MC Miller Center. University of Virginia. http://millercenter.org.

WFA *Washington's Farewell Address: In facsimile, with transliterations of all the drafts of Washington, Madison and Hamilton, Together with their Correspondence and other Supporting Documents*. Edited by Victor Hugo Paltsits. New York: New York Public Library, 1935.

INTRODUCTION

1 *more widely reprinted than the Declaration of Independence*: François Furstenburg, *In the Name of the Father* (New York: Penguin Books, 2006), 239.

2 *"a speedy death to Washington!"*: John R. Howe Jr., "Republican Thought and Political Violence in the 1790s," *American Quarterly* 19 (Summer, 1967): 149.

2 *At age sixty-four*: Ron Chernow, *Washington: A Life* (New York: Penguin Press, 2010), 437–38, 642.

2 *"growing old, his bodily health less firm"*: "Thomas Jefferson's Memorandum of Conversations with Washington, 1 March 1792," FO.

3 *"in such exaggerated and indecent terms"*: "To Thomas Jefferson from George Washington, 6 July 1796," FO.

3 *"the cares of office"*: "From George Washington to James Craik, 8 September 1789," FO.

3 *"Standing, as it were"*: "From George Washington to James McHenry, 13 December 1798," FO.

3 *"there never was a democracy yet that did not commit suicide:* "From John Adams to John Taylor, 17 December 1814," FO.

4 *"President Washington repeatedly in the act of writing"*: "Nelly Custis Lewis to Lewis Washington, January 31, 1852," FWS.

5 *"a standard to which the wise and honest can repair"*: Attributed to Washington by Gouverneur Morris, as quoted in *To Secure the Blessings of Liberty: Selected Writings of Gouverneur Morris*, ed. J. Jackson Barlow (Indianapolis: Liberty Fund, 2012), 300.

5 *"with me it has always been a maxim:* "From George Washington to James Anderson, 21 December 1797," FO.

5 *"His* public *letters alone"*: "John Jay, Miscellaneous Correspondence," in William Jay, *The Life of John Jay: With Selections from His Correspondence and Miscellaneous Papers*, vol. 2. (1833; reprint, London: Forgotten Books, 2013), 342–43.

5 *"His education had been confined"*: Henrietta Liston, in Louise V. North, ed., *The Travel Journals of Henrietta Marchant Liston: North America and Lower Canada, 1796–1800* (Lanham, MD: Lexington Books, 2014), 18.

6 *Washington was painstakingly modest*: W. W. Abbot, "An Uncommon Awareness of Self: The Papers of George Washington," *Prologue: Quarterly of the National Archives* (Spring 1999): 6–19.

6 *"a species of public property"*: "George Washington to William Gordon, October 23, 1782," in *George Washington: Writings*, ed. John Rhodehamel (New York: Penguin Books, 1997), 478.

6 *"precepts to which"*: John Marshall, *The Life of George Washington*, vol. 5 (Fredericksburg, VA: Citizens' Guild of Washington's Boyhood Home, 1926), n.p., Project Gutenberg, https://archive.org/details/thelifeofgeorgew18595gut.

7 *"best guides"*: Thomas Jefferson, "Minutes of the Board of Visitors," University of Virginia, March 4, 1825, TeachingAmericanHistory.org, http://teachingamericanhistory.org/library/document/extract-from-the-report-to-the-president-and-directors-of-the-literary-fund/, accessed August 1, 2015.

7 *"When I was a boy"*: Joseph Campbell, *The Power of Myth* (New York: Anchor, 1988), 35.

8 *"America's Political Christmas"*: "For the Columbian Centinel: A Song," *Columbian Centinel* (Boston) 24, no. 48, February 20, 1796, America's Historical Newspapers. http://infoweb.newsbank.com, accessed May 14, 2013.

10 *"The heirs of Jefferson and Madison"*: Daniel J. Boorstin, "George Washington: An American Character," presentation at the Embassy of the United States of America, London, on the occasion of George Washington's Birthday February 22, 1995.

SECTION I: THE CRISIS OF CREATION

13 *The executive mansion*: "The President's House in Philadelphia, Part II," UShistory.org, http://www.ushistory.org/presidentshouse/plans/pmhb/ph2.htm, accessed August 2, 2015.

14 *"His administration raised the nation"*: "John Jay to Richard Peters, March 29, 1811," Memoirs of the Historical Society of Pennsylvania, vol. 1, 1826.

17 *"If he does that"*: Edmund S. Morgan, *The Genuine Article: A Historian Looks at Early America* (New York: Norton, 2004), 254.

17 *"before I retire from public life"*: "From George Washington to Robert Morris, 3 June 1783," FO.

18 *"It is yet to be decided"*: "George Washington's Circular Letter of Farewell to the Army, 8 June 1783," American Revolution, 1763–83, LOC.

20 *"When I read"*: Unknown, *Thomas's Massachusetts Spy*, September 4, 1783, 4.

20 *"I looked at them"*: Douglas Southall Freeman, *George Washington*, vol. 5, *Victory with the Help of France, 1778–1783* (New York: Charles Scribner's Sons, 1952), 462–63.

20 *"With a heart full"*: As quoted in ibid., 467.

20 *Grown men cried*: Quoted in William Spohn Baker, *Washington After the Revolution: 1784–1799* (Philadelphia, 1897), 307.

22 *Over four days of celebration*: "George Washington to David Humphreys, December 26, 1786," in John C. Fitzpatrick, ed., *The Writings of George Washington from the Original Manuscript Sources, 1745–1799*. (Washington, DC: U.S. Government Print Office, 1931), 129.

22 *containing 40 eggs*: "Martha Washington's Recipe for Great Cake," GWMV.

22 *"from this moment we should"*: "Martha Washington to Mercy Otis Warren, December 26, 1789," in *Women's Letters: American from the Revolutionary War to the Present*, ed. Lisa Grunwald and Stephen J. Adler (New York: Random House, 2008), 74.

22 *his dogs' names included*: For details on Washington's dogs see vols. 2, 4, and 5, *The Diaries of George Washington*, ed. Donald Jackson and Dorothy Twohig, *The Papers of George Washington* (Charlottesville: University Press of Virginia, 1979). Also see "Soldier, Statesman, Dog Lover: George Washington's Pups," GWMV.

22 *"more permanent and genuine"*: "From George Washington to Armand, 10 August 1786," FO.

23 *"from half a pint"*: Jedidiah Morse, 1790, in William S. Baker, *Early Sketches of George Washington* (Philadelphia: Lippincott, 1893), 121, archive.org, https://archive.org/stream/earlysketchesofg00bake#page/104/mode/2up, accessed August 6, 2015.

23 *"The General with a few glasses"*: Robert Hunter Jr., *Quebec to Carolina in 1785–1786, Being the Travel Diary and Observations of Robert Hunter, Jr., a Young Merchant of London* (San Marino, CA: Huntington Library, 1948), 5.

23 *"in the company of two or three intimate friends"*: Paul Leicester Ford, *The True George Washington* (Philadelphia: Lippincott, 1896), 179.

23 *"The story so often repeated of his never laughing"*: Ibid.

24 *"To see plants rise from the Earth"*: "From George Washington to Alexander Spotswood, 13 February 1788," FO.

24 *"During our present difficulties and distress"*: "Fairfax County Resolves, 18 July 1774," FO.

24 *"we will use every means which Heaven hath given"*: "Fairfax County Resolves, 18 July 1774," FO.

25 *"a great repugnance"*: "From George Washington to John Francis Mercer, 6 November 1786," FO.

25 *"the disinclination of the individual States"*: "George Washington to Benjamin Harrison, January 18, 1784," in Jared Sparks, ed., *Writings of George Washington being his Correspondence, Address, Messages, from the Original Manuscripts*, vol. 3 (Boston: Russell, Odiorne, and Metcalf, Hilliard, Gray, 1835), 11–12.

25 *"Like a young heir"*: "George Washington to Benjamin Harrison, January 18, 1784," in Sparks, *Writings of George Washington*, 11.

26 *"If three years ago"*: "From George Washington to Henry Knox, 3 February 1787," FO.

26 *"contributed more to that uneasiness"*: "James Madison to Thomas Jefferson October 24, 1787," in *The Papers of James Madison*, vol. 1., ed. William T. Hutchinson et al. (Chicago: University of Chicago Press, 1962), 644.

26 *"We have probably had too good an opinion"*: "From George Washington to John Jay, 15 August 1786," FO.

27 *The German-born revolutionary veteran*: John R. Vile, *The Constitutional Convention of 1787: A Comprehensive Encyclopedia of America's Founding* (Santa Barbara, CA: ABC-CLIO, 2005), 490.

27 *"From thinking proceeds speaking"*: "From George Washington to John Jay, 15 August 1786," FO.

27 *"it is not my business to embark again"*: Ibid.

27 *"a liberal and energetic Constitution"*: "George Washington to James Madison, November 5, 1786," in Sparks, ed. *Writings of George Washington*, vol. 9, 206.

27 *"the sole and express purpose"*: "Report of Proceedings in Congress; February 21, 1787," AP.

27 *more than half of the fifty-five representatives*: "Delegates to the Constitutional Convention," Charters of Freedom, http://www.archives.gov/exhibits/charters/constitution_founding_fathers_overview.html, accessed July 12, 2015.

28 *"Many of the members cast their eyes"*: "Pierce Butler to Weedon Butler, March 5, 1788," in *Supplementary Records of Proceedings in Convention*, Consource, http://consource.org/document/pierce-butler-to-weedon-butler-1788-3-5/, accessed July 12, 2015.

29 *"I wish the Constitution which is offered"*: "From George Washington to Benjamin Harrison, 24 September 1787," FO.

29 *"I do not conceive"*: "From George Washington to Bushrod Washington, 9 November 1787," FO.

29 *"It is clear to my conception"*: "Undelivered First Inaugural Address: Fragments, 30 April 1789," FO.

29 *though as Congressman Elbridge Gerry slyly noted*: *Annals of Congress*, 1st session, August 15, 1789, 759.

30 *"the new constellation of this hemisphere"*: "From George Washington to Joseph Barrell, 8 June 1788," FO.

32 *"so strange a production"*: James Madison to Jared Sparks, May 30, 1827, in *The Life and Writings of Jared Sparks*, ed. Herbert B. Adams, vol. 2 (Boston, 1893), 211.

32 *"my movements to the chair of government"*: "From George Washington to Henry Knox, 1 April 1789," FO.

32 *"a mind oppressed"*: Washington, diary entry, April 16, 1789, FO.

32 *"bid adieu to the peaceful retreat"*: As quoted in Baker, *Washington After the Revolution*, 111.

32 *"They talk very loud"*: John Adams, diary entry, August 23, 1774, in *The Works of John Adams, Second President of the United States*, ed. Charles Francis Adams, vol. 2. (Boston: Charles C. Little & James Brown, 1850), 353.

33 *"There is no truth more thoroughly established*: George Washington, "Inaugural Address," April 30, 1789, National Archives and Records Administration, http://www.archives. gov/exhibits/american_originals/inaugtxt.html, accessed July 12, 2015.

34 *"This great man was agitated"*: "Journal of Senator William Maclay," April 30, 1789, LOC.

34 *"Good government, the best of blessings"*: *Maryland Gazette* (Annapolis), May 14, 1789, http://msa.maryland.gov/megafile/msa/speccol/sc4800/sc4872/001284/html/m1284-0438.html.

34 *"Few who are not philosophical spectators"*: "From George Washington to Catharine Sawbridge Macaulay Graham, 9 January 1790," *FO*.

35 *"Never was a man more egregiously disappointed"*: From Pierce Butler to James Iredell, August 11, 1789, in *Documentary History of the First Federal Congress*, vol. 16, ed. Charlene Bangs Bickford et al. (Baltimore: Johns Hopkins University Press, 2004), 1288–89.

35 *"You might search in vain"*: From John Adams to James Bridge, September 21, 1789, in *Documentary History*, vol. 17, ed. Bickford et al., 1594.

35 *"everything seems conducted"*: From John Trumbull to John Adams, June 5, 1790, in *Documentary History*, vol. 19, ed. Bickford et al., 1717.

35 *"It is truly distressing"*: From William Smith to Otho H. Williams, in *Documentary History*, vol. 19, ed. Bickford et al., 1131.

36 *"mimicry of royal forms and ceremonies"*: As quoted in B. L. Rayner, *Sketches of the Life, Writings, and Opinions of Thomas Jefferson* (New York: Francis & Boardman, 1832), 368.

37 *"I know it is very doubtful"*: As quoted in Peter R. Henriques, *Realistic Visionary: A Portrait of George Washington* (Charlottesville: University of Virginia Press, 2006), 189.

37 *"If, Sir, it is indifferent to you"*: As quoted in Mary V. Thompson, *"In the Hands of a Good Providence": Religion in the Life of George Washington* (Charlottesville: University of Virginia Press, 2008), 114.

37 *"but when he should leave us"*: *New-York Daily Advertiser*, September 4, 1789.

37 *"the distant members of the Empire"*: Ibid. May 25, 1790, in *Documentary History*, vol. 19, 1393.

40 *"a public debt is injurious"*: Madison, "The Union. Who Are Its Real Friends?," *National Gazette* (Philadelphia), April 2, 1792.

40 *"see it incorporated"*: Alexander Hamilton, *The First Report on Public Credit*, January 9, 1790.

42 *"a paper of pure"*: "From Thomas Jefferson to Thomas Mann Randolph, Jr., 15 May 1791," *FO*.

42 *"For god's sake"*: Thomas Jefferson to James Madison, July 7, 1793, in *The Works of Thomas Jefferson*, vol. 7 (1904; reprint, New York: Cosmo Classics, 2009), 436.

43 *"By making one party a check on the other"*: Madison, "Parties," in ibid., January 23, 1792.

43 *"an assumption of prerogatives"*: "To Thomas Jefferson from James Madison, 13 June 1793," *FO*.

45 *"could make it convenient"*: "To James Madison from George Washington, 19 February 1792," FO.

46 *"as would be most convenient to the public"*: James Madison, "Madison's Conversations with Washington, 5–25 May 1792," FO.

46 *"he had from the beginning found himself deficient"*: Ibid.

46 *"in the decline of his life"*: Ibid.

46 *"However novel or difficult"*: Ibid.

46 *"the conciliating influence"*: Ibid.

47 *"suggest any matters that might occur"*: Ibid.

47 *"I have not been unmindful"*: "To James Madison from George Washington, 20 May 1792," FO.

47 *"turn your thoughts to a valedictory address"*: Ibid.

48 *"I take the liberty at my departure"*: Ibid.

49 *"a simple publication in the newspapers"*: "To George Washington from James Madison, 20 June 1792," FO.

49 *"The confidence of the whole union"*: "To George Washington from Thomas Jefferson, 23 May 1792," FO.

49 *"the opinions of persons"*: "From Alexander Hamilton to George Washington, 30 July[–August 3] 1792," FO.

49 *"We must gain time"*: "To George Washington from Edmund Randolph, 5 August 1792," FO.

50 *"I can protest"*: Thomas Jefferson, *The Writings of Thomas Jefferson*, vol. 7, ed. Albert Ellery Bergh (Washington, DC: Thomas Jefferson Memorial Association, 1907), 403–4.

51 *"after a serious struggle"*: "To Alexander Hamilton from James McHenry, 20 [September] 1792," FO.

51 *"the Constitution requires"*: "Second Inaugural Address," March 4, 1793, FO.

52 *"I was no party man"*: "To Thomas Jefferson from George Washington, 6 July 1796," FO.

53 *"been born in the forests"*: Ford, *The True George Washington*, 44–45.

53 *"His person is tall"*: Ibid., 43–44, 277, 303.

54 *"Naturally grave and silent"*: James C. Nicholls and Henrietta Liston, "Lady Henrietta Liston's Journal of Washington's 'Resignation,' Retirement, and Death," *Pennsylvania Magazine of History and Biography* 95 (October 1971): 514–16.

55 *"America is free"*: Ralph Ketcham, *Framed for Posterity: The Enduring Philosophy of the Constitution* (Lawrence: University Press of Kansas, 1993), 24.

55 *"The revolution which has been effected"*: "From George Washington to Gouverneur Morris, 13 October 1789," FO.

56 *"conduct friendly and impartial"*: "Neutrality Proclamation, 22 April 1793," FO.

56 *"The liberty of the whole earth"*: "From Thomas Jefferson to William Short, 3 January 1793," FO.

57 *"a little rebellion"*: "To James Madison from Thomas Jefferson, 30 January 1787," FO.

59 *"The glorious time"*: Charlene Bangs Bickford and Kenneth R. Bowling, *Birth of the Nation: The First Federal Congress 1789–1791* (Indianapolis: Madison House, 1989), 25.

59 *"If any measure is before Congress"*: Catherine E. Hutchins, ed., *Everyday Life in the Early Republic* (Winterthur, DE: Henry Francis du Pont Winterthur Museum, 1994), 3.

59 *"In America, a great number"*: Ibid., 7.

59 *"If freedom of speech"*: From George Washington to Officers of the Army, March 15, 1783, FO.

59 *"The President was much inflamed"*: Henry Lee, *Observations on the Writings of Thomas Jefferson with Particular Reference to the Attack they Contain on the Memory of the Late Henry Lee in a Series of Letters* (Philadelphia: J. Dobson, Thomas, Copperthwait; Carey & Hart, 1839), 34.

60 *"destroy undue impressions"*: Ford, *The True George Washington*, 264.

60 *"If ever a nation"*: *Aurora*, March 23, 1796, as quoted in Marcus Daniel, *Scandal and Civility: Journalism and the Birth of American Democracy* (New York: Oxford University Press, 2009), 109.

60 *"point out one single"*: "Portius," *Aurora*, October 12, 1795.

60 *"Will not the world"*: Eric Burns, *Infamous Scribblers: The Founding Fathers and the Rowdy Beginnings of American Journalism* (New York: PublicAffairs, 2006), 323.

60 *"the greatest good"*: As quoted in Donald Henderson Stewart, *The Opposition Press of the Federalist Period* (Albany: State University of New York Press 1969), 212.

60 *"We have given him"*: Joseph J. Ellis, *Founding Brothers: The Revolutionary Generation* (New York: Knopf, 2000), 126–27.

61 *"Is our president"*: Resolution of the Democratic Society of the County of Washington, in Pennsylvania, June 23, 1794, quoted in John Ferling, *A Leap in the Dark: The Struggle to Create the American Republic* (New York: Oxford University Press, 2003), 370.

61 *"These are the times"*: Thomas Paine, "The Crisis," December 23, 1776, USHistory.org, http://www.ushistory.org/paine/crisis/c-01.htm.

62 *"The lands obtained"*: Thomas Paine, *The Political and Miscellaneous Works of Thomas*

Paine, vol. 2 (London: R. Carlile, 1819), 5, 36, Google Books, http://www.google-books.com.

62 *"The stuff was poor"*: Christopher Hitchens, "Forward," in Conor Cruise O'Brien, *First in Peace: How George Washington Set the Course for America* (Cambridge, MA: Da Capo Press, 2009), xvii.

62 *"accused of being the enemy of one Nation"*: To Thomas Jefferson from George Washington, 6 July 1796," FO.

63 *"I have a consolation"*: George Washington, in Sparks, ed., *Writings of George Washington*, vol. 10, 359.

64 *"to assist in every way"*: Harlow Giles Unger, *Noah Webster: The Life and Times of an American Patriot* (New York: Wiley, 1998), 180.

64 *"If Washington's government"*: Harlow Giles Unger, *John Marshall: The Chief Justice Who Saved the Nation* (Philadelphia: Da Capo Press, 2014), 93–94.

65 *"I have prepared the revolution"*: Ibid., 94.

65 *"the terrorism excited by Genêt"*: "John Adams to Thomas Jefferson, 30 June 1813," FO.

66 *"perhaps not improbable"*: "From George Washington to David Humphreys, 20 July 1791," FO.

67 *"We are ready"*: Harlow Giles Unger, *"Mr. President": George Washington and the Making of the Nation's Highest Office* (Philadelphia: Da Capo Press, 2013), 189.

67 *"there is no road"*: "Tully No. II, [26 August 1794]," *FO*.

69 *"originated in submission"*: Donald H. Stewart, *The Opposition Press of the Federalist Period* (Albany: State University of New York Press, 1969), 212.

69 *"kick the damned treaty to hell"*: Ibid., 214.

69 *"surrounded by an innumerable"*: As quoted in Ron Chernow, *Alexander Hamilton* (New York: Penguin Books, 2004), 487.

70 *"Firm as a majestic rock"*: "From Thomas Jefferson to James Monroe, 12 June 1796," FO.

70 *American exports increased*: David O. Stewart, *Madison's Gift* (New York: Simon & Schuster, 2015), 161

71 *"Jefferson considered Hamilton a vulgar upstart"*: James Thomas Flexner, *Washington: The Indispensable Man* (Boston: Little, Brown, 1969), 244.

71 *"political porcupine"*: As quoted in Richard Brookhiser, *Alexander Hamilton: American* (New York: Simon & Schuster, 1999), 156.

71 *"the bastard brat"*: "From John Adams to Benjamin Rush, 25 January 1806," FO.

73 *"To remain a member"*: O'Brien, *First in Peace*, 29.

73 *"flowed from principles"*: "From Thomas Jefferson to George Washington, 9 September 1792," FO.

73 *"daily pitted"*: "Thomas Jefferson to Walter Jones, March 5, 1810," Founders' Constitution, http://press-pubs.uchicago.edu/founders/print_documents/a2_2_1s14.html, accessed September 15, 2015.

73 *"How unfortunate"*: "To Thomas Jefferson from George Washington, 23 August 1792," FO.

74 *"Differences in political opinions"*: "To Alexander Hamilton from George Washington, 26 August 1792," FO.

74 *"my having decided against"*: "From George Washington to Thomas Jefferson, 6 July 1796," in *George Washington: Writings*, ed. John Rhodehamel (New York: Library of America, 1997), 951.

75 *"Were parties here divided"*: "From Thomas Jefferson to William Branch Giles, 31 December 1795," FO.

75 *"In every relation"*: "To Alexander Hamilton from George Washington, 2 February 1795," FO.

76 *"It is now generally understood"*: "From James Madison to James Monroe, 14 May 1796," FO.

76 *"He repeated it three times"*: "John Adams to Abigail Adams, 25 March 1796," AFP.

76 *"He detained me there"*: AFP, March 25, 1796.

76 *"The president does not mean"*: "To James Madison from John Beckley, 20 June 1796," FO.

77 *"remain with us"*: "To George Washington from John Jay, 18 April 1796," FO.

79 *"When last in Philadelphia"*: "To George Washington from Alexander Hamilton, 10 May 1796," FO.

79 *"As it is important"*: "To George Washington from Alexander Hamilton, 10 May 1796," FO.

79 *"known also to one"*: "From George Washington to Alexander Hamilton, May 15, 1796," in Rhodehamel, ed., *George Washington: Writings*, 938–39.

80 *"curtailed, if too verbose"*: "From George Washington to Alexander Hamilton, May 15, 1796," in Rhodehamel, ed., *George Washington: Writings*, 938–39.

80 *"All the columns"*: "To Alexander Hamilton from George Washington, 10 August 1796," FO.

81 *"Our own Jacobins"*: "From Alexander Hamilton to Angelica Church, [19–20 June 1796]," FO.

81 *"principally at such times"*: Chernow, *Alexander Hamilton*, 508.

81 *"He has often compared"*: James Thomas Callender, *The History of the United States for 1796* (Philadelphia: Snowden & McCorkle, 1797), 208.

82 *"Some of the gazettes"*: "Washington's Farewell Address, First Draft," WFA, 171.

82 *"Having no other wish"*: "To Alexander Hamilton from George Washington, 26 June 1796," FO.

82 *"deliberately to discuss"*: "John Jay to Judge Peters, March 29, 1811," WFA, 271.

83 *"I have completed"*: "From Alexander Hamilton to George Washington, 5 July 1796," FO.

83 *"I have endeavored"*: "From Alexander Hamilton to George Washington, 30 July 1796," FO.

83 *"[i]f there be any part"*: "From Alexander Hamilton to George Washington, August 10, 1796," WFA, 251.

84 *"several serious and attentive readings"*: "To Alexander Hamilton from George Washington, 25 August 1796," FO.

84 *"as one of the surest"*: "To Alexander Hamilton from George Washington, 1 September 1796," FO.

84 *"Had I health enough"*: "From Alexander Hamilton to George Washington, 5 September 1796," FO.

86 *"a wild little creature"*: Mary V. Thompson, "Eleanor 'Nelly' Parke Custis," GWMV.

86 *"the involuntary errors"*: "Enclosure: Draft of Washington's Farewell Address, [30 July 1796]," FO.

86 *"obliterated to avoid"*: John Church Hamilton, *History of the Republic of the United States of America, as Traced in the Writings of Alexander Hamilton and of His Contemporaries* (New York: Appleton, 1860), 531.

86 *"Cultivate industry"*: "From George Washington to James Warren, 7 October 1785," FO.

87 *"and requested me to bring"*: "Nelly Custis Lewis to Lewis Washington, January 31, 1852," FWS.

88 *"I do not get one paper"*: Alfred McClung Lee, "Dunlap and Claypoole: Printers and News-Merchants of the Revolution," *Journalism Quarterly* (June 1934): 160–78.

88 *"never flaunting"*: John Fanning Watson, *Annals of Philadelphia and Pennsylvania, in the Olden Time*, vol. 2 (Carlisle, PA: Applewood Books, 1830), 397.

89 *"sitting alone in the drawing room"*: "Certification of David C. Claypoole, February 22, 1826," WFA, 290.

89 *"made but few alterations"*: "Certification of David C. Claypoole, February 22, 1826," WFA, 291.

90 *"This address, whether considered"*: WFA, 56.

90 *"replete with wisdom"*: "The Following Remarks Are from an English Paper: The Resignation of General Washington," *Minerva & Mercantile Evening Adviser* (New York), vol. 4, no. 1047, January 21, 1797, 3, American's Historical Newspapers, http://infoweb .newsbank.com, accessed May 4, 2013.

91 *"unequaled by any composition"*: Sir Archibald Alison, *The Historians' History of the World*, vol. 23, *The United States*, ed. Henry Smith Williams (New York: J. J. Little, 1904), 310.

91 *"We recommend to our customers"*: WFA, 67–68.

91 *forty-five editions*: Furstenburg, *In the Name of the Father*, 239.

SECTION II: WASHINGTON'S PILLARS OF LIBERTY

95 "the pillars on which": "George Washington's Circular Letter of Farewell to the Army, 8 June 1783," AP.

95 *"four great and essential pillars"*: "From George Washington to Lafayette, 29 January 1789," FO.

97 *"the rising Empire"*: "From George Washington to Philippe de Noailles, Duc de Mouchy, 15 October 1783," FO.

98 *the population of the entire*: "Colonial and Pre-Federal Statistics," United States Census Series Z-19, http://www2.census.gov/prod2/statcomp/documents/CT1970p2-13.pdf, accessed September 15, 2015.

98 *His first land purchase*: Nicole DiSarno, "The Kanawha Tracts," GWMV.

98 *"for fertility of soil"*: George Washington, *The Diaries of George Washington*, vol. 1, *1748–1765* (Charlottesville: University of Virginia Press, 2008), 19.

98 *Over the years*: Flexner, *George Washington*, vol. 1, *The Forge of Experience* (Boston: Little, Brown, 1965), 302–3.

99 *"It is in the nature"*: Montesquieu, *The Spirit of the Laws*, trans. and ed. Anne Cohler et al. (Cambridge: Cambridge University Press, 1989), 124.

99 *there were 4 million*: "Diversity in Colonial America," University of Houston, http://www.digitalhistory.uh.edu/disp_textbook.cfm?smtID=2&psid=3585, accessed September 15, 2015.

99 *"It is hoped"*: "General Orders, 4 July 1775," FO.

100 *"Nothing but disunion"*: "From George Washington to Lieutenant Colonel Joseph Reed, 15 April 1776," FO.

100 *"The citizens of America"*: "George Washington's Circular Letter of Farewell to the Army, 8 June 1783."

101 *"Whatever measures"*: "From George Washington to The States, 8 June 1783," FO.

101 *Thirteen sovereignties*: "From George Washington to James Madison, 5 November 1786," FO.

101 *Notes on Ancient*: "Notes on Ancient and Modern Confederacies, [April–June?] 1786," FO.

102 *"became first rivals"*: Madison, "Federalist 18," in Alexander Hamilton, James Madison, and John Jay, *The Federalist Papers* (Mineola, NY: Dover, 2014), 82.

102 *Hence, the weakness*: Madison, "Federalist 18," 82.

102 *ambitious Philip*: Alexander Hamilton, *The Papers of Alexander Hamilton*, vol. 5, *June 1788–Nov. 1789*, ed. Harold C. Syrett and Jacob E. Cooke (New York: Columbia University Press, 1962), 21.

103 *"it is in the nature"*: Montesquieu, *The Spirit of the Laws*, 124.

104 *"A firm Union"*: Hamilton, "Federalist 9," in Hamilton, Madison, and Jay, *The Federalist Papers*, 37.

104 *"As the first"*: "From George Washington to James Madison, 5 May 1789," FO.

105 *"The country appears"*: "From George Washington to David Humphreys, 20 July 1791," FO.

105 *"Every citizen who enjoys"*: George Washington, "Sentiments on a Peace Establishment," in Fitzpatrick, ed., *The Writings of George Washington*, vol. 26, *1745–1799*, 44.

105 *"We may all be considered"*: "Enclosure: Madison's Draft of the Farewell Address, 20 June 1792," FO.

107 *"four sets of Indians"*: Baker, *Washington After the Revolution*, 308.

107 *"Next to the case"*: "James Madison to Thomas L. McKenney, 10 February 1826," FO.

107 *"the asylum of pacific"*: "From George Washington to Thomas Jefferson, 1 January 1788," FO.

107 *"by an intermixture"*: "To John Adams from George Washington, 15 November 1794," FO.

108 *"The West derives"*: George Washington, "Washington's Farewell Address, 1796," AP.

110 *"the palladium"*: George Washington, "Washington's Farewell Address, 1796," AP.

110 *"It is easy to foresee"*: George Washington, "Washington's Farewell Address, 1796," AP.

111 *"I was no party man myself"*: "To Thomas Jefferson from George Washington, 6 July 1796," FO.

111 *"by prudence"*: "From George Washington to Catharine Sawbridge Macaulay Graham, 9 January 1790," FO.

112 *"spirit of moderation"*: Madison, Federalist 37, and Hamilton, Federalist 1, in Hamilton, Madison, and Jay, *The Federalist Papers*, 169, 4.

112 *"He seeks information"*: "John Adams to Silvanus Bourn, 30 August 1789," in Charles Francis Adams, ed., *John Adams: Second President of the United States*, vol. 9, 561.

112 *"the only man in the U.S."*: "Thomas Jefferson's Conversation with Washington, 1 October 1792," FO.

112 *"without the great political"*: John Adams, *The Political Writings of John Adams*, ed. George W. Carey (Washington, DC: Regnery, 2001), 89.

112 *"There is a natural"*: "George Washington's Circular Letter of Farewell to the Army, 8 June 1783."

113 *"There cannot a greater"*: Joseph Addison, "Mischiefs of Party Spirit," July 24, 1711, *Spectator*, no. 125, in *Essays from Addison*, ed. J. H. Fowler (London: Macmillan, 1907), 62–63.

113 *"is but the madness"*: Alexander Pope, "Letters to and from Edward Blount, Esq., Letter LXXXV, Aug. 27, 1714," in *The Letters of Mr. Alexander Pope and Several of His Friends* (London: J. Wright, 1737), 141.

114 *"Party is a political evil"*: Henry, Viscount Bolingbroke, *The Idea of a Patriot King*, in *The Works of Lord Bolingbroke*, vol. 2 (Philadelphia: Carey & Hart, 1841), 40.

114 *"I mean the moderation"*: Montesquieu, *The Spirit of the Laws*, 155, 602, 25.

114 *"factions subvert government"*: David Hume, *Political Writings*, ed. Stuart D. Warner (Indianapolis: Hackett, 1994), 58.

114 *"Moderation"*: Hume, *Political Writings*, 58.

114 *"Both ventured on most"*: Thucydides, *The History of the Peloponnesian War*, in *The English Works of Thomas Hobbes of Malmesbury; Now First Collected and Edited by Sir William Molesworth, Bart*, 11 vols. (London: Bohn, 1839–45), vol. 8, http://oll.liberty fund.org/titles/771, accessed March 17, 2016.

114 *"who propose to take charge"*: Cicero, *On Duties*, in *Complete Works of Cicero* ([United Kingdom]: Delphi Classics, 2014), 25, 85.

115 *"By a faction"*: Madison, Federalist 10, in Hamilton, Madison, and Jay, *The Federalist Papers*, 42.

115 *"According to the classical doctrine"*: Carl J. Richard, *The Founders and the Classics: Greece, Rome, and the American Enlightenment* (Cambridge, MA: Harvard University Press, 1994), 64.

115 At twenty-three: Chernow, *Washington*, 88.

116 *"That dispassionate voice"*: Paul K. Longmore, *The Invention of George Washington* (Charlottesville: University Press of Virginia, 1999), 80.

116 *"he seems discrete and virtuous"*: Henry Wiencek, *An Imperfect God: George Washington, His Slaves, and the Creation of America* (New York: Farrar, Straus, & Giroux, 2003), 195.

117 *"may talk of patriotism"*: "From George Washington to John Banister, 21 April 1778," FO.

117 *"a great and lasting war"*: "From George Washington to John Banister, 21 April 1778," FO.

117 *"Democratical states must always* feel": "From George Washington to Lafayette, 25 July 1785," FO.

117 *"the want of harmony"*: "George Washington to Gouverneur Morris, 8 May 1779," FO.

117 *"true principles"*: Bolingbroke, *Patriot King*, 412, 406.

120 *"narrow-minded politicians"*: "From George Washington to Alexander Hamilton, 10 July 1787," FO.

120 *"I confess that there are several"*: Benjamin Franklin, *Madison Debates*, September 17, 1787, AP.

121 *"In the Constitutional Convention"*: Catherine Drinker Bowen, *Miracle at Philadelphia: The Story of the Constitutional Convention May to September 1787* (Boston: Little, Brown, 1966), xii.

121 *"The framers' aim"*: Peter Berkowitz, *Constitutional Conservatism: Liberty, Self-Government, and Political Moderation* (Stanford, CA: Hoover Institution Press, 2013), 42.

122 *"the spirit of moderation"*: Madison, Federalist 37, and Hamilton, Federalist 85, in Hamilton, Madison, and Jay, *The Federalist Papers*, 169, 431.

122 *"There are seasons in every country"*: "Publius Letter, II, [26 October 1778]," FO.

122 *"I would mount the hobbyhorse of popularity"*: "From Alexander Hamilton to Edward Carrington, 26 May 1792," FO

122 *"the violence of faction"*: Madison, Federalist 10, in Hamilton, Madison, and Jay, *The Federalist Papers*, 41.

122 *"The influence of factious"*: Federalist 10, *The Federalist Papers*, 41.

122 *"Ambition must be made"*: Madison, Federalist 51, in Hamilton, Madison, and Jay, *The Federalist Papers*, 254.

122 *"No local prejudices"*: "First Inaugural Address: Final Version, 30 April 1789," FO.

123 *"A difference of opinion"*: "From George Washington to the Governor and Council of North Carolina, 19 June 1789," FO.

123 *"It should be the highest"*: "From George Washington to the Pennsylvania Legislature, 12 September 1789," FO.

123 *"My greatest fear has been that the nation would not be sufficiently cool and moderate"*: "From George Washington to Catherine Macaulay Graham, 9 January 1790," FO.

123 *"we must drive far"*: "From George Washington to Arthur Fenner, 4 June 1790," FO.

124 *"nature's Tories and Whigs"*: "From Thomas Jefferson to William Branch Giles, 31 December 1795," FO.

124 *"was no believer"*: "To Thomas Jefferson from George Washington, 6 July 1796," FO.

124 *"It is to be"*: "To Alexander Hamilton from George Washington, 26 August 1792," FO.

125 *"How many honest"*: Joseph Addison, July 24, 1711, *Spectator* 125, in *Cato: A Tragedy and Selected Essays,* ed. Christine Dunn Henderson and Mark E. Yellin (Indianapolis: Liberty Fund, 2004), Online Library of Liberty, http://oll.libertyfund.org/titles/1229, accessed January 9, 2013.

125 *"both sides have strained"*: "To Alexander Hamilton from George Washington, 26 August 1792," FO.

125 *"one, who is of no party"*: "George Washington to Timothy Pickering 27 July 1795," in Sparks, *Writings of George Washington*, vol. 9, pp. 39–40.

125 *"I am sure the mass"*: "George Washington to John Jay 8 May 1796," in Sparks, *Writings of George Washington*, vol. 9, pp. 123–24.

126 *"He wanted to carve"*: Joseph Ellis, in *George Washington Reconsidered*, ed. Don Higginbotham (Charlottesville: University Press of Virginia, 2001), 233.

126 *"considerable changes"*: George Washington, "Farewell Address (first draft)," May 15, 1796, WFA, 168.

126 *"That party disputes"*: Ibid.

126 *"unfortunately, is inseparable"*: George Washington, "Washington's Farewell Address," 1796, AP.

126 *"They serve to organize"*: Ibid.

129 *"[l]iberty is to faction"*: Madison, Federalist 10, in Hamilton, Madison, and Jay, *The Federalist Papers*, 42.

130 *"I never felt"*: "From George Washington to James Craik, 4 August 1788," FO.

131 *"It is but an irksome"*: "From George Washington to Robert Cary & Company, 10 August 1764," FO.

131 *"Think what you do"*: Benjamin Franklin, *The Life and Writings of Benjamin Franklin*, vol. 2 (Philadelphia: McCarty & Davis, 1834), 479.

132 *"In thus pursuing"*: Longmore, *The Invention of George Washington*, 83.

133 *"deep-laid and desperate"*: As quoted in Bernard Bailyn, *The Ideological Origins of the American Revolution* (Cambridge, MA: Belknap Press of Harvard University Press, 1992), 121.

133 *"will prove the salvation"*: Chernow, *Alexander Hamilton*, 55.

133 *"to their great surprise"*: Gordon S. Wood, *The Radicalism of the American Revolution* (New York: Knopf, 1992), 91.

134 *"I think the Parliament"*: "George Washington to Bryan Fairfax, 20 July 1774," FO.

134 *Friends! Brethren! Countrymen:* Richard B. Morris and Louis L. Snyder, eds., *A Treasury of Great Reporting* (New York: Simon & Schuster, 1949), 27.

135 *"Many persons wish"*: "John Adams Diary. December 17, 1773," AFP.

135 *it took 167 continental dollars:* The Blackwell Encyclopedia of the American Revolution, ed. Jack P. Greene and J. R. Pole (Cambridge, MA: Blackwell, 1994), 364, Table 1, taken from E. J. Ferguson, *The Power of the Purse: A History of American Public Finance 1776–1790* (Chapel Hill: University of North Carolina Press, 1961), 32.

135 *"A wagon load"*: "From George Washington to John Jay, 23 April 1779," FO.

136 *"We must of necessity"*: Freeman, *George Washington*, vol. 5, 151.

136 *"placing their whole"*: "From George Washington to Benjamin Harrison, 25 October, 1779," in George Washington, *The Writings of George Washington*, ed. Worthington Chauncey Ford (New York: Putnam, 1890), n.p., Online Library of Liberty, http://oll.libertyfund.org/titles/washington-the-writings-of-george-washington -vol-viii-1779-1780.

136 *"there was never a darker hour"*: Nathanael Green to McDougall, as quoted in Freeman, *George Washington*, vol. 5, 152.

136 *"I cannot with any degree"*: "From George Washington to Lund Washington, 29 May 1779," FO.

137 *"[l]and is the most permanent"*: "George Washington to John Parke Custis, February 1, 1778," in Fitzpatrick, ed., *The Writings of George Washington*, vol. 31, *1745–1799*, 413.

137 *"The paper currency"*: "From George Washington to John Augustine Washington, June 6 [-July 6],1783," in ibid., 134–37.

137 *"makes every thing"*: Ibid.

138 *"No nation will have"*: "From George Washington to John Laurens, January 15, 1781," American Revolution, 1763–1783, LOC.

138 *"The ability of the country"*: "George Washington's Circular Letter of Farewell to the Army, 8 June 1783."

139 *"Who does not remember"*: Ibid.

139 *"a people . . . who are possessed"*: "From George Washington to Benjamin Harrison, 10 October 1784," FO.

140 *"Extend the inland navigation"*: "From George Washington to Jacob Read, 3 November 1784," FO.

140 *"Hearing little else"*: Elkanah Watson, "Two of the Richest Days of My Life," in *Experiencing Mount Vernon: Eyewitness Accounts, 1784–1865* (Charlottesville: University of Virginia Press, 2006), 25.

140 *"The earnestness"*: "To Thomas Jefferson from James Madison, 9 January 1785," FO.

141 *"Success to the navigation"*: "Mr. Hunter manuscript diary," November 16, 1785, reprinted in *West Virginia Historical Magazine Quarterly* 1–2 (1901): 61.

141 *"two charity schools"*: "From George Washington to Edmund Randolph, 30 July 1785," FO.

141 *"consider how far"*: *Annals of the Congress of the United States*, vol. 1 (Washington, DC: Gales & Seaton, 1834), vi.

142 *"Our Constitution is in actual operation"*: "Benjamin Franklin to M. Leroy, 1789," as quoted in *The Macmillan Dictionary of Political Quotations*, ed. Lewis D. Eigen and Jonathan P. Siegal (New York. Macmillan, 1993), 657.

142 *"sketch of a plan"*: George Washington, "Sketch of a Plan of American Finance," October 1789, TeachingAmericanHistory.org, http://teachingamericanhistory.org/library/document/sketch-of-a-plan-of-american-finance/, accessed July 7, 2014.

142 *"power without revenue"*: "Republican Philadelphia: The First Bank," USHistory.org. http://www.ushistory.org/gop/tour_firstbank.htm.

142 *"influence is not government"*: George Washington to Henry Lee, October 31, 1786, in Sparks, ed., *Writings of George Washington*, vol. 9, 204.

142 *"getting money from the states"*: Alexander Hamilton, "The Continentalist No. IV, [30 August 1781]," FO.

142 *He was determined*: Chernow, *Alexander Hamilton*, 297.

144 *"When the country had drained"*: As quoted in Fergus M. Bordewich, *The First Congress: How James Madison, George Washington, and a Group of Extraordinary Men Invented the Government* (New York: Simon & Schuster, 2016), 170.

144 *"our public credit"*: "From George Washington to David Humphreys, 20 July 1791," FO.

145 *"If duties are too high"*: Alexander Hamilton, *The Federalist Papers, No. 21*, AP.

145 *"to restrain persons"*: *Votes and Proceedings of the House of Representatives of the Province of Pennsylvania Beginning the Fourteenth Day of October, 1767*, vol. 6 (Philadelphia: Henry Miller, 1776), 215.

145 *When it was over*: Gerald Carson, "A Tax on Whiskey? Never!," *American Heritage*, http://www.americanheritage.com/content/tax-whiskey-never?page=4, accessed March 17, 2016.

145 *"Nothing can more promote"*: "Washington's Sixth Annual Message to Congress," November 1, 1794, Washington Papers, http://gwpapers.virginia.edu/documents/washingtons-sixth-annual-message-to-congress/.

146 *"whether foreign commerce"*: "From George Washington to James Warren, 7 October 1785," FO.

146 *"I cannot avoid reflecting"*: From George Washington to Marquis de Lafayette, August 15, 1786, TeachingAmericanHistory.org, http://teachingamericanhistory.org/library/document/letter-to-marquis-de-lafayette-5/, accessed September 15, 2015.

146 *whose book:* Jeffry H. Morrison, *The Political Philosophy of George Washington* (Baltimore: Johns Hopkins University Press, 2009), 10; Alan B. Krueger, "The Many Faces of Adam Smith: Rediscovering 'The Wealth of Nations,' " *New York Times*, August 16, 2001.

147 *"the spirit of trade"*: "From George Washington to James Warren, 7 October 1785," FO.

147 *"cherish public credit"*: George Washington, "Washington's Farewell Address," 1796, AP.

147 *"avoiding occasions of expense"*: Ibid.

150 *"I am in want of money"*: "Robert Morris to Benjamin Harrison, Jr., 1795," in Charles Rappleye, *Robert Morris: Financier of the American Revolution* (New York: Simon & Schuster, 2010), 502.

150 *"My money is gone*: Ibid., 507.

152 *"Of all the animosities"*: "From George Washington to Edward Newenham, 20 October 1792," FO.

152 *"In the winter of '77"*: Mason Locke Weems, *The Life of George Washington; with Curious Anecdotes Equally Honorable to Himself, and Exemplary to His Young Countrymen* (Philadelphia: Joseph Allen, 1837), 183.

153 *"I owe it to truth"*: "From Bishop William White to Reverend B.C.C. Parker, 28 November 1832," in Sparks, ed., *Writings of George Washington*, vol. 11, 408.

153 *"I considered it my duty"*: "Letter by Reverend James Ambercrombie, 29 November 1831," as submitted by William L. Stone in "Washington as a Church Member: Original Letter by His Pastor, Dr. James Ambercrombie," *Presbyterian Banner*, vol. 89, July 24, 1902.

153 *"he had received"*: Ibid.

154 *"being in that language"*: [Diary entry, July 3, 1791], FO; John A. Schutz and Douglas Adair, eds., *A Virtuous Heretic: The Spur of Fame: Dialogues of John Adams and Benjamin Rush, 1805–1813* (Indianapolis: Liberty Fund, 2001), 76.

154 *"No man, who is profligate"*: "From George Washington to the General Assembly of the Presbyterian Church, 30 May–5 June 1789," FO.

155 *"prudence, temperance, fortitude, and justice"*: James T. Kloppenberg, *The Virtues of Liberalism* (New York: Oxford University Press, 1998), 5.

155 *"ridiculous and childish custom"*: "General Orders, 5 November 1775," FO.

155 *"not suppose that Washington"*: As quoted in Ford, *The True George Washington*, 83.

155 *"more of an institution"*: Freeman, *George Washington*, vol. 2, 387.

155 *"there was for him no rock"*: Ibid., 397.

156 *"There exists in the economy"*: George Washington, "First Inaugural Address of George Washington," April 30, 1789, AP.

156 *"The consideration that human"*: "From George Washington to the Protestant Episcopal Church, 19 August 1789," FO.

156 *Masonic Lodge*: Alexander Immekus, "Freemasonry," GWMV.

157 *"God preserve"*: As quoted in Longmore, *The Invention of George Washington*, 116.

157 *"My Dearest"*: "George Washington to Martha Washington, 18 June 1775," FO.

157 *"May that God"*: "George Washington to Lieutenant General Thomas Gage, 19 August 1775," FO.

157 *"Providence—to whom we are infinitely"*: Quoted in Moncure D. Conway, "The Religion of George Washington," in *The Open Court: A Weekly Magazine Devoted to the Work of*

Conciliating Religion with Science, vol. 3 (Chicago: Open Court Publishing Company, 1889–1890,1896),

157 *"We shall have equal occasion"*: Immekus, "Freemasonry."

158 *"I now make it my earnest"*: "George Washington's Circular Letter of Farewell to the Army, 8 June 1783."

158 *"religious bondage shackles"*: "Champion of Religious Freedom," James Madison's Montpelier, http://www.montpelier.org/james-and-dolley-madison/james-madison/champion-of-religious-freedom, accessed March 17, 2016.

158 *"the Constitution of the U.S."*: Ibid.

158 *"It would be peculiarly"*: George Washington, "First Inaugural Address of George Washington," April 30, 1789, AP.

159 *"increased by slow degrees"*: "From Lawrence Washington to Mr. Hanbury, n.d.," in Sparks, *Writings of George Washington*, vol. 2, 481.

160 *"No man's sentiments"*: "From George Washington to George Mason, 3 October 1785," FO.

160 *"If they are good workmen"*: Mary V. Thompson, "Islam at Mount Vernon," GWMV.

160 *"A religious sect"*: Madison, Federalist 10, in Hamilton, Madison, and Jay, *The Federalist Papers*, 47.

160 *"If I could have entertained"*: "From George Washington to the United Baptist Churches of Virginia, May 1789," FO.

161 *"as mankind becomes more liberal"*: "From George Washington to Roman Catholics in America, c.15 March 1790," FO.

161 *"It is now no more"*: "From George Washington to the Hebrew Congregation in Newport, Rhode Island, 18 August 1790," FO.

161 *"May the children"*: Ibid.

162 *Washington referred*: George Tsakiridis, "Vine and Fig Tree," GWMV.

164 *"every American considers"*: Hutchins, *Everyday Life in the Early Republic*, p. 18.

165 *"bind it in your Bible"*: Furstenberg, *In the Name of the Father*, 52.

166 *"That Washington was not a scholar"*: "From John Adams to Benjamin Rush, 22 April 1812," FO.

166 *"mind was great"*: "From Thomas Jefferson to Walter Jones, 2 January 1814," FO.

166 *"his talents were rather"*: David Humphreys, *Life of General Washington* (Athens: University of Georgia Press, 2006), 52.

166 *"I have had but little"*: As quoted in Morrison, *The Political Philosophy of George Washington*, 6.

167 *"read men by business"*: Hugh Jones, quoted in Daniel J. Boorstin, *The Americans: The Colonial Experience* (New York: Random House, 1958), 304.

167 *"I conceive a knowledge"*: "From George Washington to Jonathan Boucher, 9 July 1771," FO.

168 *At the end*: "Take Note! George Washington the Reader," GWMV.

168 *Young George enjoyed*: Morrison, *The Political Philosophy of George Washington*, 78.

170 *"We ought not"*: "From George Washington to John Armstrong, 26 March 1781," FO.

170 *"The best means"*: "From George Washington to George Chapman, 15 December 1784," FO.

170 *"The arts and sciences"*: "George Washington to Joseph Willard, 22 March 1781," in Sparks, ed., *Writings of George Washington*, vol. 7, 459.

170 *"The foundation of our empire"*: "George Washington's Circular Letter of Farewell to the Army, 8 June 1783."

171 *"dogs, horses, and guns"*: "From George Washington to Jonathan Boucher, 16 December 1770," FO.

171 *"To be acquainted"*: "From George Washington to Jonathan Boucher, 2 January 1771," FO.

172 *"in the composition"*: "George Washington to Eleanor 'Nelly' Parke Custis, March 21, 1796," Presidential Series, Papers of George Washington, University of Virginia, http://gwpapers.virginia.edu/documents/george-washington-to-nelly-custis-21 -march-1796/, accessed September 15, 2015.

172 *"Love is a mighty"*: "From George Washington to Elizabeth Parke Custis, 14 September 1794," FO.

172 *With 95 percent of Americans*: "Population: 1790 to 1990," U.S. Census Bureau, https:// www.census.gov/population/censusdata/table-4.pdf.

173 *"the business of education"*: Benjamin Rush, "Of the Mode of Education Proper in a Republic," 1798, Founders' Constitution, http://press-pubs.uchicago.edu/founders/ documents/v1ch18s30.html, accessed September 15, 2015.

173 *"Knowledge is in every country"*: "From George Washington to the United States Senate and House of Representatives, 8 January 1790," FO.

174 *"This power should"*: *Annals of Congress*, House of Representatives, 1st Congress, 2nd session (May 3, 1790), 1604.

174 *"the further children"*: Annals of Congress, House of Representatives, 4th Congress, 2nd session (December 1796), 1697.

174 *"It has always been"*: "From George Washington to the Commissioners of the District of Columbia, 28 January 1795," Founding.com: A Project of Claremont University, http://www.founding.com/founders_library/pageID.2224/default.asp.

175 *"There is scarcely"*: Humphreys, *Life of General Washington*, 35.

175 *"I must study"*: "From John Adams to Abigail Adams, 12 May 1780," AFP.

176 *"Proceed, great chief"*: As quoted in Wiencek, *An Imperfect God*, 207.

176 *"I thank you"*: "From George Washington to Phillis Wheatley, 28 February 1776," FO.

176 *"those bards"*: "From George Washington to Lafayette, 28 May 1788," FO.

177 *"The propriety of"*: "To Thomas Jefferson from George Washington, 15 March 1795," FO.

177 *"I have regretted"*: "Alexander Hamilton from George Washington, 1 September 1796," FO.

178 *"you will observe"*: "Alexander Hamilton to George Washington, 5 September 1796," FO.

179 *"There will several"*: Ibid., FO.

182 *"To promote literature"*: "To George Washington from Washington Academy Trustees, 12 April 1798," FO.

182 *Washington set aside*: "George Washington's Last Will and Testament, 9 July 1799," FO.

182 *"the establishment of"*: Ibid.

184 *"essential principles"*: Thomas Jefferson, "First Inaugural Address," March 4, 1801, AP.

185 *"Sir, I take"*: "John Adams to the president of Congress, 10 February 1784," FO.

185 *"My politics"*: Felix Gilbert, "The English Background of American Isolationism in the Eighteenth Century," *William and Mary Quarterly* (1944): 142.

186 *"Such was the complication"*: As quoted in Francis Parkman, *Montcalm and Wolfe* (Boston: Little, Brown, 1902), 16.

186 *"The militia of this country"*: "George Washington's Circular Letter of Farewell to the Army, 8 June 1783."

186 *"a standing army"*: As quoted in David O. Stewart, *The Summer of 1787: The Men Who Invented the Constitution* (New York: Simon & Schuster, 2002), 222.

187 *"No foreign enemy"*: Vile, *The Constitutional Convention of 1787*, 30.

187 *"to be prepared"*: "From George Washington to the United States Senate and House of Representatives, 8 January 1790," FO.

187 *"when foreign nations"*: "From George Washington to Lafayette, 18 June 1788," FO.

187 *"Nations are not influenced"*: "From George Washington to Lafayette, 15 August 1786," FO.

189 *"Any submission to"*: Thomas Paine, "Common Sense," in Paine, *Collected Writings: Common Sense, The Crisis, Rights of Man, The Age of Reason, Pamphlets, Articles, and Letters* (New York: Library of America, 1995), 27.

189 *"Not even Spain"*: "From John Adams to the President of Congress, No. 48, 18 April 1780," FO.

189 *"The future interest"*: *Journal of the Continental Congress, 1774–1789*, vol. 24 (Washington, DC: U.S. Government Printing Office, 1922), 394.

189 *"I was opposed"*: "From George Washington to John Ellis, 10 July 1783," FO.

190 *"The duty and interest"*: "The Proclamation of Neutrality, 1793," AP.

191 *"If you consult"*: Horatius No. II, [July 1795], FO.

191 *"If the Jay Treaty"*: Samuel Flagg Bemis, "John Quincy Adams and George Washington," *Proceedings of the Massachusetts Historical Society*, 3rd Series, 67 (October 1941–May 1944): 373–74.

191 *"it would be a war"*: Bemis, "John Quincy Adams and George Washington," 377–78.

191 *"to keep the United States"*: George Washington to Patrick Henry, October 9, 1795, in Fitzpatrick, ed., *The Writings of George Washington*, 918.

192 *"My policy has been"*: George Washington to Gouverneur Morris, December 22, 1795, in ibid.

192 *"Nothing but his weight"*: John Quincy Adams, "To Sylvanus Bourne, London, December 24, 1795," in *Writings of John Quincy Adams*, vol. 1, ed. Worthington Chauncey Ford (New York: Macmillan),1913.

192 *"Mr. Jefferson likes"*: Walter A. McDougall, *Promised Land, Crusader State: The American Encounter with the World since 1776* (New York: Houghton Mifflin, 1997), 42.

193 *"Our countrymen"*: "From Thomas Jefferson to Elbridge Gerry, 21 June 1797," FO.

195 *"I have always"*: George Washington to James Monroe, August 25, 1796, in Sparks, ed., *Writings of George Washington*, vol. 11, 167.

195 *"the cause of virtue"*: "Address to the Inhabitants of Bermuda, 6 September 1775," FO.

196 *"I do not conceive"*: "From George Washington to Bushrod Washington, 9 November 1787," FO.

SECTION III: THE AFTERLIFE OF THE IDEA

199 *"The advice he gives"*: Jacob Hiltzheimer, *Extracts from the Diary of Jacob Hiltzheimer*, ed. Jacob Cox Parsons (Philadelphia: Wm. F. Fell, 1893), 234.

199 *"This advice is a text book"*: "From W. V. Murray to Unknown, 14 July 1797," New York Public Library Archives and Manuscripts, New York.

200 *In December*: Jasper Dwight, "A Letter to George Washington, President of the United States: Containing Strictures on his Address of the Seventeenth of September 1796, notifying his Relinquishment of the Presidential Office," Philadelphia, 1796, FWS. Jasper Dwight was the pen name of William Duane. For more information on this pamphlet and other attacks on Washington by the press see James D. Tagg, "Benjamin Franklin Bach's Attack on George Washington," *Pennsylvania Magazine of History and Biography* 100 (April 1976): 191–230.

200 *"dangerous incendiary"*: Kim T. Phillips, "William Duane, Philadelphia's Democratic Republicans, and the Origins of Modern Politics," *Pennsylvania Magazine of History and Biography* 101 (July 1977): 368.

200 *"will serve as a signal"*: Fisher Ames to Oliver Wolcott, September 26, 1796, in *Memoirs of the Administrations of Washington and John Adams, Edited from the Papers of Oliver Wolcott*, vol. 1, ed. George Gibbs (New York: W. Van Norden, 1846), 384.

201 *"an advocate for"*: Tunis Wortman, "A Solemn Address to Christians and Patriots" (New York, 1800), Consource, http://www.consource.org, accessed May 1, 2015.

202 *"He has for eight years"*: Henrietta Liston Journal, March 5, 1797, in *The Travel Journals of Henrietta Marchant Liston: North America and Lower Canada, 1796–1800*, ed. Louise V. North (New York: Lexington Books, 2014), 17, 19.

202 *"Methought I saw"*: "John Adams to Abigail Adams, 5 March 1797," AFP.

202 *"[a]gricultural pursuits and rural"*: "From George Washington to Buchan," 4 July 1797, FO.

202 *"as if I had"*: "From George Washington to David Humphreys, 26 June 1797," FO.

203 *expanding his whiskey*: Michael Beschloss, "Washington, The Whiskey Baron," *New York Times*, February 14, 2016.

203 *"I shall view"*: "From George Washington to David Humphreys, 26 June 1797."

203 *"men who were"*: "I. Thomas Jefferson to Philip Mazzei, 24 April 1796," FO.

203 *"one of the most detestable"*: Peter R. Henriques, *Realistic Visionary* (Charlottesville: University of Virginia Press, 2006), 122.

203 *"insanity in the extreme!"*: Washington, "Remarks on Monroe's 'View of the Conduct of the Executive of the United States," in Ford, ed., *The Writings of George Washington*, vol. 13, 467, 480, 476, 478.

204 *"It has always"*: "George Washington's Last Will and Testament," July 9, 1799, FO.

205 *"in a central part"*: Ibid.

205 *"a plan devised"*: Ibid.

205 *"like even to think"*: "From George Washington to Alexander Spotswood, 23 November 1794," FO.

206 *"he had made"*: "Notes of a Conversation with Edmund Randolph, [after 1795]," FO.

206 *"I can clearly"*: As quoted in Wiencek, *An Imperfect God*, 352.

206 *"the unfortunate condition"*: Humphreys, *Life of George Washington*, 78.

207 *slave labor force*: Kenneth Morgan, "George Washington and the Problem of Slavery," *Journal of American Studies* 34 (August 2000): 279–301.

207 *"expressly forbid the sale"*: "George Washington's Last Will and Testament, 9 July 1799," FO.

208 *"a classic 'textbook' case"*: White McKenzie Wallenborn, M.D., "George Washington's Terminal Illness: A Modern Medical Analysis of the Last Illness and Death of George Washington," Papers of George Washington, http://gwpapers.virginia.edu/history/articles/illness/, accessed July 6, 2015.

209 *So the tincture*: Ibid.

209 *"Doctor, I die hard"*: Tobias Lear, "The Last Illness and Death of General Washington," SeacoastNH.com, http://www.seacoastnh.com/famous-people/tobias-lear/death-of-george-washington, accessed June 14, 2015.

209 *"do not let"*: Ibid.

210 *"His example"*: John Adams, "Death of George Washington," December 19, 1799, MC.

210 *Readings of the Farewell*: Furstenberg, *In the Name of the Father*, 43.

210 *"of approximately 2,200"*: Ibid., 28.

210 *"Our father and friend"*: Robert Allen, "Eulogy of George Washington," December 29, 1799, UShistory.org, http://www.ushistory.org/presidentshouse/history/alleneulogy.htm, accessed July 12, 2015.

211 *"an oracle of political truth"*: Timothy Bigelow, " A Eulogy on the Life, Character, and Services of Brother George Washington," February 11, 1800, in *Eulogies and Orations on the Life and Death of General George Washington First President of the United States of America* (Boston: Manning & Loring, 1800), 137.

211 *"Let the infant cherub"*: Furstenberg, *In the Name of the Father*, 42

213 *"Every difference of opinion"*: Jefferson, "First Inaugural Address," March 4, 1801, AP.

213 *"If there be any"*: Jefferson, "First Inaugural Address."

213 *"kindly separated by nature"*: Ibid.

214 *"attempts to disorganize"*: James Madison, "Second Inaugural Address, [March 4,] 1813," FO.

214 *"a conspiracy in New England"*: Matthew Carey, *The Olive Branch: or Faults on Both Sides, Federal and Democratic* (Philadelphia: Matthew Carey, 1815), 9.

214 *"the restoration of harmony"*: Ibid., 20.

216 *"She has, in the lapse"*: John Quincy Adams, "Speech on Independence Day," July 4, 1821, MC.

217 *"Washington's Farewell is full"*: Daniel Webster, "The Character of Washington," February 22, 1832, in *Speeches and Other Proceedings at the Public Dinner in Honor of the Centennial Anniversary of Washington* (Washington, DC: Jonathan Elliot, 1832), 8.

217 *"From the president's speech"*: Andrew Jackson to Robert Hays, December 16, 1796, in *The Papers of Andrew Jackson*, vol. 1, *1770–1803*, ed. Sam B. Smith and Harriet Chappell Owsley (Knoxville: University of Tennessee Press, 1980), 103.

218 *"Our Federal Union"*: Andrew Jackson, "President Jackson's Proclamation Regarding Nullification," December 10, 1832, AP.

219 *"The necessity of watching"*: Andrew Jackson, "Farewell Address," March 4, 1837, TeachingAmericanHistory.org, http://teachingamericanhistory.org/library/docu ment/farewell-address-3/, accessed July 5, 2015.

222 *"That man does not"*: As quoted in Chernow, *Alexander Hamilton*, 508.

223 *"The unnecessary* buzz": Judge Peters to John Jay, February 14, 1811, in Henry Johnson, ed., *John Jay, The Correspondence and Public Papers of John Jay*, vol. 4, *1794–1826* (New York: Putnam, 1893), 344, Online Library of Liberty, http://oll.libertyfund.org/ti tles/2330, accessed April 21, 2015.

223 *"The history"*: "John Jay to Judge Peters, March 29, 1811," WFA, 270.

223 *"That Address was to be"*: Ibid., 268–69.

225 *"With respect to his"*: "Thomas Jefferson to Judge Johnson, June 12, 1823," in Thomas Jefferson Randolph, ed., *Memoirs, Correspondence, and Private Papers of Thomas Jefferson, Late President of the United States*, vol. 3 (London: Henry Colburn & Richard Bentley, 1829), 379.

225 *"ought to claim"*: "James Madison to Thomas Jefferson, June 27, 1823" in *Letters and Other Writings of James Madison*, vol. 3, *1816–1828* (New York: R. Worthington, 1884), 323.

227 *Original of Washington's Farewell*: *Sunbury American*, November 24, 1849.

228 *"What is to become"*: *Congressional Globe*, 31st Congress, 1st session, January 29, 1850.

228 *"Amidst the discordant"*: Ibid.

229 *"This is but"*: Ibid., January 24, 1850.

229 *"merely a scheme"*: Ibid., January 29, 1850.

230 *"We certainly venerate"*: "Washington's Farewell Address," *Dollar Newspaper*, January 30, 1850.

230 *"There is a wide difference"*: "Washington's Farewell Address," *Lewisburg Chronicle* (Pennsylvania), February 6, 1850.

232 *"Some of you delight"*: Abraham Lincoln, "Cooper Union Address," February 27, 1860, National Park Service, http://www.nps.gov/liho/learn/historyculture/cooperunion address.htm, accessed July 23, 2015.

233 *"You say you are conservative"*: Ibid.

234 *"that immortal Farewell Address"*: "Memorial of the mayor and other citizens of Philadelphia, praying that George Washington's Farewell Address may be read to both houses of Congress and to the army and navy of the United States on the 22d of February, January 31, 1862," RG 46, *Records of the United States Senate*, National Archives, http://www .archives.gov/global-pages/larger-image.html?i=/legislative/features/washington/ images/philadelphia-l.jpg&c=/legislative/features/washington/images/philadelphia. caption.html, accessed July 23, 2015.

234 *"the President of the United States"*: "General Order 16, February 18, 1862," in *A Compilation of the Messages and Papers of the Presidents*, vol. 6, *1861–1865*, ed. James D. Richardson (New York: Bureau of National Literature and Art, 1897), 105.

236 *"Supposing he was doing his duty"*: Abraham Lincoln to attorney general 2/16/1863, *Collected Works of Abraham Lincoln*, vol. 6.

236 *"the bastard flags"*: As recounted in Adam J. Gaffney, "Recollecting Union: 'Rebel Flags' and the Epideictic Vision of Washington's Farewell Address," *Western Journal of Communications* 79 (2015): 328.

236 *"our policy of non-intervention"*: William H. Seward, "To Mr. Dayton, May 11, 1863," in *Papers Relating to Foreign Affairs, Accompanying the Annual Message of the President*, part 1 (Washington, DC: U.S. Government Printing Office, 1864), 668.

236 *"Never in the history"*: Seward, "To Mr. Dayton," 338.

236 *"a magnificent chapter"*: As recounted in Gaffney, "Recollecting Union," 327–47.

236 One Confederate delegate: William F. B. Vodrey, "George Washington: Hero of the Confederacy?," *American History Magazine*, October 2004.

237 *"On this the birthday"*: Jefferson Davis, "Second Inaugural Address," February 22, 1862, Papers of Jefferson Davis, Rice University, https://jeffersondavis.rice.edu/Content. aspx?id=107, accessed July 24, 2015.

237 Envelopes issued by the Confederate: Furstenburg, *In the Name of the Father*, 101.

237 Moss secretly carried: Christine A. Smith, "George Washington's Last Will and Testament: An American Odyssey," *Winterthur Portfolio* 38 (Winter 2003): 185.

238 *"containing all the principles"*: "A Speech by the President: He Defies the Radicals," *Fayetteville Observer* (Tennessee), March 8, 1866, Chronicling America, http://chronicl ingamerica.loc.gov. 23 October 2013.

239 One textbook: Emma Willard, *Abridged History of the United States* (Philadelphia: A. S. Barnes, 1844), 266.

239 *"the despotism which"*: "George Washington—Rebel," *Daily Constitutionalist*, February 22, 1867.

239 *"secular Sabbath"*: "The Twenty-Second of February," *Indianapolis Sentinel*, vol. 26, no. 53, February 22, 1877, America's Historical Newspapers, http://infoweb.newsbank .com, accessed June 10, 2013.

239 *a sermon declared*: "Trinity Baptist Church," *New York Herald*, February 22, 1869.

239 *Celebrations of his birthday:* "Washington's Birthday," *New York Herald*, February 23, 1873.

240 *the* Herald *suggested*: Forrest G. Wood, *Black Scare: The Racist Response to Emancipation and Reconstruction* (Berkeley: University of California Press, 1968), 124.

240 *"The utterances today"*: Worthington C. Ford, "Washington's Farewell Address," *Harper's Weekly*, September 19, 1896.

241 *"the scrupulous avoidance"*: Grover Cleveland, "First Inaugural Address," Bartleby, http://www.bartleby.com/124/pres37.html.

241 *"Today the United States"*: Richard Olney, "Guiana Boundary Dispute," in *Appletons' Annual Cyclopaedia and Register of Important Events of the Year 1895*, new series, vol. 20 (New York: Appleton, 1896), 748.

241 *"Though the nation"*: Olney, "International Isolation of the United States," Harvard College, March 1898.

243 *"Following the precepts"*: Quoted in *Washington's Farewell Address and Webster's First Bunker Hill Oration*, ed. Charles Robert Gaston, PhD (Boston: Ginn, 1906), 52.

245 *"The circumstances which"*: Woodrow Wilson, "The First President of the United States," *Harper's New Monthly Magazine* 93, November 1896, 863.

245 *"It would be an irony"*: As quoted in David Milne, *Worldmaking: The Art and Science of American Diplomacy* (New York: Farrar, Straus & Giroux, 2015), 83.

245 *"isolated as we are"*: As quoted in George Herring Jr., "James Hay and the Preparedness Controversy, 1915–1916," *Journal of Southern History* 30 (November 1964): 386.

246 *"the ocean barrier"*: Congressional Record, 63rd Congress, 3rd session, 1915, 1610.

246 *"forgotten the sound"*: John Milton Cooper, *The Vanity of Power: America Isolationism and World War I, 1914 to 1917* (Santa Barbara, CA: Greenwood, 1969).

246 *While the term*: Brooke L. Blower, "From Isolationism to Neutrality: A New Framework for Understanding American Political Culture, 1919–1941," *Diplomatic History* 38 (2014): 345–76, first published online May 29, 2013, http://dh.oxfordjournals.org/content/38/2/345, accessed October 10, 2015.

246 *"I still believe"*: Cooper, *The Vanity of Power*, 118–19.

246 *"any sort of alliances"*: Ibid.

247 *"We are participants"*: Woodrow Wilson, "Address Delivered at the First Annual Assemblage of the League to Enforce Peace: 'American Principles,' " American Presidency Project, http://www.presidency.ucsb.edu/ws/?pid=65391, accessed August 1, 2015.

247 *"While I am far"*: Henry Cabot Lodge, "Washington's Policies of Neutrality and

National Defense," Washington Association of New Jersey at Morristown, New Jersey, February 22, 1916.

248 *"The chief argument"*: Lodge, "Washington's Policies of Neutrality and National Defense."

248 *"I am proposing"*: Woodrow Wilson, "Peace Without Victory," *American Experience*, http://www.pbs.org/wgbh/amex/wilson/filmmore/fm_victory.html, accessed August 1, 2015.

249 *"no alliances, no leagues"*: Lodge, "Washington's Policies of Neutrality and National Defense."

249 *"no superstition in regard"*: Lodge, "The President's Plan for World Peace," speech before the U.S. Senate, February 1, 1917, in *War Addresses 1915–1917 by Henry Cabot Lodge* (New York: Houghton Mifflin, 1917), 272, Google Books, http://books.google.com.

250 *"not surprised to note"*: Cooper, *The Vanity of Power*, 201.

250 *only 54 representatives*: Ibid.

250 *"Patriotic exercises should"*: Superintendent of Public Instruction of the Commonwealth of Pennsylvania, *Report for the Year Ending July 1, 1918* (Harrisburg, PA: J. L. L. Kuhn, 1918), vi.

250 *In Brooklyn, eighth graders*: Albert J. Levine, "A Study in Economy of Learning History and Civics," *Atlantic Educational Journal* 12, no. 1 (1916): 296.

251 *Seventy-three percent of French troops*: "WWI Casualty and Death Tables," U.S. Department of Justice, https://www.pbs.org/greatwar/resources/casdeath_pop.html, accessed February 10, 2015.

252 *"I will consent"*: As quoted in Richard Hofstadter, "Wilson, the Intransigent," *New Republic*, August 6, 1945.

253 *"Should a war"*: Madison, Federalist 41, in Hamilton, Madison, and Jay, *The Federalist Papers*, 200.

253 *"That could have been said"*: Arthur H. Vandenberg, *If Hamilton Were Here Today: American Fundamentals Applied to Modern Problems* (New York: Putnam's, 1923), 352.

253 *"was not the astigmatized"*: Vandenberg, *If Hamilton Were Here Today*, 353–54.

254 *"Liberty is crumbling"*: Herbert Hoover, *Addresses Upon the American Road, 1933–1938* (New York: Charles Scribner & Sons, 1938, 235); Herbert Hoover Presidential Library and Museum, Published Writings of Herbert Hoover, http://www.ecommcode.com/hoover/ebooks/displayPage.cfm?BookID=B3&VolumeID=B3V1&PageID=241, accessed July 23, 2015.

255 *"despite what happens"*: Franklin D. Roosevelt, "Address at San Diego Exposition, San Diego, California, October 2, 1936," APP.

256 *"bow our heads"*: As quoted in Ronald H. Carpenter, *Father Charles E. Coughlin: Surrogate Spokesman for the Disaffected* (Westport, CT: Greenwood, 1998), 169.

256 *"Mr. Republican"*: Robert A. Taft, "Russia and the Four Freedoms Russian War

Strengthens Arguments Against Intervention," Radio Address. June 25, 1941, in *The Papers of Robert A. Taft, 1939–1944* (Kent, OH: Kent State University Press, 2001), 253.

256 *"Who is pushing":* Dorothy Thompson, "An Open Letter to Anne Lindbergh," *Look,* March 1941, 11.

257 *"My Fellow Christian Americans":* German American Bund, *Free America: The German American Bund at Madison Square Garden, February 20, 1939* (New York: A.V., 1939), 1–2.

257 *"George Washington, whose birthday":* Ibid.

259 *"The best British Ambassador":* As quoted in Lynne Olson, *Those Angry Days: Roosevelt, Lindbergh, and America's Fight Over World War II, 1939–1941* (New York: Random House, 2013), 124.

260 *"lack of sincerity and directness":* Raymond Moley, *27 Masters of Politics* (New York: Funk & Wagnalls, 1949), 41.

262 *"the assumption by this President":* Wendell Willkie, Address Accepting the Presidential Nomination in Elwood, Indiana, August 17, 1940.

262 *"a third term":* "No Third Term, Republican National Committee, Washington, DC, 1940, http://www.gilderlehrman.org/history-by-era/new-deal/resources/campaigning-against-franklin-roosevelt's-third-term-1940.

263 *"Partisan politics ought":* As quoted in *CQ Press Guide to Congress,* 7th edition, vol. 1 (Los Angeles: Sage, 2013), 222.

263 *"His allegiance stopped":* Vandenberg, *If Hamilton Were Here Today,* 353.

263 *"Throughout my years":* As quoted in Matthew Spalding and Patrick J. Garrity, *A Sacred Union of Citizens: George Washington's Farewell Address and the American Character* (Lanham, MD: Rowman & Littlefield, 1996), 165.

263 *"It was a long way to Europe":* Harry S. Truman, *Where the Buck Stops: The Personal and Private Writings of Harry S. Truman,* ed. Margaret Truman (New York: Warner Books, 1989), 187–88.

264 *"the only thing new":* Truman, *Memoirs* (New York: Doubleday, 1955), 102.

265 *"Washington was my hero":* Dwight D. Eisenhower, *At Ease: Stories I Tell to Friends* (New York: Doubleday, 1967), 40–41.

265 *"You know that General MacArthur":* Garry Wills, *Nixon Agonistes: The Crisis of the Self-Made Man* (New York: First Mariner Books), 122.

266 *"those who so glibly":* "Dwight D. Eisenhower to Henry A. Wallace, February 22, 1957," Henry A. Wallace Collection, University of Iowa Libraries, Iowa Digital Library, http://digital.lib.uiowa.edu/cdm/ref/collection/wallace/id/48780, accessed August 1, 2015.

266 *"I've often felt":* "Dwight D. Eisenhower to Henry A. Wallace," February 22, 1957.

266 *"I have no patience":* Dwight D. Eisenhower, "Ike Takes a Look at the GOP," *Saturday Evening Post,* April 21, 1962, 19.

266 *"The middle of the road"*: Eisenhower, "Remarks at the Republican National Committee Breakfast," July 27, 1960, in *Public Papers of the Presidents of the United States, Dwight D. Eisenhower, 1960–1961* (Washington, DC: U.S. Government Printing Office, 1911), 246.

266 *"I don't care whether entangling alliances"*: Walter Isaacson and Evan Thomas, *The Wise Men: Six Friends and The World They Made* (New York: Simon & Schuster, 1986), 447.

266 *"As I read this"*: Margaret Chase Smith, inscription, February 22, 1949, http://www. senate.gov/artandhistory/history/resources/pdf/MCSMithPage.pdf.

267 *"I want to say something"*: Charles J.G. Griffin, "New Light on Eisenhower's Farewell Address," *Presidential Studies Quarterly* 22 (Summer 1992): 470.

267 *"I was struck by its relevance"*: Frederic Fox to Dwight D. Eisenhower, April 5, 1960, http://www.eisenhower.archives.gov/research/online_documents/farewell_ad dress/1960_04_05.pdf, August 23, 2015.

269 *"Only an alert"*: Eisenhower, "Farewell Address," also known as "Military-Industrial Complex Speech," January 17, 1961, AP.

270 *"All of you who"*: John F. Kennedy, "Remarks at a Reception Marking African Freedom Day," Drawing Room State Department Auditorium, Washington, D.C., April 15, 1961, APP.

271 *"The one division"*: Lyndon B. Johnson, "Remarks in Harrisburg at a Dinner Sponsored by the Pennsylvania State Democratic Committee," September 10 1964, APP.

271 *"I think all Americans"*: Lyndon B. Johnson, "Remarks at a Dinner Honoring Senator Everett McKinley Dirksen, November 20 1967, APP.

272 *"The problem is to stand"*: Ibid.

272 *"[it] was also Washington*: Lyndon B. Johnson, "Remarks at the Dedication of the Smithsonian Institution's Museum of History and Technology," January 22, 1964, APP.

273 *"The principal burden"*: Wills, *Nixon Agonistes*, 490–92.

275 *"The electronic era"*: Gerald Ford, "Remarks at the Annual Congressional Breakfast of the National Religious Broadcasters," January 28,1975, APP.

276 *"Freedom, it has been said"*: Ronald Reagan, "Remarks and a Question-and-Answer Session with the Students and Faculty at Moscow State University," May 31, 1988, APP.

276 *"Because they know that liberty"*: Ibid.

276 *"In George Washington's first draft"*: William J. Clinton: "Remarks to the Opening of the National Summit on Africa," February 17, 2000, APP.

277 *"The first thing"*: Jeff Shesol, interview with the author, February 26, 2016.

279 *"the personal and the political"*: Lin Manuel Miranda, interview with the author, March 5, 2016.

279 *"It's the most audacious"*: Miranda, interview.

287 *"to be partisan"*: Walter Lippmann, *The Essential Lippmann: A Political Philosophy for Liberal Democracy*, ed. Clinton Rossiter and James Lare (Cambridge, MA: Harvard University Press, 1982), 207.

ILLUSTRATION CREDITS

INDEX

ABOUT THE AUTHOR

John Avlon is the Editor-in-Chief and managing director of *The Daily Beast* and a CNN political analyst. He is the author of *Independent Nation* and *Wingnuts* as well as an editor of the anthology *Deadline Artists: America's Greatest Newspaper Columns*. He won the National Society of Newspaper Columnists' award for Best Online Column in 2012. He served as chief speechwriter for New York City Mayor Rudy Giuliani, and his essay "The Resilient City" concluded the anthology *Empire City: New York Through the Centuries*, winning acclaim as "the single best essay written in the wake of 9/11." He lives with his wife, Margaret Hoover, and their two children in New York City.